PAINLESS WINDOWS
SECOND EDITION

D1358408

A HANDBOOK
FOR SAS® USERS

JODIE
GILMORE

Comments or Questions?

The authors assume complete responsibility for the technical accuracy of the content of this book. If you have any questions about the material in this book, please write to the author at this address:

SAS Institute Inc.
Books By Users
Attn: Jodie Gilmore
SAS Campus Drive
Cary, NC 27513

If you prefer, you can send e-mail to sasbbu@sas.com with "comments for Jodie Gilmore" as the subject line, or you can fax the Books by Users program at (919) 677-4444.

The correct bibliographic citation for this manual is as follows: Gilmore, Jodie, *Painless Windows: A Handbook for SAS Users, Second Edition,* Cary, NC: SAS Institute Inc., 1999. 360 pp.

Painless Windows: A Handbook for SAS Users, Second Edition

Table of Contents

 ## Learning to Do Windows

2 Performing the Basic SAS® Software Tasks under Windows

3 Editing and Working with Files

4 Submitting SAS® Code and Generating Output

5 Printing

6 Adjusting Your Windows Environment

7 Managing SAS® Files

8 Customizing Your Start-up Files and SAS® System Options

9 Using Batch Mode

10 Executing DOS Commands and Windows Applications from Your SAS® Session

11 Sharing Data between Your SAS® Session and Other Windows Applications

12 Using SAS/CONNECT® Software to Connect Your PC to Other Computer Systems

Appendix 1 | Troubleshooting

Appendix 2 | Creating a Print File

Appendix 3 | Becoming Familiar with the Windows Explorer

Glossary

Index

Welcome to Version 7 of the SAS® System for Windows

What This Book Is

Painless Windows: A Handbook for SAS Users, Second Edition is a task-oriented book about Version 7 (and subsequent releases) of the SAS System under Microsoft Windows. The book does not assume the user grew up using Windows.

Note

The term "Windows" refers to Windows 95 (and subsequent versions such as Windows 98) and Windows NT in the rest of this book. Where there is a difference between the two systems (Win95/98 vs WinNT), the specific system is mentioned. Version 7 of the SAS System does not run under earlier versions of Windows (such as Windows 3.1).

This book assumes that you are familiar with some version of the SAS System but not with Version 7 of the SAS System or with Windows. It also acknowledges that you may not even like Windows but that you have to use SAS software under Windows to do part of your job. In this book, you learn to use key features of base SAS software to accomplish certain tasks under Windows. Example tasks include

- opening a file that contains SAS code

- submitting SAS code

- using the Output Delivery System (ODS)

- using the SAS Explorer to manage files

- saving changes to your SAS code

- printing output from your SAS code.

The book also touches briefly on some other components of the SAS System, including SAS/AF and SAS/CONNECT software.

You also learn how to get around in Windows. For example, the first chapter shows you how to slow down your mouse and how to redisplay an application you want to use after it has disappeared behind several other applications. The chapters include many screen shots, showing what your display should look like while you are filling out dialog boxes and using menus.

What Software You Need

The information in this book assumes you have Microsoft Windows 95, Microsoft Windows 98, Microsoft Windows NT (Version 4.0 or later), or a subsequent version of Windows.

Also, the examples and discussion throughout this book assume you have Version 7 (or a subsequent release) of the SAS System for Windows. If you have an earlier version of the SAS System, you should read

Painless Windows 3.1: A Beginner's Handbook for SAS Users

if you have Windows 3.1 and/or Release 6.11 of the SAS System.

Painless Windows: A Handbook for SAS Users

if you have Windows 95 or Windows NT and/or Release 6.12 of the SAS System.

What This Book Is Not

This book is not a comprehensive guide to using Windows. For example, it does not discuss how to tune Windows performance or discuss using the Control Panel to add serial ports to your system. Nor is this book a guide to SAS software itself. It assumes you know what a DATA step is, that you have used PROC PRINT, and that you know the difference between a system option and a statement option. If you need a guide to using SAS software in general or need more information on Windows, refer to "Further Reading" later in this chapter.

This book is not meant to replace SAS Institute reference documentation. It does not show you every nuance of the tasks it discusses, nor does it show you every way to perform a task. Also, there are aspects of Version 7 of the SAS System that this book does not cover. For example, it does not cover using e-mail or advanced OLE features. For nitty gritty details, turn to SAS Institute's reference guides and online documentation.

Finally, this book is not an installation guide. SAS Institute provides comprehensive installation instructions along with the software. If you need installation assistance, contact your on-site SAS System consultant, ask your company's help desk, or review the documentation that came with your SAS software.

Book Overview

This book contains 12 chapters and three appendices. The chapters are task-oriented and progress from simple tasks such as opening and closing files to more complicated tasks such as using SAS/CONNECT software to connect your PC to other computers. In addition, this book contains a main table of contents, individual chapter tables of contents, and an index. Use these tools to quickly find what you are looking for. If you encounter a term with which you are unfamiliar, check the "Glossary."

Graphics: This book contains many pictures of menus and screens. Because Windows is a highly-customizable operating system, your menus and screens may not look exactly like those shown in this book. However, you should still be able to use the graphics to orient yourself.

V7 Hilites: and **FasTip:** sections: Many sections begin with a V7 Hilites section that summarizes the relevant new features of Version 7 of the SAS System. (These features will also apply to subsequent releases of the SAS System.) FasTips give bare-bones information on performing a task. If you have performed the task before and need a quick reminder, check these first. FasTips do not appear in Chapters 8–12 and the appendices, as these chapters cover complex tasks that cannot be summarized in a few words.

Version 7 Highlights

If you have used Version 6 of the SAS System under Windows, you may want to use the following table to find the major changes to Version 7 of the SAS System. You should also scan the rest of the book for the V7 Hilites sections, which summarize both major and minor changes to Version 7 of the SAS System.

Feature	Section and/or Chapter
SAS Explorer interface	"Becoming Familiar with the SAS Explorer Window" Chapter 2
	"Customizing the SAS Explorer" Chapter 6
New Help interface	"Getting Help" Chapter 2
Results window—a graphical output manager	"Looking at the Output" Chapter 2
My Favorite Folders	"Using the My Favorite Folders Feature" Chapter 2
HTML-formatted output	"Generating Different Kinds of Output with the Output Delivery System (ODS)" Chapter 4
	"Printing HTML SAS Output" Chapter 5
	"Using the Output Delivery System (ODS) in Batch Mode" Chapter 9
New information about using the Forms subsystem	"Using SAS Print Forms" Chapter 5
New Preferences and tool customization dialog boxes	Chapter 6
New SAS data library and file management features	Chapter 7
New interface to SAS/AF BUILD windows	"Understanding Object Linking and Embedding (OLE)" Chapter 11
New SAS/CONNECT features	Chapter 12

Terminology Changes

This book uses new terminology for some SAS System concepts, as shown in the following table:

Old Term	New Term
libref	library reference
fileref	file shortcut
SAS data set	SAS table
variable	column
observation	row

Typographical Conventions

This book uses several typefaces to convey particular information. For example, menu items are in one typeface, while SAS code is in another. The following list gives the purpose of each typeface used:

Bold: Boldface is used to set off elements in windows and dialog boxes, such as menu choices and field names.

monospace: Monospace is used for SAS code and operating system commands.

italics: Italics are used in SAS code to indicate user-supplied values.

What You Should Read

If you are a neophyte Windows user, you should read Chapters 1 and 2 thoroughly. They give you a survival kit of information that you need to understand the rest of the book. If you have used the SAS System under Windows, but are new to Version 7, read the V7 Hilites section at the beginning of the sections that describe the tasks you want to do.

Further Reading

Because this book is a beginner's guide, it does not contain information on complex tasks, nor does it cover all features of either the SAS System or Windows. Check the following list for books you may want to have on hand for further research. The list is by subject.

SAS System Documentation: The following books are about the SAS System. This is not a complete list; check the SAS Institute *Publications Catalog* or the SAS Institute's World Wide

Web page (http://www.sas.com) for additional titles. Books with (SUP) after their titles are published through the SAS Institute's SAS User Publishing program.

Note

SAS Institute also provides online documentation, called SAS OnlineDoc.

Base SAS Software:

100 Essential SAS Software Concepts (SUP)

Getting Started with SAS Software, First Edition

Introducing the SAS System, Version 6, First Edition

Quick Start to Data Analysis with SAS (SUP)

SAS Applications Programming: A Gentle Introduction (SUP)

SAS Language and Procedures: Introduction, Version 6, First Edition

SAS Language and Procedures: Usage, First Edition

SAS Language and Procedures: Usage 2, First Edition

SAS Language: Reference, Version 6, First Edition

SAS Procedures Guide, Version 6, Third Edition

The Little SAS Book: A Primer, Second Edition (SUP)

SAS/AF Software:

Getting Started with the FRAME Entry: Developing Object-Oriented Applications, Second Edition

SAS Screen Control Language: Reference, Version 6, Second Edition

SAS Screen Control Language: Usage, Version 6, First Edition

SAS/AF Software: Usage and Reference, Version 6, First Edition

Other Useful SAS System Books:

Master Index to SAS System Documentation, Version 6, Fourth Edition

Microsoft Windows Environment: Changes and Enhancements to the SAS System, Release 6.11

SAS Companion for the Microsoft Windows Environment, Version 6, Second Edition

SAS Software: Abridged Reference, Version 6, First Edition

SAS Software: Changes and Enhancements, Release 6.10

SAS Software: Changes and Enhancements, Release 6.11

SAS Technical Report P-242, SAS Software: Changes and Enhancements, Release 6.08

SAS/CONNECT Software: Usage and Reference, Version 6, Second Edition

Note

You can find changes and enhancements documentation for Version 7 in the online help under the **What's New** topic, and also at the Institute's Web page (http://www.sas.com).

Microsoft Windows Documentation: The following books, listed in alphabetical order, are about Windows. Check your local bookstore and library for additional titles.

Windows 95 Books:

Alan Simpson's Easy Guide to Windows 95

Denny Goodman's Windows 95 Handbook

Field Guide to Microsoft Windows 95

Inside Windows 95

Introducing Microsoft Windows 95

Learn Windows 95 (a video)

Mastering Windows 95

PC Guide for Windows 95

The Complete Idiot's Guide to Windows 95

The Little Windows 95 Book

The Mother of All Windows 95 Books

The Ultimate Microsoft Windows 95 Book

Voodoo Windows 95: Mastery Tips and Masterful Tricks

Windows 95 for Dummies

Windows 95 Made Easy

Windows NT Books:

The ABCs of Windows NT Workstation 4

The Complete Idiot's Guide to Windows NT Workstation 4.0

Inside Windows NT

Keys to Learning Windows NT

Learn Windows NT in a Day

Microsoft Windows NT Step by Step

Teach Yourself... Windows NT

Using Windows NT Workstation 4.0

Windows NT: A Practical Guide

Windows NT Answer Book

Windows NT 4 for Dummies

Windows NT: Inside and Out

Windows NT Quick Reference Guide

Windows NT: The Complete Reference

Working with Windows NT

1 Learning to Do Windows

Making the Mental Adjustment

If you are used to a command-line-driven environment like OS/390 (formerly referred to as MVS) or CMS, the mouse- and menu-driven Windows environment can be overwhelming. Instead of typing a command, you now have to point and click or remember some obscure key sequence. Instead of an uncluttered screen, you now have to worry about scroll bars, icons, colors, and layered windows.

This chapter helps you make the mental adjustment to the Windows environment by defining some common terms, showing you how to take control of your mouse, showing you how to move and resize windows, and explaining how files are stored on the PC.

How Windows Works

Windows is an operating system, like VMS or CMS. But instead of issuing commands at a prompt, you work with files and start applications using a "graphical user interface" (GUI). This interface includes windows, dialog boxes, icons, buttons, and other items. Usually, you use a mouse to interact with the GUI, although you also use the keyboard.

Windows supports a "DOS mode," where you can run older, DOS-based applications from the DOS prompt. However, Windows 95 and Windows NT are not themselves DOS-based applications.

To work with applications under Windows, you use the Windows desktop, and in particular, the **Start** button. The **Start** button is a Windows component that organizes all your Windows applications into groups and makes interacting with the operating system easier. Some applications, such as Microsoft Paint and Microsoft Write, come with Windows; other applications you install separately—such as the SAS System.

Note

It is possible to use alternatives to the Windows desktop and even to use a version of the Windows 3.1 Program Manager. However, this book assumes that you are using the standard Windows desktop.

Unlike many operating systems, Windows can do several things at once. For example, in DOS, if you submitted a command, you had to wait for that command to finish before you could do anything else. With Windows, you can submit a command, and that command operates in the background—enabling you to start another process.

In particular, you can have several "instances" of a program open at once. Therefore, you can start multiple SAS sessions, all running at the same time.

Note

Only the first SAS session started uses the SASUSER.PROFILE catalog. Subsequent sessions use a temporary profile catalog called WORK.PROFILE.

Terms You Should Know

Every operating system has its own jargon, and Windows is no exception. If you have used a different windowing environment, such as X Windows under UNIX, some of the terms are familiar. But you should scan this section anyway, to see if there are discrepancies between how you understand a term and how this book uses it.

The Glossary at the end of this book provides a more complete list of terms used with the SAS System for Windows. The following alphabetical list gives you a head start so that you can read this chapter without referring to the Glossary constantly.

active window: the application or part of an application that is ready to accept input.

application: a program with its attendant windows. Examples include the SAS System, Microsoft Word, and Netscape.

click: to press a mouse button once. Unless otherwise stated, click means to press the left mouse button.

Clipboard: a Windows component that is like an online pegboard—a place to store something until you need it again. Typically, the Clipboard is used to store text and graphics that you want to copy somewhere else.

close: to shut down an individual window or an entire application.

dialog box: a type of window that solicits information from you. Usually, you must supply this information before you can continue using an application.

double-click: to quickly press a mouse button twice in a row (usually the left mouse button).

desktop: your screen, where all applications appear.

icon: a pictorial representation of something, such as a window or file.

mouse: the hand-held device you use to select and manipulate applications and text. The mouse activates the mouse pointer on the screen.

point: to move the mouse pointer over an item on the screen, such as a menu choice, a word, or an icon.

popup menu: a context-sensitive menu that appears when you click the right mouse button.

program group: a collection of applications available from the **Programs** selection of the **Start** button menu. Examples of program groups include **Accessories** and **The SAS System**.

right-click: to press the right mouse button once. Usually, right-clicking displays a context-sensitive menu called a popup menu.

Start button: the button in the lower-left corner of the screen labeled "Start". Clicking on this button enables you to launch applications, alter configuration settings, access Windows help files, and perform other tasks.

Taskbar: a list of all open applications, located by default across the bottom of the Windows desktop.

Becoming Familiar with the Windows Desktop

When you start Windows, the Windows desktop appears. That may be all that happens, or other applications may start, depending on how your system is configured. The Windows desktop keeps a list of all open applications. This list is displayed across the bottom of the screen and is called the Taskbar. The active application's name is highlighted; to move to a different application, click on the application's name in the Taskbar.

Figure 1.1 shows a sample Windows desktop. The Taskbar indicates that two applications are open: SAS and Microsoft Word. Your desktop may look slightly different than the one in Figure 1.1.

Figure 1.1   Sample Windows Desktop with Taskbar

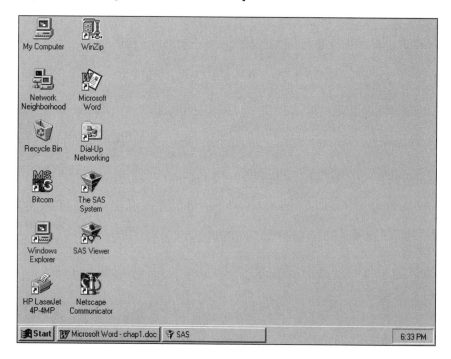

Besides the Taskbar, two more useful components of the Windows desktop are the **Start** button and the Recycle Bin.

- The **Start** button is located in the lower-left corner of the Windows desktop. You use it to start applications and manage your Windows session. See "Starting Applications" later in this chapter.

- The Recycle Bin is a temporary storage area for files deleted (when you use the Windows Explorer to delete them). See "Restoring Deleted Files" in Appendix 3 for more information.

Windows Geography

The applications and windows you see as you work with Windows have many things in common. This section familiarizes you with the "lay of the land" under Windows. Figure 1.2 shows some of the standard window elements.

Figure 1.2 Standard Window Elements

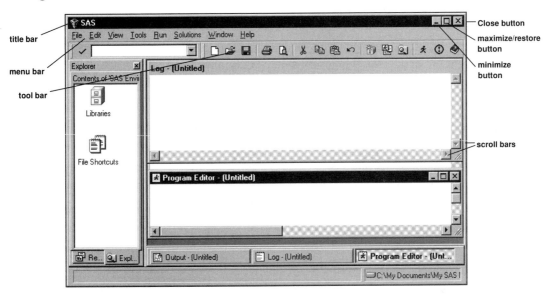

A brief description of each element in Figure 1.2 follows; "Getting to Know the SAS System Interface" in Chapter 2 presents more details on these and other window elements specific to the SAS System.

Title Bar: Each window has a title bar that tells the name of the window. In this case, the title bar at the top tells you the application is SAS. Each individual window also has a title bar, such as the Log window and the Program Editor window. As well as providing the title of the application, the title bar is also the "handle" for moving windows, as discussed later in this chapter.

Menu Bar: If you are used to nonwindowing environments, you are familiar with giving operating system commands. In Windows, you often use the menu bar to issue these commands. For example, instead of typing "save example1.sas" on a command line, you click on **File**, then on **Save**. While this may seem awkward at first, it does provide the advantage of not having to remember command syntax.

Use the following guides as you browse the menus:

- If a menu choice has an arrow after it, that means there is another layer of choices.

- If a menu choice has an ellipsis after it, that means clicking on it opens a dialog box.

- If there is no symbol after the menu choice, clicking on that choice executes a command, such as SAVE.

- Shortcut keys are listed to the right of menu choices. Instead of using the menus, you can press the shortcut keys to achieve the same result. For example, CTRL-S is the shortcut key for SAVE.

Tool Bar: Another method of issuing commands under Windows is to use the graphical tool bar. For example, to save a file in the SAS System, click on the icon that looks like a computer disk. Most applications, including the SAS System, allow you to define your own tools; this enables you to customize your environment and work efficiently.

Scroll Bars: Most windows provide both horizontal and vertical scroll bars. These enable you to move left, right, up, and down in the window. Clicking on the up arrow moves the view up, clicking on the down arrow moves the view down. Similarly, clicking on the left arrow moves the view left, and clicking on the right arrow moves the view right. To move larger distances, click in the scroll bar area instead of on the arrows. "Scrolling" in Chapter 3 provides more detailed information on using scroll bars.

Minimize Button: Click on the minimize button (the left-most of the three buttons in the top-right corner of a window) to cause the window to shrink to an icon. If you minimize an entire application, the window disappears from the desktop; to restore the application, click on its name in the Taskbar. Typically, only the active window shows the minimize button.

Maximize/Restore Button: The middle button in the top-right corner of the window does double duty. If it appears as a single box (as it is in Figure 1.2), clicking on it causes the window to take up the whole screen (that is, maximize). If it appears as two layered boxes, clicking on it causes the window to restore to the size it was before it was maximized. Typically, only the active window shows the maximize button.

Close Button: The Close button is the right-most button in the top-right corner of a window, and is an X. Clicking on it closes the application or window. Typically, only the active window shows the Close button.

Taking Control of Your Mouse

While using Windows with only a keyboard is possible, it is more efficient to use a mouse also. But often, people unfamiliar with the mouse are frustrated by having the pointer move too quickly, not being able to double-click properly, and other problems caused by lack of practice. However, using the mouse does not have to be a rat race! Windows provides a way to slow the mouse down, adjust the double-click rate, and in general let you take control of your mouse.

Using the Mouse Buttons: Most mice have two or three buttons. The left button is used to "click" on things—icons, filenames, options, and so on. The right mouse button is reserved for special tasks, such as opening popup menus. If your mouse has a middle button, you can pretty much ignore it, although some software applications (including the SAS System) let you associate commands with the middle mouse button. Figure 1.3 shows the standard, right-handed definition of the mouse buttons.

Note

If your mouse is a left-handed mouse, the left and right buttons are switched. The "left button" is always the button under your index finger.

Figure 1.3 Mouse Button Diagram

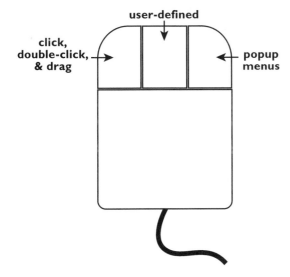

Adjusting How Your Mouse Works: To adjust how your mouse works, follow these steps:

1. Click on the **Start** button, then on **Settings**. When the second-level menu appears, click on **Control Panel**.

2. When the Control Panel appears, double-click on the **Mouse** icon. The Mouse Properties dialog box opens. Figure 1.4 shows a sample Mouse Properties dialog box.

Figure 1.4 Sample Mouse Properties Dialog Box

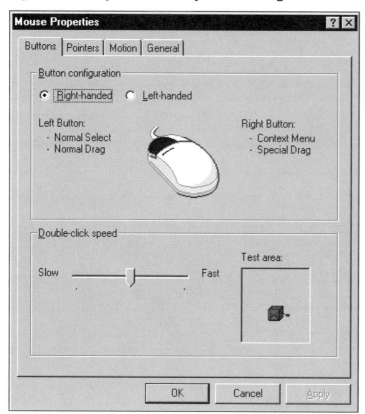

3. There are four tabs in the Mouse Properties dialog box. The top tab is **Buttons**. On this tab, you can adjust the mouse's double-click speed and the left- or right-handed configuration of your mouse.

4. New Windows users usually prefer a slower double-click speed. In the **Double-click speed** area, place your mouse pointer over the slider, hold the left mouse button down, and drag the mouse pointer so that the slider moves to the left (toward **Slow**). Release the mouse pointer and double-click on the jack-in-the-box icon in the **Test** area to see if you like the new speed. If your double-click is successful, the icon shows a jack-in-the-box pop out. Double-clicking again closes the jack-in-the-box.

5. If you are left-handed, click next to **Left-handed** in the **Button configuration** area. The text next to the mouse explains what function each mouse button has—if you choose this option, the button under your left index finger (originally the "right" mouse button) becomes the "left" mouse button and vice versa.

6. To slow your mouse down so that you can follow it more easily with your eyes, click on the **Motion** tab at the top of the Mouse Properties dialog box. In the **Pointer speed** area, place your mouse pointer over the slider, hold the left mouse button down, and drag the mouse pointer so that the slider moves to the left (toward **Slow**). Release the mouse pointer; now move the mouse pointer, to see if you like the new speed.

7. To make the mouse pointer easier to find on the screen when you move the mouse, you may want to use "pointer trails." To enable this feature, click on **Show pointer trails** in the **Pointer trail** area. Now when you move your mouse pointer, the mouse leaves a brief trail of pointers behind.

Depending on your mouse driver (the software that controls your mouse), you may also see other options, such as changing the mouse pointer to a larger size.

When you are happy with your selections, click on **OK**. This closes the Mouse Properties dialog box. To close the Control Panel, click on **File** in the Control Panel menu, then click on **Close**.

As you become more adept with your mouse, return to the Mouse Properties dialog box and adjust the settings again to fit your new skill level.

Using Your Mouse to Communicate with Applications: Your mouse is the primary method of communicating with Windows applications, although you also use function keys and keyboard sequences. You need to master several skills with the mouse:

Pointing	Pointing involves moving the mouse pointer until it is directly on top of something, such as an icon or a menu choice. In some cases, pointing causes Windows to take an action. For example, in the **Start** button menu, simply pointing (without clicking) to a menu item opens the submenu.
Clicking	Clicking involves pressing and releasing the left mouse button once. Usually, you click on something to select (that is, highlight) it.
Right-clicking	Right-clicking involves pressing and releasing the right mouse button once. Usually, you right-click on something to display a context-sensitive menu.
Double-clicking	Double-clicking involves pressing the mouse button twice in rapid succession. Usually, you double-click on something to activate it (such as starting an application from an icon).
Dragging	Dragging involves holding the mouse button down while you move the mouse around. Usually, you drag an object to move it (such as moving window borders or text in a text editor).

Practice Using Your Mouse: One way to practice using your mouse is to use the tutorial that comes with Windows. To access this tutorial, click on the **Start** button, then click on **Help** in the **Start** button menu. In the window that appears, double-click on **Tour: Ten minutes to using Windows**. You must have your Windows CD-ROM to use this tutorial.

Learning the Basic Survival Kit

There are several things you should know before you start using Windows extensively. For example, how do you start applications? When you are done with them, how do you close them? What if you want to use a new application but do not want to close the others? Learning the answers to these and a few other questions helps you work more efficiently under Windows.

Starting Applications: An easy way to start an application is by clicking on its name in the **Programs** menu and submenus, accessed by clicking on the **Start** button.

When you click on the **Start** button, a menu appears, as shown in Figure 1.5.

Figure 1.5 Start Button Menu

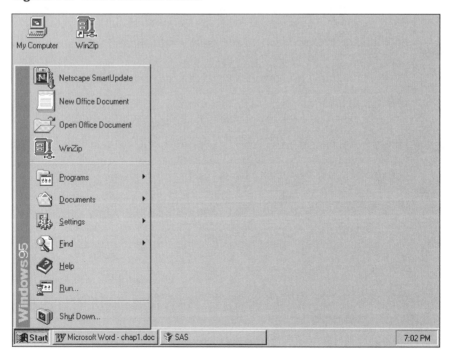

To start an application, such as the SAS System, click on the **Programs** item in the **Start** button menu. A second menu appears, as shown in Figure 1.6.

Figure 1.6 Programs Menu from the Start Button

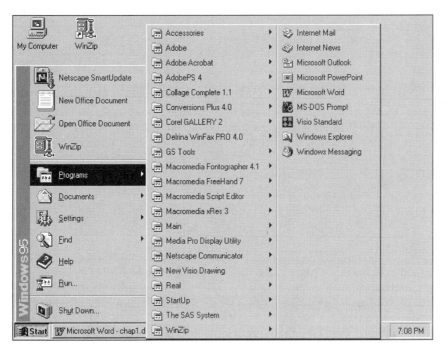

This menu shows the program groups available on your system, such as **Accessories** and **StartUp**.

- **Accessories** contains handy applications supplied by Microsoft and installed with Windows. Example accessories include Paint (a drawing program) and WordPad (a text editor).

- **StartUp** contains applications you want to start automatically every time you start Windows.

Your desktop may show other groups, such as **The SAS System** and **Microsoft Office**, depending on what software is installed on your PC.

Note

> Most of the time, merely placing the mouse pointer over the text is sufficient to select it in a menu, but not always. And clicking doesn't hurt anything. Therefore, in many places, this book says "click on **Programs**" or gives other similar instructions.

Program groups in the **Programs** menu that are followed by a right arrow contain subgroups. Clicking on the main group displays the subgroup. Take a moment to investigate all program groups on your desktop, to see what applications are available to you. To close the **Programs** menu system without starting an application, click outside of the menus.

 Closing Applications: The easiest way to close applications is to click on the Close button. This is the X in the upper-right corner of an application's main window. Sometimes, you also have to confirm that you want to exit the application. (For example, by default the SAS System prompts you with the question "Are you sure you really want to terminate the SAS session?")

Two other methods of closing an application include

- clicking on the **File** choice in the application's menu bar and then clicking on **Exit** or **Close**

- right-clicking on the application's name in the Taskbar and clicking on **Close**.

Managing Several Open Applications at Once: One of the nice things about Windows is that you can use several applications at the same time. But you have only one screen, so the open windows are layered. The window that is "on top" is usually the active window. To make another window active, you must somehow get to it.

Suppose you have started the SAS System, and now you want to open Microsoft Word, without ending your SAS session. Follow these steps to start Word:

1. Click on the **Start** button.

2. Click on **Programs** in the **Start** button menu, then on **Microsoft Office**. When the third-level menu appears, click on **Microsoft Word**. (Your menu path to the Microsoft Word program may be somewhat different, depending on how Word was installed.)

Now two applications are open at once: the SAS System and Word.

Here are some ways you can return to your SAS session:

- click on **SAS** on the Taskbar.

- press ALT-ESC to toggle through all open applications.

Using Dialog Boxes: To communicate with most Windows applications, you must use dialog boxes. These are interactive ways to give commands and information to an application. When you adjusted your mouse settings, you were using a dialog box. Dialog boxes have many features in common, such as the following:

- Clicking on **OK** or **Close** applies your changes and closes the dialog box.

- Clicking on **Cancel** closes the dialog box without having any other effect.

- Sometimes you can type a value into a field—this is called a text-entry field.

- If there are several choices for a field value, clicking on a down arrow displays a list of choices—click on one of the choices to change the field value. This is called a drop-down list box.

- Other times, the entire list of choices is displayed in a list box; use the scroll bars to navigate the list. Click on a choice to select it.

- If there are options that can be on or off, clicking in the box or button by the option toggles its value. If a box has an 'x' in it, or if a round button is filled in, the option is on. The difference between check boxes (square boxes) and radio buttons (round buttons) is as follows:

  - you can choose several options in a list of check boxes

  - options with radio buttons are mutually exclusive.

- Many dialog boxes offer a context-sensitive help button near the upper-right corner of the dialog box. Clicking on this button changes the mouse pointer to an arrow with a question mark beside it. Now click on the part of the dialog box you want more information on. The help information is displayed in a window. Click again anywhere to close the instructions. Occasionally, instead of the context-sensitive help button, you may see a button labeled **Help**.

- In dialog boxes that list files, you may see four useful icons. Click on the icon to activate it.

  - 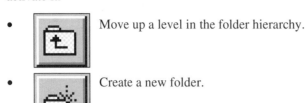 Move up a level in the folder hierarchy.

  - Create a new folder.

  - List folders and files with no details.

  - List folders and files with details such as file description, creation date, and so on.

Figure 1.7 shows an example dialog box that displays many of these features.

Figure 1.8 shows another dialog box with more features.

Figure 1.7 Standard Dialog Box Features

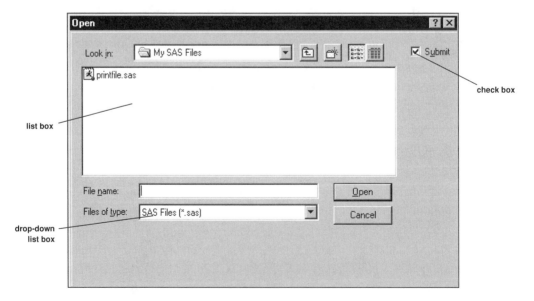

Figure 1.8 More Standard Dialog Box Features

Controlling How Programs Work: The icons you see on the desktop are not magic. They are pictorial representations of operating system commands and command options. When you install an application such as the SAS System, the installation utility adds the icon to the appropriate program group in the **Programs** menu and associates certain commands and options with the icon. These commands control the location of the program's executable file (such as SAS.EXE) and other aspects of running the program. This collection of commands constitutes the application's "properties."

You can change an application's properties by using the Properties dialog box. "Altering the Properties of the SAS System Icon" in Chapter 8 gives some examples of how to change SAS System properties.

Moving and Resizing Windows: Sometimes the default size or position of a window is not satisfactory. You've already learned about the minimize and maximize buttons, but you can also move windows or cause them to shrink and grow.

To move a window, place the mouse pointer in the title bar of the window. Now hold the mouse button down. Drag the mouse, and the entire window follows it. Release the mouse button when the window is where you want it.

To resize the window, place the mouse pointer on the edge of the window. The pointer turns into a horizontal, vertical, or diagonal double-headed arrow (depending on whether the mouse pointer is positioned on a side, the top or bottom, or a corner of the window, respectively). Hold the mouse button down and drag the mouse—the window edge follows the pointer—until the window is the size you want. Resize a window in both the vertical and horizontal directions at once by placing the mouse pointer over a corner of the window. In this case, the pointer turns into a diagonal double-headed arrow.

To practice resizing windows, double-click on the Recycle Bin icon on the Windows desktop. Now make the Recycle Bin window narrow, then tall, then back to its original size. Close the Recycle Bin by clicking on its Close button.

Note

You cannot resize a maximized window except to minimize it.

Shutting Down Windows: You can choose to leave Windows running all the time, even when you are away from your desk. Or, you may want to turn your computer off. Never turn off your computer without properly shutting down Windows.

To shut down Windows, click on the **Start** button, then click on **Shut Down** (at the bottom of the **Start** button menu). A dialog box appears, asking what type of shut-down you want to use. Click on **Shut down the computer?** and press Enter. Windows shuts down, and the screen displays a message that it is now safe to turn your computer off.

Handy Keyboard Shortcuts

Table 1.1 provides a list of handy keyboard shortcuts for performing tasks in the Windows environment. Refer to this table as you read the rest of the book—if you do not want to use the mouse for a task, use the keyboard shortcut listed in the table.

Table 1.1 Keyboard Shortcuts

Keyboard Shortcut	Action
ALT-Enter	Opens the Properties dialog box for an icon
CTRL-ESC	Opens the Start button menu
ALT-ESC	Toggles through all open applications
ALT-TAB	Toggles between the two last-used applications
TAB	Moves the cursor from field to field in dialog boxes
SHIFT-TAB	Moves the cursor backward through fields in dialog boxes
Backspace	In file list windows, such as the SAS Explorer, Windows Explorer, or Open dialog boxes, moves you up one level in the file hierarchy

The menus also provide a type of keyboard shortcut, called hotkeys. These are the underlined letters you see in each of the menu choices. If the menu is open, pressing the hotkey is equivalent to clicking on a menu choice.

To open a menu without using the mouse, press the ALT key. This highlights the first item in the menu bar. Once the highlight is in the menu bar, use your arrow keys to move to the menu item you want, and press Enter to execute the command. Or, type the letter that is underlined in the menu.

Note

The hotkey is not always the first letter of the menu choice.

Understanding How Files Are Stored and Named

V7 Hilites: SASUSER and WORK subfolders are no longer created. By default, the SASUSER data library corresponds to C:\My Documents\My SAS Files, and the WORK data library corresponds to C:\DOS\Temp\Temporary SAS Files.

The SAS configuration file is no longer named CONFIG.SAS – the new name is SASV7.CFG.

SAS files have new long file extensions (no longer limited to three characters).

If you are coming from a UNIX or VMS background, you are familiar with the hierarchical structure of folders, subfolders, and files under Windows. But if you are familiar with OS/390, CMS, or VSE, you may be used to a different file structure. It is important to understand how Windows files are stored and named before you begin to use SAS software to create and manage files.

Note

The terms folder and directory are synonymous.

Understanding the Windows File Structure: Under Windows, individual files have a filename and an extension. Think of a file as a collection of information, where the filename describes the information and the extension describes the format of the information. For example, MEMO.TXT is a memo and is in plain ASCII text format. HOUSE.TIF is a picture of a house in the TIFF bitmap format.

Windows supports long filenames—that is, you can use a total of 255 characters for the filename. In addition, filenames and extensions can contain spaces, quotation marks, and other characters not allowed in filenames under many other operating systems.

Examples of valid filenames are CONFIG.SYS, DECEMBER'S REPORT.TXT and JOAN & TOM.DOC. The following characters are not allowed in filenames: / \ : ; ? " < > | *.

Understanding Truncated Filenames: If you intend to use files under Windows and other operating systems that do not support long filenames, be aware that the long filename may be truncated to eight characters, replacing certain characters (such as commas and spaces) with underscores (_) and extra characters with a tilde (~) and a numeral. Table 1.2 shows four examples of long and truncated filenames (assuming the files are stored in the same folder). For example, if you issue the DIR command in a DOS session, the files will be listed with their truncated names.

Table 1.2 Long and Truncated Filenames

Long Name	Truncated Name
DECEMBER'S REPORT.TXT	DECEMB~1.TXT
DECEMBER'S BILLS.TXT	DECEMB~2.TXT
THAT'S ALL.TXT	THAT'S~1.TXT
X,Y.TXT	X_Y~1.TXT

The last file, X,Y.TXT, has the ~1 added, even though the filename is short. This is because of the substitution of the underscore for the comma.

Note

> Windows supports long file extensions (that is, they are not limited to three characters). However, when a filename is truncated, the long file extension is truncated to the first three characters.

Understanding Files and Folders: Files are grouped together in folders. (In previous versions of Windows and DOS, the term directory was used. Directory and folder are synonymous.) Folders can contain subfolders as well as files. For example, you might have a folder called BILLS, and within that folder you have some miscellaneous files along with two subfolders, PAID and OVERDUE. In turn, these subfolders contain files for each individual bill.

Your root folder is the top-level folder that contains all other subfolders and files. Usually, this is called C:\ and is the default folder when you boot your PC. The C:\ folder can contain many subfolders, which can contain other subfolders, and so on.

Figure 1.9 shows a sample folder hierarchy.

Figure 1.9 Sample Folder Hierarchy

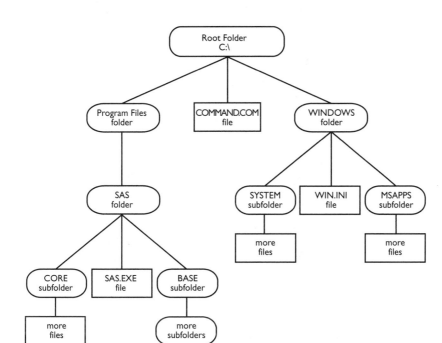

Understanding Drives: Another concept you need to understand is drive. While the root folder is referred to as C:\, the drive is referred to as C:. Your computer may have several drives—the hard drive might be C:, the 3 1/2" floppy drive might be A:, and if you have a CD-ROM drive, it might be designated D:. If you are on a network, you probably have access to many drives. To find out how your system is organized, use the Windows Explorer, which is discussed later in this chapter.

Understanding Common File Extensions: Some file extensions are associated with particular applications. For example, files with an extension of .SAS are SAS programs, while files with a .DOC extension are usually Word files. Table 1.3 gives some common file extensions.

Table 1.3 Common File Extensions

Text Files		SAS Files	
Extension	**File Type**	**Extension**	**File Type**
SAS	SAS code	SAS7BDAT	SAS table
DAT	raw data files	SAS7BNDX	SAS data file index
TXT	ASCII text files	SAS7BCAT	SAS catalog
LST	SAS output	SAS7BPGM	SAS stored program
LOG	SAS log files	SAS7BVEW	SAS data view
		SAS7BACS	SAS access descriptor

Using Wildcard Characters: Like most operating systems, Windows accepts wildcard characters in filenames when you are performing file maintenance (such as deleting, moving, or searching). Table 1.4 lists the wildcard characters Windows accepts.

Table 1.4 Wildcard Characters

Character	Meaning
*	replaces any number of characters
?	replaces a single character

To show how these wildcard characters work, here are a few examples:

PROG*.SAS   finds PROG1.SAS and PROGRAM2.SAS

PROG?B.SAS   finds PROG1B.SAS but not PROG11B.SAS

REVENUE.*   finds REVENUE.SAS and REVENUE.DAT

Understanding How SAS Files Are Stored under Windows: As a SAS user, you already know about the various types of SAS files and that these files are stored in SAS data libraries. Under Windows, the concept of a SAS data library is loosely analogous to that of a folder, with the addition of the concept of SAS engines. An example will help illustrate this.

Suppose you have two folders, C:\REPORTS and C:\INCOME. In the REPORTS folder, there are some Version 7 SAS tables. In the INCOME folder, you also have Version 7 SAS tables but also some Version 6 SAS tables. To access these three categories of tables, you would set up three SAS data libraries. Two of the data libraries would point to the INCOME folder, but each of these libraries would contain only those tables accessed by the appropriate SAS engine.

Note

In this book, "table" is used in place of "data set," and "row" and "column" replace "observation" and "variable."

You can also concatenate several folders into one SAS data library. See Chapter 7 for more information on managing SAS data libraries.

Knowing the Important Files and Folders: Certain files, folders, and subfolders are important to you as a SAS software user. Table 1.5 gives some of these and briefly describes their purpose.

Table I.5 Important SAS Files and Folders

Default Filename	Purpose
SAS.EXE	is the executable program that runs the SAS System.
SASV7.CFG	contains the configuration options for your SAS session.
AUTOEXEC.SAS	contains start-up statements you want to execute when you begin a SAS session.
C:\My Documents\My SAS Files subfolder	corresponds to your SASUSER SAS data library, and contains your SAS profile catalogs, key definitions, tool definitions, and so on.
C:\DOS\Temp\SAS Temporary Files subfolder	contains your WORK SAS data library. The WORK library for a SAS session is created as a subfolder of the C:\DOS\TEMP\SAS Temporary Files folder, in the form TD#####.

Note

The pathnames for the SASUSER and WORK SAS data libraries in Table 1.5 are the default locations; these can be changed during SAS installation.

Using Filenames in SAS Statements and Commands: When you type the name of folders, subfolders, and files in SAS statements and commands, such as on the Command bar or in dialog boxes, separate the folder, subfolder, and filename with a backslash. For example, the following INCLUDE command references a file named MEDICALREPORT.DAT in a folder called MYDATA, which is a subfolder of the root folder on the C: drive:

```
INCLUDE 'C:\MYDATA\MEDICALREPORT.DAT'
```

This is called the full pathname for the file, which states explicitly where the file is stored. When in doubt, specify the full pathname for files; while there are rules for how the folder and file extension default, it is always safe to specify the full pathname.

Defining File Shortcuts and Library References: One of the most common uses of the full pathname is when you use the FILENAME and LIBNAME statements to define file shortcuts (called filerefs in Version 6 of the SAS System) and library references (called librefs in Version 6 of the SAS System) in your SAS programs. Here is an example of each of these statements, using the full pathname for the file or folder:

```
filename misc 'c:\misc\qtr1.dat';
libname inv 'c:\sas\invoices';
```

Note

> If the filename contains spaces or other punctuation such as a single quotation mark, use double quotation marks in SAS statements such as FILENAME and LIBNAME.

Testing Your Survival Kit

Now that you understand a little bit about how Windows works, you are ready to see if you can "do Windows." Try the next chapter, which walks you through most of the fundamental tasks involved in using base SAS software. After you've done the first two or three exercises, you'll see that "doing Windows" is not that hard after all. And even if you never like Windows, at least you will not feel like you're looking through frosted glass while you work.

Performing the Basic SAS® Software Tasks under Windows

Getting Ready for the Tutorial

Because of the tutorial nature of this chapter, it does not show you every aspect of every task—there are many ways to edit a file, for example; this chapter shows only a few techniques. But if you master the techniques in this chapter, you can then learn new techniques as you go along, using the online help, other manuals, and so on.

Now that you understand Windows' file-naming conventions, can double-click, and can open and close applications, you are ready to apply these skills to using the SAS System. Most of this chapter is a tutorial. You should try each exercise so that you get a feel for how the SAS System works under Windows.

The following sections are not tutorial, but they do provide important information. If you are new to Version 7 of the SAS System for Windows, you should read these sections.

- "Getting to Know the SAS System Interface"

- "Getting Help"

- "Becoming Familiar with the SAS Explorer Window"

- "Using the My Favorite Folders Feature"

Before you begin the exercises in this chapter, you should close Windows and bring it up again, so that you have a "pristine" environment to work in. (For more information on closing Windows, see "Shutting Down Windows" in Chapter 1.)

Starting Your SAS Session

FasTip: Click on the **Start** button. Click on **Programs**, then on **The SAS System**. Now click on **The SAS System for Windows V7**.

To start the SAS System, click on the **Start** button, then on **Programs**, then on **The SAS System**. Now click on **The SAS System for Windows V7**. Figure 2.1 shows a sample **Start** menu, with the pointer over **The SAS System for Windows V7**. Your display should look similar to this before you start this exercise. (Your display may not be identical to Figure 2.1 because you may have different software installed.)

Figure 2.1 Starting the SAS System

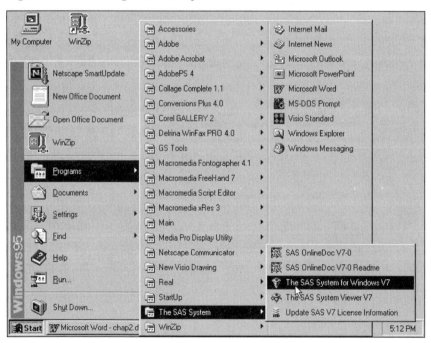

The SAS System logo appears, followed by the Log, Program Editor, and SAS Explorer windows. Figure 2.2 shows how these SAS windows look. Typically, there are some notes in the Log window that state your site number, version number, and other site-specific information.

Figure 2.2 Initial SAS Windows after Start-up

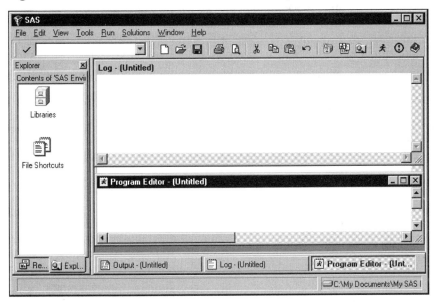

While you can proceed directly with the rest of the tutorial, starting with "Accessing the SAS Sample Library," consider reading the next two sections before proceeding.

Note

Under Windows 95 and Windows NT, you can have more than one SAS session running at once. The number of sessions is limited only by the amount of RAM (random-access memory) your computer has.

Getting to Know the SAS System Interface

V7 Hilites: SAS Explorer and Results windows offer a graphical interface to the SAS System.

Most windows have new menus and tools.

The Command bar is now resizeable.

There is a Window Bar at the bottom of the SAS workspace, that works like the Windows Taskbar.

While the basic geography of the SAS System, such as the Log, Program Editor, and Output windows, is the same across operating systems, you need to know some windowing terminology to fully understand the SAS System for Windows. Here is a brief orientation session.

Note

Many aspects of the appearance and behavior of the SAS System are configurable. The discussion that follows assumes that you are using the defaults for the various features. If you are using someone else's system, and it has been configured to differ from the defaults, ask the machine's owner to reset the features to the default behavior before you read the rest of this chapter.

SAS Workspace: The large window that has "SAS" across the top and contains all open SAS windows is called the SAS workspace. The SAS workspace is like a container for your SAS session—in general, everything you do in your SAS session—opening new windows, interacting with dialog boxes, and so on—occurs inside the SAS workspace.

Title Bar: Across the top of the SAS workspace is the title bar. Every window inside the SAS workspace also has a title bar.

Scroll Bars: Down the right side of a window is a scroll bar that enables you to move up and down in the windows. The scroll bar at the bottom of a window lets you move left and right across the screen.

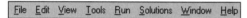

Menu Bar: Just under the title bar is the SAS System main menu. Here you find commands to open and save files, print, submit code, change system options, invoke other parts of the SAS System, and ask for help.

Command Bar: Under the menu bar, on the left, is a white box—this is the Command bar, and it is where you type SAS commands. If you are coming from OS/390 or CMS, use the Command bar like the command line in those operating systems. To activate the Command bar, point to it with the mouse and click. To return to a SAS window, click in the window. (Alternatively, you can press F11 to move the cursor to the Command bar; press ESC to return the cursor to the active SAS window.)

The Command bar remembers the commands that you have issued in your SAS session and keeps a list of them. If you want to repeat a command, click on the down arrow by the Command bar to display a reverse order list of recently issued commands. Click on the command you want. This copies the command to the Command bar. Once the Command bar contains the command you want to issue, click on the check mark to the left of the Command bar to execute the command, or press Enter. The command list is saved from one SAS session to the next.

As you type in the Command bar, the SAS System uses an "auto complete" feature to guess what you are going to type, based on commands you have already entered. If the command that appears in the Command bar after you type a few letters is correct, simply press Enter.

You can resize the Command bar by placing the mouse pointer over the vertical double-bar that appears to the right of the Command bar (the pointer turns into a double-headed arrow). Drag this bar to the left, making the Command bar smaller. You may need to do this in order to see all the tools on the tool bar.

See "Customizing the Tool Bar and Command Bar" in Chapter 6 for information on customizing the Command bar.

Tool Bar: To the right of the Command bar is the tool bar. This is a graphical menu, where clicking on an icon executes a command (such as save, print, or help). Each window in the SAS System has its own tool set (except for the Log, Program Editor, and Output windows, which all use the same tools). The tool bar icons change when you make a new window active.

By default, there are 15 tools on the tool bar for the Program Editor window—if you do not see all 15, try resizing the Command bar to leave more room for tools, as described previously.

See "Customizing the Tool Bar and Command Bar" in Chapter 6 for information on customizing the tool bar.

Minimize and Maximize/Restore Buttons: There are three buttons in the upper-right corner of the SAS workspace and the active SAS window. The left-most and middle buttons control the size of the window:

- The left-most button is the minimize button. Click on this to shrink the window to an icon. To get the window back, click on **Window** in the SAS System main menu, then click on the name of the minimized window.

- The middle button is the maximize/restore button. It's action depends on the button's shape:

  - When the button is a single window icon, clicking on this button makes the window take up the whole display—that is, it maximizes the window.

  - When a window is maximized, the maximize button becomes the restore button. In this case, the button shows two layered windows. Clicking on the restore button makes the window return to its original size.

 Close Button: The Close button is the X icon in the upper-right corner of an application's workspace. Not only does the SAS workspace have a Close button, but so does the active SAS window. Click on the Close button to close a window.

Context-Sensitive Menus: Notice that the Log and Program Editor windows do not have individual menu bars. That is because the selections available in the main menu change, depending on which window is active. If you click in the Log window, its title bar is highlighted. It is now the active window. If you click on **Edit** in the main menu, you see that, for example, **Undo** is grayed out—this is not a valid command in the Log window. But if you click in the Program Editor window and then look at the **Edit** menu, **Undo** is available.

Popup Menus: Another way to see the menus for a particular window is to right-click in the window. The menu that appears is called a popup menu. For example, Figure 2.3 shows the first layer of the popup menu for the Log window.

Figure 2.3 Popup Menu for the Log Window

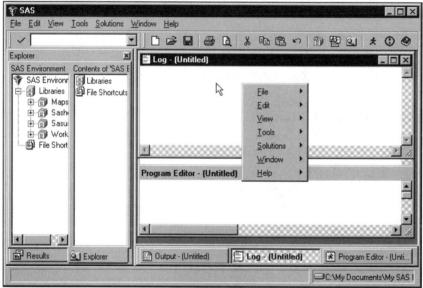

If you activate a menu by mistake, click outside the menu, anywhere in the SAS workspace. This closes the menu; now try again.

Window Bar: A quick way to access open SAS windows, the Window Bar (located across the bottom of the SAS workspace) works like the Taskbar on the Windows desktop. Click on the window's name in the Window Bar to jump to that window.

Docking Area: By default, the Results and SAS Explorer windows are "docked" (that is, anchored) in the left side of the SAS workspace and cannot be moved to other places in the workspace. See "Looking at the Output" and "Becoming Familiar with the SAS Explorer" later in this chapter for descriptions of the Results and SAS Explorer windows, respectively. The callout in Figure 2.4 shows the docking area.

Figure 2.4 Docking Area

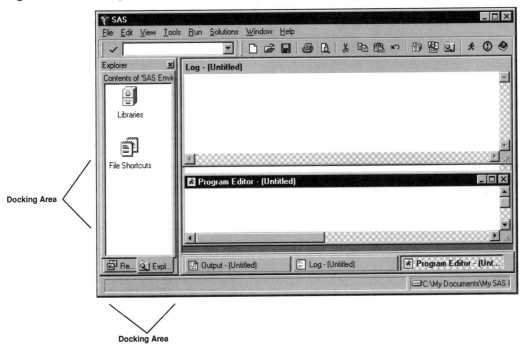

Practice Using the SAS Menus: Use the following exercise to practice using the menus:

1. Make the Program Editor window active by clicking anywhere within it.

2. Click on **Window** in the SAS System main menu.

3. Click on **Output**. This takes you to the Output window.

4. Click the right mouse button in the Output window. The popup menu appears.

5. Click on **Window**, then on **Program Editor**. Now both the Output and Program Editor windows are visible.

6. To return to the default appearance, right-click in the Program Editor window, click on **Window**, then on **Log**.

Other SAS System Workspace Features: At the bottom of the SAS workspace are some useful items:

- In the lower-left corner is a status bar, which displays brief help messages about various tools and the results of SAS commands.

- If you place your mouse pointer over a tool in the tool bar and wait a bit, a "screen tip" appears below the tool that tells you what the tool does.

- In the lower-right corner is a folder icon with a folder name after it. This icon tells you which folder the SAS System is using as its working folder. "Changing the SAS Working Folder" in Chapter 3 provides more information.

Getting Help

V7 Hilites: The **Using This Window** feature provides help on the active window (for most windows).

New tutorials offer help in learning about SAS for Windows.

World Wide Web connection gives you access to even more help.

FasTip: Click on the Help icon on the SAS tool bar (accesses the **Using This Window** feature).

While this book only scratches the surface of using the SAS System for Windows, all the information you could possibly want is at your fingertips—or at least at your mouse pointer. So, before continuing with the tutorial, read this section to familiarize yourself with the SAS Help system.

The fastest way to obtain help while using the SAS System is to click on the Help icon on the SAS tool bar. This opens a window that provides information about the active window. Or, access more detailed help by using the **Help** menu.

Also, many dialog boxes offer context-sensitive help. To access it, click on the Help icon located in the upper-right corner of the dialog box. Click on this icon, then click on a field or button in the dialog box to display an explanation of the dialog box feature. To close the explanation, click anywhere outside the explanation. A few dialog boxes also contain a **Help** button.

Online documentation for the SAS System is available on a separate CD-ROM; contact SAS Book Sales at sasbook@sas.com for more information on obtaining a copy of *SAS OnlineDoc*.

Using the Help Menu: If you click on the **Help** menu item in the SAS System main menu, you see the choices illustrated in Figure 2.5.

Figure 2.5 SAS System Help Menu

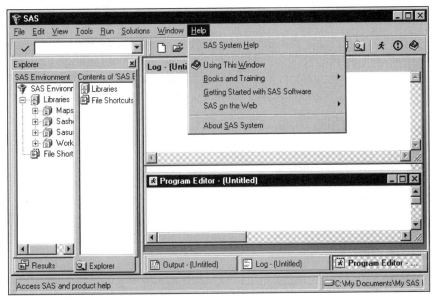

Here is an explanation of the **Help** menu choices you may use most often:

- **SAS System Help** opens the **Welcome to SAS Software** topic. Also displayed are the contents of the entire SAS Help system, from which you can choose an appropriate topic.

- **Using This Window** opens a help file for the active window. Also displayed are the contents of the entire SAS Help system, from which you can choose an appropriate topic.

Note

Some windows, such as the SPELL windows, do not have **Using This Window** help available.

- **Books and Training** offers access to online SAS documentation, if it is installed, and to tutorials about using the SAS System.

- **Getting Started with SAS Software** accesses a tutorial that you can use to become familiar with the SAS System for Windows.

- **SAS on the Web** gives you the capability to access even more help, assuming you are already connected to the World Wide Web (SAS does not provide the connection).

Practice opening the various **Help** menu items by clicking on them, then close the resulting windows by clicking on their Close buttons.

How the SAS Help System Is Organized: The information in the SAS Help system is organized from general to specific. By making choices in the SAS System Help windows, you progress through the layers toward the specific topic or task that you are interested in (this is sometimes referred to as "drilling down").

When you open a SAS System Help window, the topics are listed in the left pane of the window, and the information is presented in the right pane. Across the top of the window are some navigational and other tools.

Navigating Topic Lists: Topic lists include two types of icons:

- Topics represented by book icons expand and list that topic's subtopics when you double-click on them. The book icon you double-clicked on "opens." If you double-click on the book icon again, the book icon closes and the list of subtopics disappears.

- Double-clicking on question mark icons displays the topic information.

Figure 2.6 shows a sample topic list that illustrates both types of icons.

Figure 2.6 Sample Topic List

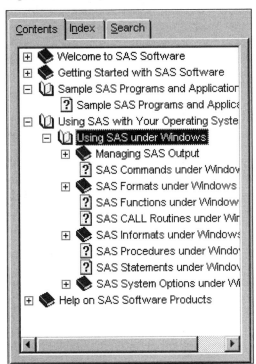

Navigating the SAS Help System: In the topic information, you may see highlighted text. These highlighted text strings are called "links." When you move the mouse pointer over a link, the pointer turns into a hand. Clicking on a link takes you to more information on that topic.

Use the tools at the top of the SAS System Help window to navigate the SAS Help system. Here is a description of the most commonly used tools:

Hide   suppresses the topic list pane. When you choose this tool, it changes to
             Show. Clicking on **Show** displays the topic list again.

Back   takes you back one link.

Home   takes you to the **Welcome to SAS Software** topic (the "start" of the SAS
             Help system topics).

Print   prints the current topic on the default printer.

Options   displays a list of various options you can use to customize the SAS Help system.

Performing a Text Search: You can search the SAS Help system for text strings. This is useful if you do not know what the topic is called, but you know the information for that topic contains a certain word. To perform a text search, click on the **Search** tab in the topic list pane of the SAS System Help window. Now fill in the information on the **Search** tab. Type the search string in the text entry field at the top of the **Search** tab, then click on **List Topics**. Once the topic list on the **Search** tab shows the topic that you want, double-click on the topic to display it.

Accessing the SAS Sample Library

To continue with the rest of the tutorial, you must first have a SAS program to work with. One easy way to start a program is to choose a similar program from the SAS Sample Library. Follow these steps to copy a SAS program from the SAS Sample Library:

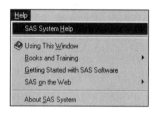

1. In the main SAS System menu, click on **Help→SAS System Help**.

2. In the topic list in the left pane of the SAS System Help window, double-click on **Sample SAS Programs and Applications**. When the topic expands, click on **Sample SAS Programs and Applications**.

3. Scroll the topic window (right pane) down until you see the **Base SAS** link; click on this link.

4. Click on **Basic Dataset Manipulations**.

5. To highlight just the program you want, click at the beginning of the first comment line. (You will not see an insertion point.) Now scroll down until you see the final RUN statement of this example (just before the next topic, **Biorhythm Cycle Plots**). Hold the Shift key down while you click at the end of this RUN statement. All the example should now be highlighted. (If it is not, scroll back up to the top of the code and try again.)

6. To copy the code to the Clipboard, right-click in the topic window (right pane) and click on **Copy**.

7. Close the SAS System Help window by clicking on its Close button.

8. Click in the Program Editor window to make it active.

9. Make sure the cursor is at the beginning of the first line of the Program Editor window; now click on **Edit** in the main SAS System menu, then click on **Paste**. The sample program appears in the Program Editor window.

Editing a File

Now that you have your SAS program in the Program Editor window, you can make changes. For example, you may want to delete the large comment section and add your own comments.

Highlighting a Large Chunk of Text: Sometimes you may want to work with a large chunk of text. An easy way to do this is to highlight it using the mouse. For example, you can highlight the large comment section at the beginning of the file, then delete it. Click at the beginning of the first line. Now hold the left mouse button down and drag the mouse pointer toward the bottom of the window. As you drag the mouse, the highlight follows. Stop dragging and release the mouse button when the entire comment section is highlighted. To delete the highlighted text, click on **Edit** in the SAS System main menu, then on **Clear**. The highlighted text disappears.

Note

> The text may scroll quickly when dragging; you may have to repeatedly scroll down and up (still holding the mouse button down) until just the text you want is highlighted.

Undoing Changes: If you accidentally delete something, don't panic—you can undo it. For example, to regain the comments you just deleted, click on **Edit** in the SAS System main menu, then on **Undo** (or press CTRL-Z). The comment section reappears.

Adding a Line: To add a line, click at the end of the line preceding the new one, then press RETURN. Now type your new text, such as

```
/* My own data manipulation code */
```

There are many other editing features of the Program Editor window. You can toggle between insert mode (the default) and overstrike mode, search for and replace text, do a spell check, and so on. Chapter 3 goes into more detail on editing files.

Submitting a File

V7 Hilites: Most code-submission menu choices now are located under **Run** in the SAS System main menu.

FasTip: Click on **Run→Submit**.

Now that you have the code looking the way you want, submit it. Methods of submitting code abound—you can use a function key, the tool bar, the menus, or commands.

For this exercise, we'll use the menus. To submit the code, be sure the Program Editor window is active. Then, click on **Run** in the SAS System main menu, then on **Submit**. The code is submitted, the Program Editor window clears, notes appear in the Log window, the Output window appears, and the Results window pops to the top in the left side of the SAS workspace. (See "Looking at the Output" later in this chapter for more information on the Results window.) Figure 2.7 shows what the last page of the output looks like.

Figure 2.7 Last Page of Output from the Data Manipulation Program

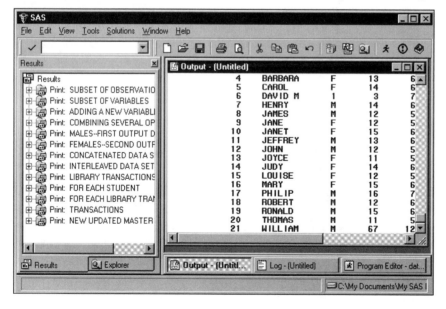

Note

> If your code contains an error, the Output and Results windows may not appear. If this happens, examine the notes in the Log window to see where the error is.

 To return to the Program Editor window, click on the SAS Programming Windows icon in the tool bar.

Chapter 4 provides more information on submitting SAS code in a variety of ways.

Recalling Code to the Program Editor

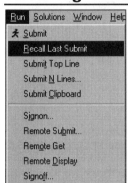

V7 Hilites: The **Recall Last Submit** menu choice is under **Run** on the SAS System main menu.

FasTip: Click on **Run→Recall Last Submit**.

If your output is not correct, recall your code, edit it, and resubmit it. To recall the last submitted program to the Program Editor, be sure the Program Editor is the active window. Then, click on **Run** in the SAS System main menu, then click on **Recall Last Submit** (or press F4).

Looking at the Output

V7 Hilites: New Results window offers easy access to SAS output.

FasTip: Click on the **Results** tab in the SAS workspace Window Bar.

When your output appears in the Output window, the Results window appears adjacent to the Output window. To access the Results window at other times, click on **Results** in the Window Bar. Figure 2.8 shows the Results window adjacent to the DATAMANIP output.

Note

> In the Figure, the Results window has been resized so that more of the text is visible.

Figure 2.8   Results and Output Windows after Submitting the DATAMANIP Program

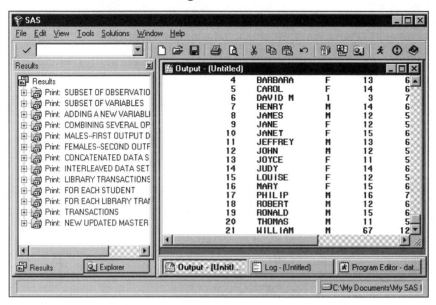

Each procedure in your program that creates output is listed in the Results window. The output is organized into folders, subfolders, and items within those folders that represent individual pieces of the output. Because the DATAMANIP program generated only simple PROC PRINT steps, that is all that is listed.

To better understand how the Results window works, submit the following program:

```
data test;
    do i = 1 to 150;
        group = (i > 50);
        x = normal(123);
        y1 = uniform(123);
        y2 = uniform(567);
        output;
    end;
run;
proc print;
    title 'Print Step';
run;
proc means;
    by group;
    title 'Means Step';
run;
```

Figure 2.9 shows the Output and Results windows for this code.

Figure 2.9 Another Example of the Results Window

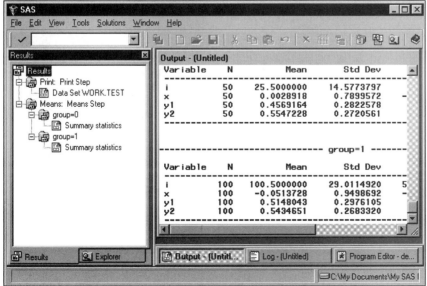

Click on the plus signs to expand the **Print Step** and **Means Step** folders; then click on the plus signs to expand the subfolders. When everything is expanded, the Results window looks like Figure 2.10.

Figure 2.10 Results Window with All Output Nodes Expanded

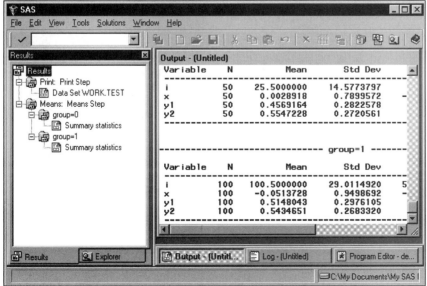

To jump directly to the Group 1-related output, click on the **Summary statistics** item under the **group=1** folder.

Navigating in the Results Window: Navigating in the Results window works the same as navigating in other folder-oriented windows:

- Click on a plus sign to expand the view of an output.

- Click on a minus sign to collapse the view.

- Double-click on an output line to view that piece of the output. The Output window scrolls to the appropriate place.

- Press the Backspace key to move up one level in the Results folder hierarchy.

You can use the Results window to manage your output. For example, you can rename, delete, save, and print the output. Each of these tasks is explained in the next few sections.

Renaming Output: To rename a piece of your output from the Results window, right-click on the output that you want to rename. In the popup menu, click on **Rename**. When the Rename dialog box appears, provide the new name in the **Description** field and click on **OK**.

Deleting Output: To delete a piece of output, right-click on the output node that you want to delete, then click on **Delete** in the popup menu. The output is deleted both from the Results window and the Output window. You can delete only the highest level of output; you cannot delete individual pieces of output listed under a higher-level node.

If you clear the Output window by clicking on **Edit** in the SAS System main menu, then on **Clear all**, the Results window is cleared as well.

Saving Output: To save a piece of your output from the Results window, right-click on the output that you want to save. In the popup menu, click on **Save As**. When the Save As dialog box appears, provide the new name in the **File name** field and click on **OK**.

Printing Output: To print a piece of your output from the Results window, right-click on the output that you want to print. In the popup menu, click on **Print**. The output is sent to your default printer. See Chapter 5 for more details about printing.

Note

When you print from the Results window, the print dialog box does not appear. Therefore, be sure your printer and page setup options are set before you choose **Print** in the Results window popup menu.

Determining the Properties of Your Output: Your output has several properties associated with it, such as a template, date modified, and beginning and ending Output window line numbers. To see the properties for a particular piece of output (such as what template a piece of output uses), right-click on the output's name in the Results window, then click on **Properties**. This opens the Properties window for that piece of output. Figure 2.11 shows the properties for the **Summary statistics** piece of output for Group 1.

Figure 2.11 Properties for a Piece of Output

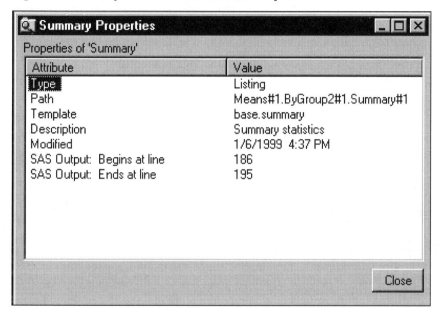

Note

For more information on templates, see "Generating Different Kinds of Output Using the Output Delivery System" in Chapter 4.

Printing the Output

V7 Hilites: You can now print from either a SAS window such as Output or from the Results window.

FasTip: Click on the Print icon on the SAS tool bar.

Printing the Entire Output Window: To print all output displayed in the Output window, click on **Window** in the SAS System main menu, then on **Output**. This makes the Output window active. Now click on **File** in the SAS System main menu, then on **Print** (or press CTRL-P). The Print dialog box appears, similar to the one shown in Figure 2.12.

Figure 2.12 Print Dialog Box

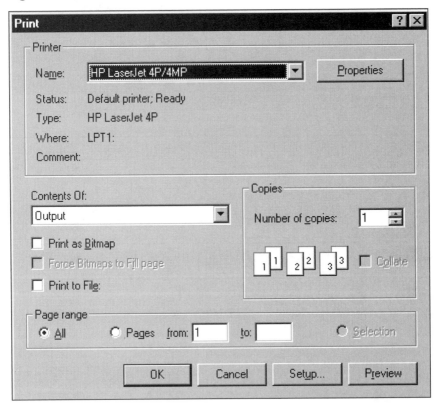

Click on **OK** to send the contents of the window to your default printer.

Printing Only a Portion of the Output: You can also print the output from the Results window, which enables you to have more control over which portions of your output to print. For example, to print only the Group 0-related output from the example in the previous section, right-click on **Group=0** in the Results window, then click on **Print** in the popup menu.

Note

Printing from the Results window bypasses the Print dialog box. Before printing from the Results window, be sure your printer is configured properly.

Chapter 5 provides more detail about printing.

Saving a File

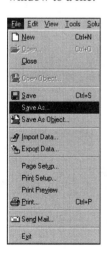

V7 Hilites: Default location for saved files is C:\My Documents\My SAS Files.

FasTip: Click on the Save icon on the SAS tool bar.

Besides printing your output (or code or log), you also might want to save the contents of the window to a file.

Because you have not saved your SAS program before, you must give the file a name. Make the Program Editor window active. (If it does not contain your code, recall it by clicking **Run** in the SAS System main menu, then clicking on **Recall Last Submit**.) Now click on **File** in the SAS System main menu, then on **Save As**. The Save As dialog box opens. Figure 2.13 shows a sample Save As dialog box.

Figure 2.13 Sample Save As Dialog Box

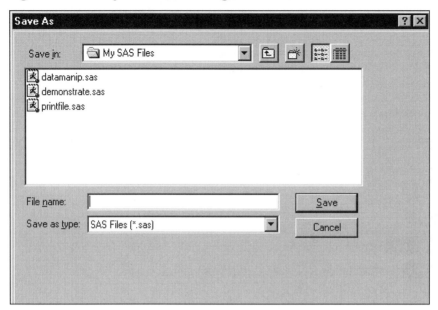

Type the name that you want to use for the file in the **File name** field—we'll use DATAMANIP.SAS. If you do not specify the full pathname, the file is stored in the SAS working folder. In this case, the working folder is C:\My Documents\My SAS Files (as indicated by the **Save in** field).

Click on **Save**; the file is saved and the dialog box closes.

"Saving an Existing File" and "Saving a New File" in Chapter 3 explain further how to use the Save As dialog box.

Becoming Familiar with the SAS Explorer Window

Version 7 of the SAS System offers a new way to organize and access the components of the SAS environment, such as SAS windows and applications, SAS data libraries, SAS program files, SAS catalogs, and SAS tables, through the SAS Explorer window.

Note

Windows also offers an Explorer. See Appendix 3 for information on using the Windows Explorer.

The SAS Explorer window is "object-oriented." So, instead of typing a command or traversing a menu path, you click, double-click, and right-click on icons that represent various SAS System items. The following sections show you the highlights of using this new interface to the SAS System.

Opening the SAS Explorer Window: When SAS starts up, a SAS Explorer window opens by default, on the left side of your SAS session. (This window is "docked"—see "Resizing the SAS Explorer Window" later in this chapter for more details.) By default, the SAS Explorer window shows the components of the SAS environment represented by large icons. For example, Figure 2.14 shows the default SAS Explorer window that appears when you start the SAS System.

Figure 2.14 Initial SAS Explorer Window, Using Large Icons

To switch to a view that is more like the Windows Explorer, (which uses a two-pane approach), click on **View** in the SAS System main menu, then on **List**. Click again on **View**, and then click on **Show Tree**. Figure 2.15 shows what this view looks like.

Figure 2.15 SAS Explorer Window, Using the List/Tree View

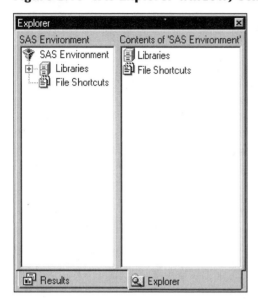

Note

The left and right panes of the SAS Explorer window in Figure 2.15 have been resized so that all the contents are visible.

Note

The rest of this book assumes that you are using the list/tree display in the SAS Explorer.

 You can have multiple instances of the SAS Explorer window open at the same time. To open another SAS Explorer window, click on the Explorer icon on the SAS tool bar.

 You can also open the SAS Explorer window by clicking on **View** in the SAS System main menu, then on **Explorer**.

To differentiate between the various instances of SAS Explorer windows, the title bar contains a number, as shown in Figure 2.16.

Figure 2.16 Multiple Instances of the SAS Explorer Window

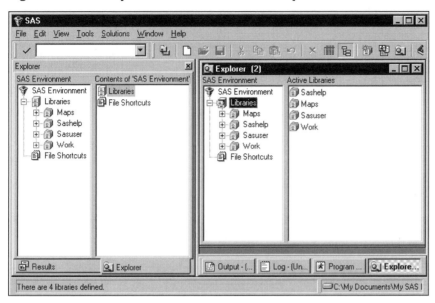

The following sections illustrate some of the tasks that you can perform from the SAS Explorer window.

Navigating in the SAS Explorer Window: When you first open the SAS Explorer window, you see two icons: **Libraries** and **File Shortcuts**. Double-clicking on an icon changes the view to show the contents of the icon on which you double-clicked.

If you use the tree view instead of the list view, you can tell a folder has subfolders if the folder has a plus sign next to it. Clicking on a plus sign expands the view to include subfolders.

Figure 2.17 shows the SAS Explorer window in tree view after the **Libraries** folder has been expanded.

Figure 2.17 SAS Explorer Window with the Libraries Folder Expanded

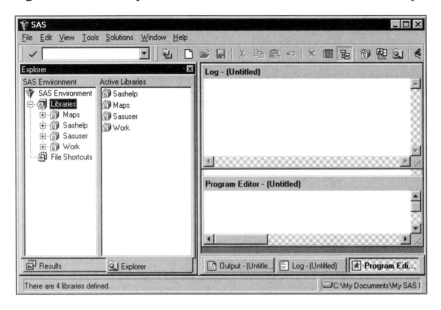

To see the contents of a subfolder, click on it—the contents of the subfolder are listed in the right pane of the SAS Explorer window. For example, Figure 2.18 shows the SAS Explorer window after you click on the **SASUSER** subfolder.

Figure 2.18 SAS Explorer Window with SASUSER Catalog Expanded

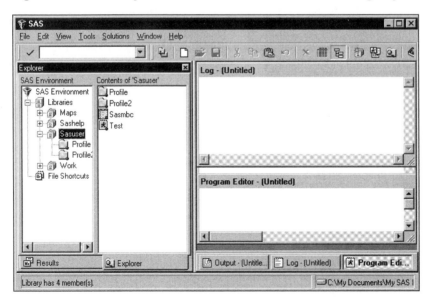

- To access an item that is listed in the right pane of the window, double-click on the item. The action taken depends on the item. For example, double-clicking on a table name opens the VIEWTABLE window.

- To collapse a folder view, click on the minus sign next to the folder.

- To move up a level in the SAS Explorer window folder hierarchy, click on the Up One Level icon on the SAS tool bar. The keyboard shortcut for the Up One Level tool is the Backspace key.

To familiarize yourself with this new interface to the SAS System, take a few moments to explore the various folders to see what is stored where.

Moving and Copying Files: You can use the SAS Explorer window to move or copy files from one place to another. For example, suppose you decide you want the CLASS2 table created by the DATAMANIP program to be permanent. It currently is stored in the WORK data library. To see this, expand the **Libraries** folder in the SAS Explorer window, then click on **Work**. In the right pane of the window, you see the CLASS2 table, as shown in Figure 2.19.

Figure 2.19 Preparing to Copy the CLASS2 Table in the SAS Explorer Window

![Screenshot of the SAS Explorer window showing the Libraries folder expanded with Maps, Sashelp, Sasuser, Work, and File Shortcuts. The Contents of 'Work' pane shows B, Both, C, Class, Class2 (highlighted), D, E, Females, Library, Males, Newclass, Newlib, and Transact. The right side shows Log - (Untitled) and Program Editor - datamanip.sas windows.]

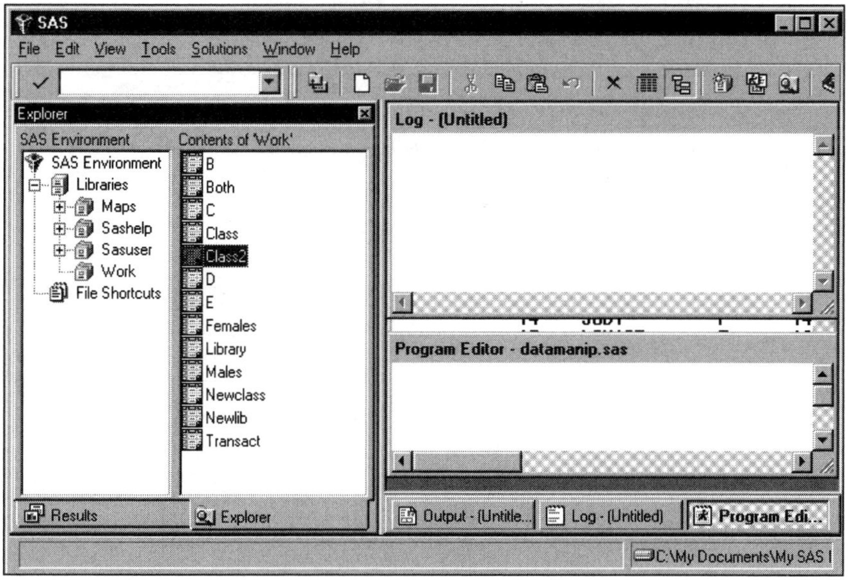

To move this file to the SASUSER data library, click on the table in the right pane of the window, so it is highlighted. Now drag the table into the left pane of the window until the mouse pointer is over the SASUSER data library. Release the mouse button, and expand the view of the SASUSER data library. The CLASS2 table has been moved (deleted) from the WORK data library and inserted into the SASUSER data library.

If you want to copy a table (or other item), use the right mouse button to drag the file. When you release the mouse button, you are prompted whether you want to move or copy the item. Select **Move** or **Copy** (or **Cancel**) as appropriate.

Renaming Files: Suppose you want to rename the B table (created by the DATAMANIP program) to SecondTable. To do so, display the contents of the **Work** folder, then right-click on B in the right pane of the SAS Explorer window. When the popup menu appears, click on **Rename**. A dialog box appears, as shown in Figure 2.20.

Figure 2.20 Rename Dialog Box Accessed from the SAS Explorer Window

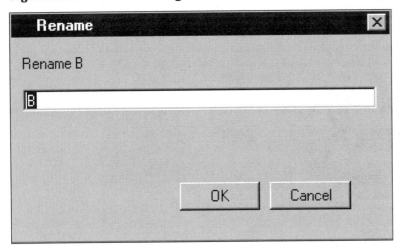

Type the new name in the text entry field and click on **OK**.

Deleting Files: Deleting files works similarly to renaming files. To delete the E table, right-click on the table name in the right pane of the SAS Explorer window. When the popup menu appears, click on **Delete**. To complete the delete, click on **OK** in the Delete Confirmation dialog box when it appears. To cancel the delete, click on **Cancel**.

Creating a File Shortcut: You can use the SAS Explorer window to create file shortcuts (known as filerefs in Version 6 of the SAS System). To create a shortcut, follow these steps:

1. Back up in the SAS Explorer hierarchy (if necessary) until the **File Shortcuts** icon appears in the left pane of the SAS Explorer window.

2. Right-click on **File Shortcuts** in the left pane of the SAS Explorer window.

3. In the popup menu, click on **New File Shortcut**. The New File Shortcut dialog box appears, as shown in Figure 2.21.

**Figure 2.21 New File Shortcut Dialog Box Accessed from the SAS Explorer
Window**

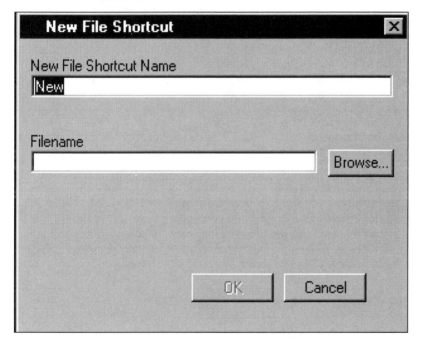

4. Type the file shortcut name in the **New File Shortcut Name** field. For this example, type

    FILEREF1.

5. Type the full physical pathname for the file in the **Filename** field. For this example, type

    ```
    C:\My Documents\My SAS Files\datamanip.sas
    ```

Note

> You can click on the **Browse** button to access the Open dialog box, which enables you to find the file in your list of folders and files. Chapter 3 describes how to use the Open dialog box.

6. When the **New File Shortcut Name** and **Filename** fields contain the right information, click on **OK**.

The new file shortcut is now listed in the right pane of the SAS Explorer window. You can now use this file shortcut in your SAS programs. To test it, type the following in the Program Editor window and submit it:

```
%include fileref1;
```

The DATAMANIP.SAS file is submitted.

You can also drag and drop the file shortcut onto the Program Editor window, which includes the text file into the Program Editor window, but does not submit the code.

File shortcuts are temporary, and do not last from one SAS session to the next.

Refreshing the SAS Explorer Information: If you add or delete files outside of the SAS System, or otherwise change the information that is listed by the SAS Explorer window, you may need to "refresh" the SAS Explorer information. To do so, make the SAS Explorer window active. Now, click on **View** in the SAS System main menu, then on **Refresh**.

Getting More Information out of the SAS Explorer Window: You may need more information than is shown by default in the SAS Explorer window. There are two ways of gaining further information.

First, you can choose the detailed view instead of the list view. To change from list view to detailed view, click on **View** in the SAS System main menu, then on **Details**.   Now the right pane of the SAS Explorer window shows more information about every file, including **Name**, **Size**, **Type**, **Description**, and **Modified** (the date and time the file was last modified). To see all of this information, you may have to scroll right in the window. Figure 2.22 shows a sample of the detailed view (the SAS Explorer window has been enlarged so that more information is visible).

Figure 2.22 Detailed View in SAS Explorer Window

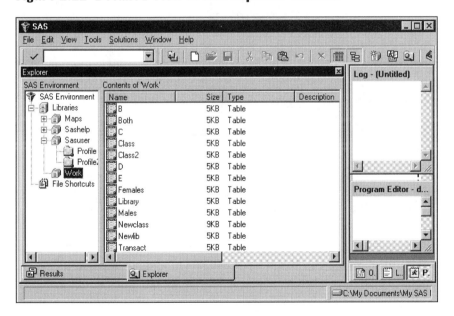

Note

To return to the less-detailed view, click on **View** in the SAS System main menu, then on **List**.

Another way of gaining more information about a file or object is to right-click on it (in either the right or left pane of the SAS Explorer window), then click on **Properties** in the popup menu. The Properties dialog box appears. The information displayed in the Properties dialog box varies, depending on what type of item you selected.

For example, display the contents of the WORK data library, and right-click on the CLASS table, then click on **Properties** in the popup menu. A dialog box similar to Figure 2.23 appears.

Figure 2.23 General Properties for a SAS Table

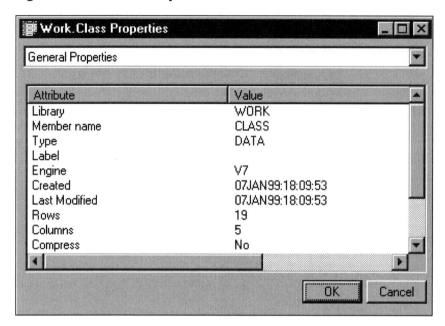

The general properties are displayed by default. You can click on the down arrow next to the top field and select other types of properties. For example, Figure 2.24 shows the **Engine/Host Information** for the CLASS table. To close this Properties dialog box, click on **OK**.

Figure 2.24 Engine/Host Properties for a SAS Table

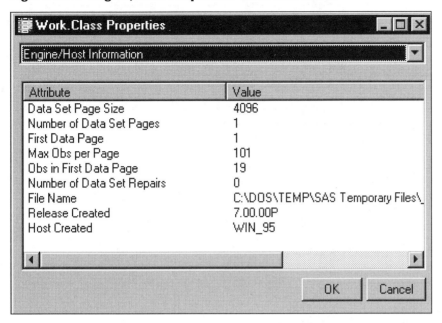

You can display properties for any item displayed in the SAS Explorer window.

To close the Properties dialog box, click on **OK**, **Close**, or **Cancel**.

Sorting Your Files: To sort your files, select the detailed view, as described in the previous section. Now click on a column head, such as **Type** or **Name**. The files are sorted in ascending order by the column you selected. To reverse the sort, click on the column head again.

Resizing the SAS Explorer Window: By default, the SAS Explorer window (as well as the Results window) is "docked" (that is, anchored) in the left side of the SAS workspace. While you can make the entire window or individual panes wider or narrower, you cannot move, maximize, or minimize these windows. To be able to move, maximize, or minimize the SAS Explorer window, follow these steps:

1. Click in the SAS Explorer window so that it is active.

2. Click on **Window** in the SAS System main menu, then click on **Docked**.

Note

Follow similar steps to undock the Results window.

Now you can move, maximize, or minimize the SAS Explorer window. It is possible to change your preferences so that no windows are docked; see Chapter 6 for more information.

Note

Subsequent instances of the SAS Explorer window are not docked, even if the original instance is.

Saving the Format of the SAS Explorer Window: If you prefer the detailed view to the list view, for example, it is cumbersome to have to turn on the detailed view every time you open a SAS Explorer window. You can save the view settings. To do so, follow these steps:

1. Get the window looking like you want it and make sure the SAS Explorer window is active.

2. Click on **Tools→Options→Preferences** in the SAS System main menu, then click on the **General** tab.

3. Select the **Save settings on exit** option.

4. Click on **OK**.

Now the appearance of the SAS Explorer (and all other SAS windows) is saved when you close SAS, so they look the same the next time you start SAS up.

Customizing the SAS Explorer Window: You can customize the SAS Explorer window. For example, you can change the default action for double-clicking on SAS files, or add the Favorite Folders folder to the SAS Explorer window. See "Customizing the SAS Explorer" in Chapter 6 for more details.

Using the My Favorite Folders Feature

The SAS System offers a way to view your external files from the SAS System using the SAS Explorer window interface and the Windows concept of "favorite folders." Favorite folders are folders that you access often. You can define as many favorite folders as you want.

To open a window that contains your favorite folders (as well as the contents of the rest of your computer file system, such as the C: drive and any floppy drives you have installed), click on **View** in the SAS System main menu, then on **My Favorite Folders**. A new SAS Explorer window appears, as shown in Figure 2.25.

Figure 2.25 My Favorite Folders Window

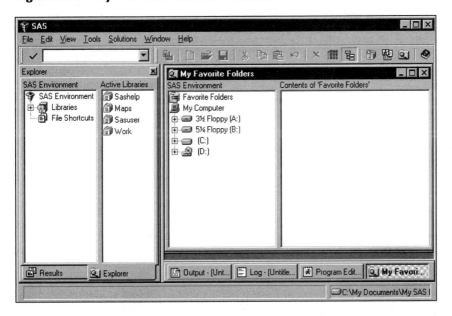

By default, there are no folders listed under the **Favorite Folders** folder. To create a new favorite folder, right-click on **Favorite Folders** in the left pane of the window. In the popup menu, click on **New Favorite Folder**. The New Favorite Folder dialog box appears, as shown in Figure 2.26.

Figure 2.26 New Favorite Folder Dialog Box

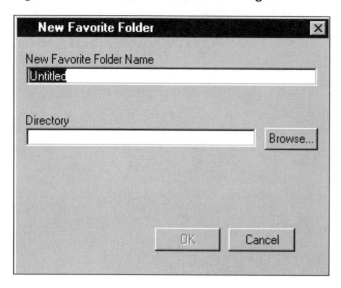

Type a name for the folder in the top text entry field, and type the full physical pathname of the folder in the second text entry field. (If you do not know the full pathname, click on the **Browse** button and navigate to the folder you want in the Select dialog box, then click on **OK**). When the text entry fields contain the right information, click on **OK**. The new folder is now listed under Favorite Folders in the SAS Explorer window. The name you give the favorite folder is a logical reference to the actual physical folder, just as a library reference is a logical pointer to the physical location of a SAS data library.

Note

Although you can view the contents of your hard drive and floppy drives from the My Favorite Folders window, you cannot manage these files in any way (such as copying, deleting, or renaming). See Appendix 3 for information on how to use the Windows Explorer to perform these tasks.

Renaming a Favorite Folder: Should you decide to change the name of a favorite folder, right-click on the folder name. In the popup menu, click on **Rename Favorite Folder**. Type the new name in the Rename Favorite Folder dialog box and click on **OK**. Remember—this does not rename the actual physical file but only the logical reference that you have associated with the file.

Deleting a Favorite Folder: To delete a favorite folder, right-click on the folder name. In the popup menu, click on **Delete Favorite Folder**. When prompted whether you are sure you want to delete the folder, click on **OK**. Remember that deleting a favorite folder from the SAS Explorer window does not delete the actual physical folder—it just deletes the logical reference to the folder.

Displaying Your Favorite Folders when SAS Starts Up: By default, the SAS Explorer window that is displayed when the SAS System starts up does not show Favorite Folders. If you'd like to see your favorite folders in this window, see "Customizing the SAS Explorer" in Chapter 6.

Ending Your SAS Session

FasTip: Click on the SAS workspace Close button.

To end your SAS session, click on the SAS workspace Close button. When a dialog box prompts you for whether you really want to end the session, click on **OK**. The SAS System shuts down, and you are returned to the Windows desktop.

Note

> If you had text in SAS Text Editor windows, such as the Program Editor or NOTEPAD windows, you are prompted to save the text in those windows before your SAS session ends. You can choose not to save the text at that point.

Placing the SAS System on the Desktop

Although not strictly necessary, you may find it useful to have a SAS System icon on the desktop. That way, you can simply double-click on the icon to start the SAS System instead of having to use the **Start** button menus. A copy of a program icon is called a shortcut.

To place a SAS System shortcut on the desktop, follow these steps:

1. Right-click in a blank area of the desktop.

2. When the popup menu appears, click on **New**, then on **Shortcut**.

3. The Create Shortcut dialog box appears. In the **Command line** field, type the following:

    ```
    c:\Program Files\Sas\Sas.exe system-options
    ```

    where *system-options* are any SAS System options that you want to use (such as CONFIG and AUTOEXEC). (If you chose a nondefault location for the SAS executable files during SAS installation, use this pathname instead.)

4. Click on **Next**.

5. In the next dialog box that appears, type a name for the shortcut that you are creating. For example, you could type

    ```
    Shortcut to SAS
    ```

6. Click on **Finish**. Figure 2.27 shows how the desktop looks after the shortcut is created—the mouse pointer is on the SAS System shortcut.

Figure 2.27 Windows Desktop with a SAS System Shortcut

7. If necessary, use the mouse to drag the **Shortcut to SAS** icon on the desktop so that it is positioned where you want it.

Now you can double-click on the **Shortcut to SAS** icon on the desktop to start the SAS System, without having to navigate the **Start** button menus.

Note

Each shortcut that you create has its own properties, such as a command line and working directory. When you change one shortcut's properties, the changes do not apply to other shortcuts to the same program.

Deciding Where to Go from Here

If you use the SAS System for Windows only occasionally and all you do is submit a file, look at the output, and print or save it, you may not need to read much more of this book. However, this chapter has scratched only the surface of Version 7 of the SAS System—it is a powerful, flexible tool if you are willing to explore it. You can create your own tool bar icons, use the SAS System to access data in other applications, and so on.

Why not be adventuresome? Read Chapter 3, which explains more about using the SAS Program Editor window, and perhaps Chapter 5, about printing. Or, read Chapter 12 if you'd like to download some files from your mainframe. Take another look at the Table of Contents at the beginning of this book, and see what topics interest you—each chapter opens another panoramic view on Version 7 of the SAS System for Windows.

3 Editing and Working with Files

Introduction

This chapter shows you how to use the SAS Text Editor to edit files and how to perform other tasks involving files such as opening and saving files. Becoming familiar with the shortcuts and capabilities of the SAS Text Editor makes your work more efficient and less frustrating. While this chapter uses the Program Editor window to illustrate file editing techniques, you can use these techniques in any SAS Text Editor window (such as the NOTEPAD window and the SOURCE window in SAS/AF software).

Note

> You do not have to use the SAS Text Editor to edit your files—you can use a different Windows text editor. See "Using a Different Text Editor" later in this chapter for more information.

Moving the Cursor

The basic tools for moving the cursor are your arrow keys. Keyboards differ, but you should have at least one set of arrow keys—up, down, left, and right. If your keyboard has a numeric keypad, you can use the arrow keys on the pad as well.

Note

To use the keypad arrow keys, NumLock must be off. Check your keyboard for a NumLock key, and see if the NumLock indicator light is on. If so, press the NumLock key once to turn it off.

The basic increments of cursor movement are

- by character

- by line

- by word

- by page.

Moving Character by Character: The left and right arrow keys move the cursor one character at a time to the left and right.

Moving Line by Line: The up and down arrow keys move the cursor up and down one line.

The Home key moves your cursor to the beginning of a line of text; the End key moves your cursor to the end of a line of text.

Moving Word by Word: Use the Control key with the left and right arrow keys to move the cursor from word to word.

CTRL-LeftArrow moves the cursor one word to the left; CTRL-RightArrow moves the cursor one word to the right.

Moving Page by Page: The PageUp and PageDown keys scroll the active window one full page up and down respectively. The size of the page is relative to the size of the window.

Moving to the Top and Bottom of a File: Using the Control key with the PageUp and PageDown keys moves your cursor to the first and last characters of your file:

- To move to the first character, press CTRL-PageUp.

- To move to the last character, press CTRL-PageDown.

Note

CTRL-Home is equivalent to CTRL-PageUp, and CTRL-End is equivalent to CTRL-PageDown.

Undoing Changes

FasTip: Click on the Undo icon on the SAS tool bar.

Before you start editing a file, it is good to know how to undo your changes, especially while you are learning to use the mouse and the editing commands.

To undo a change, such as a line deletion or insertion of text in the wrong place, click on **Edit** in the SAS System main menu, then on **Undo** (or press CTRL-Z). This undoes the last thing you did (except for irreversible actions, such as saving or printing a file). Choosing **Undo** several times in a row undoes recent changes in reverse order.

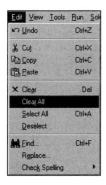

Another way of undoing changes is to clear the Program Editor (click on **Edit** in the SAS System main menu, then click on **Clear all**) without saving the file. Now open the file again—the changes you made were not saved, so the original file is the same as it was.

You may want to keep backup files, in case you make a mistake that you cannot fix, such as overwriting a file.

Note

No change that you make to your file is permanent until you save the file. See "Saving a File" in Chapter 2 and "Saving Files" later in this chapter for more information on how to save your file.

Marking Text

V7 Hilites: SHIFT-click now extends a mark.

ALT-click causes the next drag to mark a rectangular block of text.

To mark text means to highlight one or more characters, usually in preparation for moving, copying, or deleting the text.

Clearing a Mark: Before you become adept at marking text, you may highlight too much or too little. Clicking the mouse button anywhere in the window clears the mark so that you can start over. (This is different than in some other Windows applications such as Notepad and Word, where moving the cursor with the arrow keys clears the mark. With the SAS Text Editor, moving the arrow keys without the Shift key held down has no effect on the mark.)

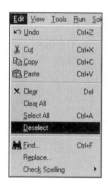

You can also use the menus to clear a mark. Click on **Edit** in the SAS System main menu, then click on **Deselect**.

Using the Mouse to Mark Text: You can use either your mouse or the keyboard to mark text. Here is the basic procedure for highlighting with the mouse:

1. Click on the first character of the section that you want to highlight.

2. Hold down the mouse button and drag the mouse until all the text that you want to include is highlighted.

3. If you need to go beyond the edge of the window, drag the mouse pointer over the edge of the window, and the window scrolls. However, it scrolls quite quickly—you may have to practice a bit before you get it to stop exactly where you want.

4. Release the mouse button when all the text that you want to mark is highlighted.

More techniques you may find helpful include

- Double-clicking in the middle of a word highlights that word.

- Holding down the SHIFT key while clicking extends a mark (equivalent to dragging to extend the mark).

- Holding down the CTRL key while clicking on a line of text highlights the entire line.

- Holding down the ALT key while dragging the mouse pointer or clicking highlights a rectangular block (column) of text. Alternatively, hold the ALT key down and click anywhere in the window. The next drag will then highlight a rectangular block of text.

Using the Keyboard to Mark Text: If you prefer to use the keyboard to mark text, place the cursor over the first character of the section you want to mark. Now hold the Shift key down, and use the cursor movement keys to extend the mark. For example, pressing Shift-CTRL-LeftArrow extends the mark one word to the left, and Shift-CTRL-PageDown extends the mark to the end of the file.

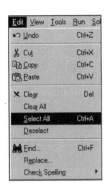

Marking All Text: If you want to select all of the text in the window, click on **Edit** in the SAS System main menu, then click on **Select all**.

Deleting Text

V7 Hilites: CTRL-Delete now deletes the rest of a word after the cursor, not the entire line of text.

FasTip: Mark the text, then press the Delete key.

To clear an entire window (even the Log window), click on the New icon on the SAS tool bar.

As with moving the cursor, you can delete by character, by word, or by line. You can also delete all the text in the window. In addition, you can choose to delete text by using keys on the keyboard or by using the menus.

Deleting a Single Character: To delete a single character, press Backspace or Delete. Here is the difference between the two:

- The Backspace key deletes the character immediately before the cursor position.

- The Delete key deletes the character under the cursor.

Deleting a Word: To delete a word, double-click on the word, then press Delete. To delete the rest of a word after the cursor, press CTRL-Delete.

Deleting Lines of Text: To delete all the characters in the line after the cursor position (except the carriage return), press ALT-Delete.

To delete a large chunk of text, first mark the text, then press Delete.

Using the Menus to Delete Text: Instead of pressing the Delete key to delete marked text, you can use the menu. Click on **Edit** in the SAS System main menu, then click on **Clear**.

Be careful—if you select **Clear all** instead, the entire window is cleared. If this happens to you, immediately click on **Edit**, then on **Undo**. The text reappears.

Replacing Old Text with New Text: You can replace old text with new text by first marking the text that you want to replace, then beginning to type the new text. The old text is deleted, and the new text appears as you type.

Clearing an Entire Window: You can clear the text from a window in several ways. Here are two methods:

-  For text-editing windows, such as the Program Editor, click on **File** in the main SAS System menu, then click on **Clear all**.

- For any SAS window, including the Log and Output windows, click on the New icon in the SAS tool bar. If you are clearing a text-editing window, you are prompted to save before the window is cleared.

Cutting Text

FasTip: Mark the text, then press CTRL-X.

Cutting text is not the same as deleting it. When you delete text, it is gone. If you cut the text, it is placed on the Clipboard for future use. You can then paste the text somewhere else in a SAS window or in another application such as Excel or Word.

To cut text, first mark it. Then click on **Edit** in the SAS System main menu, then click on **Cut** (or press CTRL-X). The text disappears from the SAS window and is placed on the Clipboard.

The Clipboard can hold only one section of text at a time. That is, if you cut one portion of text, then cut a second portion of text, the Clipboard contains only the second portion of text.

Copying Text

FasTip: Mark the text, then press CTRL-C.

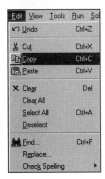

If you want to reuse text but do not want to delete it from its original position, copy it instead of cutting it. First, mark the text. Now click on **Edit** in the SAS System main menu, then click on **Copy** (or press CTRL-C). The text is placed on the Clipboard but remains in its original position as well. A side effect of copying text is that the mark is cleared.

The Clipboard can hold only one section of text at a time. That is, if you copy one portion of text, then copy a second portion of text, the Clipboard contains only the second portion of text.

Pasting Text

V7 Hilites: Pasted text now replaces marked text.

FasTip: Place the cursor at the insertion point and press CTRL-V.

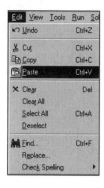

If you have cut or copied text, you can paste it elsewhere in a SAS window or even in another Windows application such as WordPad. To paste text into a SAS window, position your cursor where you want the new text to appear—the text appears after the cursor. Now click on **Edit** in the SAS System main menu, then click on **Paste** (or press CTRL-V). The text is pasted into the SAS window. The text is not deleted from the Clipboard, so you can paste it several times in a row if you want.

If you mark text before you paste, the marked text is replaced with the pasted text.

Inserting Text

FasTip: Position the cursor and type.

If you want to type new text in a file, position your cursor where you want the new text to appear. If you are in insert mode, the text appears in front of the existing text. If you are in overstrike mode, the text replaces the existing text.

The shape of the cursor indicates whether you are in insert or overstrike mode:

- A block cursor indicates overstrike mode.

- A thin cursor indicates insert mode.

To switch between the two modes, press the Insert key.

If you want to replace a chunk of text with new text, mark the text, then start typing. When you type, the marked text is deleted and the new text replaces it.

If you want to append text to a file without opening it, type the new text in the Program Editor window, then use the Save As dialog box to append to the file, as described in "Saving an Existing File" later in this chapter.

Scrolling

The scroll bars on the right side and bottom of the window can help you scroll. You control how much the window scrolls by how you use the scroll bars.

Scrolling Line by Line: To scroll line by line, click repeatedly on the up and down arrows.

Scrolling Character by Character: To scroll character by character horizontally, click repeatedly on the left and right arrows.

Scrolling by Larger Amounts: To smoothly scroll vertically or horizontally, drag the square block inside the scroll bar. Release the mouse button when you have scrolled to where you want to be.

To jump vertically through a file, click in the vertical scroll bar. Clicking above the square block jumps your cursor toward the top of the window; clicking below the square block jumps your cursor toward the bottom of the window. Use the horizontal scroll bar in the same way to move left and right by large amounts.

Remember that you can also use the PageDown and PageUp keys alone and in combination with the Control key to scroll your file.

Setting Tab Stops in the Program Editor Window

By default, the tab stops in the Program Editor window are set to every eight spaces. Many times, you may want tab stops at a different place (such as every three spaces). To set new tab stops in the Program Editor window, issue the following command from the Command bar:

```
:tan ; :d
```

Replace *n* in the command with the number of spaces that you want between tab stops.

If you want the tab stop settings to be remembered between SAS sessions, issue the WSAVE command from the Command bar (make sure the Program Editor window is active when you issue this command).

Dragging and Dropping Text between SAS Windows

FasTip: Use the left-button drag for the default action.

Use the Control key plus the left mouse button for copying.

Use the right mouse button to get a move/copy prompt.

After you mark some text, you can drag it to another place in the same window or to another SAS window. As you recall, dragging is done by holding down the mouse button and moving the mouse. Dropping is when you release the mouse button when the pointer is in the destination window.

Why Drag and Drop?: Why would you want to drag and drop text? Suppose you have some code in the NOTEPAD window that you want to submit. By using drag and drop, you can move the text to the Program Editor window without opening any menus.

How to Drag and Drop Text: Here is the basic procedure for dragging and dropping text:

1. Mark the text you want to move and release the mouse button.

2. Place the mouse pointer over the marked text and hold the mouse button down.

3. Drag the pointer to the destination window and release the mouse button.

You must hold the mouse button down for a second or so before you begin dragging. Otherwise, the mark is changed instead of the text being dragged.

Note

It is also possible to move text from your SAS session to another Windows application and vice versa. Both the SAS window and the target application must be visible at the same time. To accomplish this, resize the SAS workspace as described in "Moving and Resizing Windows" in Chapter 1.

Interpreting the Mouse Pointer: You can drag text from any SAS window to any SAS window that supports text input. For example, you can drag and drop text from the Output window to the Program Editor window but not to the Log window. The mouse pointer indicates which windows accept dropped text:

*   If the pointer is over a window that accepts text, the pointer turns into a little box (with or without a + sign next to it).

*   If the pointer is over a window that does not accept text, the pointer turns into a "no" icon—a circle with a bar through it.

Whether or not the pointer has a + sign next to it tells you that the text is moved or copied:

- If the pointer has a + sign next to it, the text is copied from one window to the other.

- If the pointer has no + sign next to it, the text is moved (that is, deleted) from the original window.

Controlling Whether the Text is Copied or Moved: To control whether the text is copied or moved, use the Control key and either the left and right mouse button, as follows:

- If you hold the Control key down while dragging, the text is always copied. Be sure that you release the Control key after you release the mouse button. You must first begin to drag, then press and hold the Control key. (If you press the Control key before beginning to drag, the mark is extended instead of the text being copied.)

- If you use the right mouse button to drag the text, you are prompted whether you want to move or copy the text when you release the mouse button at the insertion point.

Use Table 3.1 to help you determine how to control the copying and moving of text.

Table 3.1 Copying and Moving Text with the Mouse

Key and/or Button	Has the Following Result
Left Mouse Button	moves text from text-editing window to text-editing window
	copies text from non-text-editing window to text-editing window
Control + Left Mouse Button	copies text
Right Mouse Button	prompts you with a dialog box with **Move** and **Copy** choices. If the destination window is the Program Editor, the dialog box also offers a **Submit** choice.

Searching for Text

V7 Hilites: **Edit** menu no longer contains a **Repeat Find** choice (use CTRL-R instead).

FasTip: Click on **Edit→Find**.

Press CTRL-R for repeat find.

If you have a long program in the Program Editor window and want to find some text, it may be faster to use the Find feature than to scroll through the window. To search for text, click on **Edit** in the SAS System main menu, then click on **Find**. The Find dialog box appears, as shown in Figure 3.1.

Figure 3.1 Find Dialog Box

Controlling the Search Parameters: Type the word that you want to find (such as an option name, a table name, or some other keyword) in the **Find What** field. The search is case insensitive unless you click on the **Match Case** option.

If the **Find What** field contains the word data, by default the search finds both lines containing "DATA A" and "proc datasets". If you want to find only the whole word "data", use the **Match Whole Word Only** option.

Controlling the Search Direction: By default, the search starts at the cursor position and continues forward (down) through the file. If you want to search backward from the cursor position, click on the **Up** option.

Performing the Search: When you have the options set to your satisfaction, click on **Find Next**. The cursor jumps to the next instance of the word that you wanted to find, and the dialog box closes. If no such word is found, the message area at the bottom of the SAS workspace displays a message: `WARNING: No occurrences of "word" found.`

Note

> The search function does not find the occurrence of a word that the cursor is in.

Repeating a Search: If you want to search repeatedly for a word, either open the Find dialog box again—it remembers the last search you performed—or press CTRL-R.

Note

> The search stops at the end of the file. If you want to start searching again at the top, press CTRL-R once more.

Replacing Text

FasTip: Click on **Edit→Replace**.

Replacing one string of text with another works similarly to finding text. Click on **Edit** in the SAS System main menu, then click on **Replace**. The Replace dialog box appears, as shown in Figure 3.2.

Figure 3.2 Replace Dialog Box

Replace	? X
Find What:	Find Next
Replace With:	Replace
☐ Match Whole Word Only Direction	Replace All
☐ Match Case ○ Up ● Down	Cancel

Type the search string in the **Find What** field and the replacement string in the **Replace With** field.

Controlling the Search and Replace Parameters: Many of the options in the Replace dialog box are similar to the ones in the Find dialog box. For example, the replacement is case insensitive unless you click on the **Match Case** option. The default direction of the search is down; to change this, click on the **Up** option. The Replace dialog box remembers this direction and retains it for the remainder of your SAS session, unless you change it again. If you want to ensure that only entire instances of the search string are replaced, click on the **Match Whole Word Only** option.

Performing the Replacement: When you have the options set to your satisfaction, click on **Replace**. The SAS System finds the first instance of the search string and replaces it.

Caution

> The SAS System does not prompt you for the replacement. Undo an erroneous replacement by clicking on **Edit** in the SAS System main menu, then click on **Undo** (or press CTRL-Z).

Repeating Replacements: The Replace dialog box does not stay open after it replaces the text. To replace the next instance, open the Replace dialog box again and click on **Replace**. The Replace dialog box does remember what search you performed last time and retains the text strings in the text entry fields.

If you prefer, use the RCHANGE command from the Command bar to repeat replacements. You are not prompted for the replacement.

Getting Prompted for Replacements: There is no "prompt before replace" option in the Replace dialog box. To simulate a prompt, press CTRL-R to perform the repeat-find operation. To do the actual text replacement, open the Replace dialog box again and click on **Replace**.

Replacing All Occurrences of a String: To replace all instances of the search string at once, click on **Replace All** in the Replace dialog box, instead of on **Replace**. Be careful when using **Replace All**—you are not prompted for the replacements, so you might replace a lot of things accidentally if the original string occurs in places that you did not expect. If you find that you've used the Replace All feature unadvisedly, click on **Edit** in the SAS System main menu, then on **Undo** to reverse all the changes at once.

Spell Checking Your Program

V7 Hilites: **Replace** and **Remember** commands are now in the **Tools** menu (when the SPELL window is active).

File menu no longer offers a **Cancel** choice for the SPELL: Suggestions window.

FasTip: Click on **Edit→Check Spelling→Spell All Suggest**.

The SAS System includes a spell checker. To access this feature, click on **Edit** in the SAS System main menu, then on **Check Spelling**. This opens another menu as shown in Figure 3.3.

Figure 3.3 Spell Check Menu

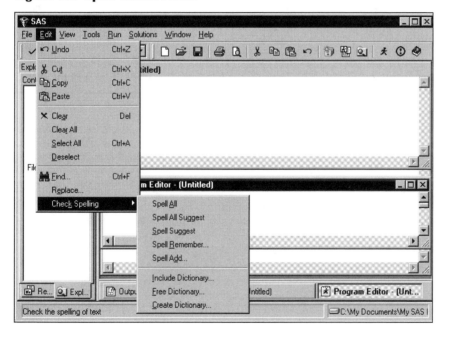

Generating a Misspelled Word List: To generate a list of unrecognized words and their corresponding line numbers, click on **Spell All** in the second-level spell-check menu. The SPELL: Unrecognized Words window opens with the list. Figure 3.4 shows a sample SPELL: Unrecognized Words window.

Figure 3.4 SPELL: Unrecognized Words Window

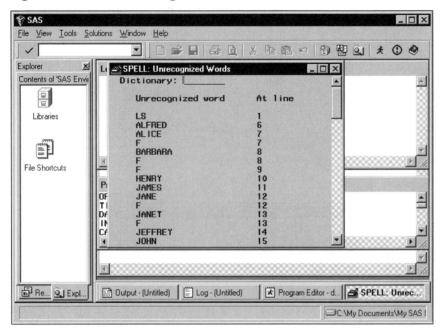

To close the SPELL: Unrecognized Words window, click on its Close button.

Letting the SAS System Make Spelling Suggestions: If you click on **Spell All Suggest** instead of **Spell All** in the second-level spell-check menu, the SPELL: Suggestions window appears. This window lists the first unrecognized word, the dictionary being used, and the suggestions for the misspelled word. Figure 3.5 shows a sample SPELL: Suggestions window.

Figure 3.5. SPELL: Suggestions Window

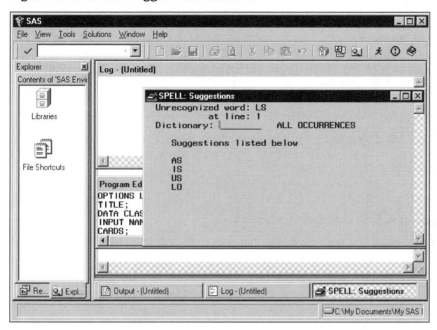

To implement one of the suggestions, click on the word with the correct spelling. Then click on **Tools** in the SAS System main menu, then click on **Replace**. Alternatively, use the TAB key to move the cursor to the correct spelling, then press Enter to highlight your choice. Now issue the REPLACE command from the Command bar. Only that occurrence is corrected.

If you want all occurrences of that misspelling corrected, highlight the correct spelling, then click on **ALL OCCURRENCES** before you do the replace. The message area of the SAS workspace tells you how many occurrences were replaced.

Ignoring Suggestions: If you do not want to take action on a word, click on the Close button of the SPELL: Suggestions window. It moves to the next word.

Canceling the Suggestion Process: To cancel the whole process of spell checking and suggesting corrections, issue the CANCEL command from the Command bar.

Adding Words to the Dictionary: You can add words to the default dictionary so that they are not flagged as misspelled in future spell checks. You can also create auxiliary dictionaries. These techniques work in both the SPELL: Unrecognized Words window and the SPELL: Suggestions window.

To add a word to the default dictionary, click on the word, or use the TAB key to move the cursor to the word, and press Enter to highlight it in the SPELL: Unrecognized Words window. This step is not necessary in the SPELL: Suggestions window. Now click on **Tools** in the SAS System main menu, then on **Remember**. Or, issue the REMEMBER command from the Command bar. From now on, that word is not flagged as misspelled.

To create an auxiliary dictionary, place your cursor in the **Dictionary** field and type a dictionary name. If one does not exist, create a new name, such as MYDICT. The name must be a valid SAS name. This creates an entry MYDICT.DICTIONARY in your SASUSER.PROFILE catalog. In the SPELL: Unrecognized Words window, all REMEMBER commands now affect the auxiliary dictionary, not the default dictionary. In the SPELL: Suggestions window, you must set the dictionary for each change; otherwise the REMEMBER command affects the default dictionary.

To return to using the default dictionary, click in the **Dictionary** field and use your Delete and Backspace keys to clear this field. Now press Enter. The field is blank, and all REMEMBER commands now affect the default dictionary.

Changing the SAS Working Folder

V7 Hilites: Default working folder is now C:\My Documents\My SAS Files.

FasTip: Double-click on the folder icon in the lower-right corner of the SAS workspace.

When you start a SAS session, the SAS System uses a default folder called the SAS working folder. This folder is where the SAS System looks for files, stores files, and so on. For Version 7, the default working folder is C:\My Documents\My SAS Files. You can use the folder lists in dialog boxes such as Open and Save As to change folders when you open and close files. But if all your files reside in a particular folder, it may be more efficient to change the working folder instead of changing the folder in the dialog boxes.

Note

> If you chose a different folder than C:\My Documents\My SAS Files during SAS installation, the folder that you chose will be your default working folder.

The working folder is displayed in the lower-right corner of the SAS workspace. For example, in Figure 3.6 the mouse pointer is near the working folder name (C:\SASPROJ).

Figure 3.6 Working Folder Displayed in the SAS Workspace

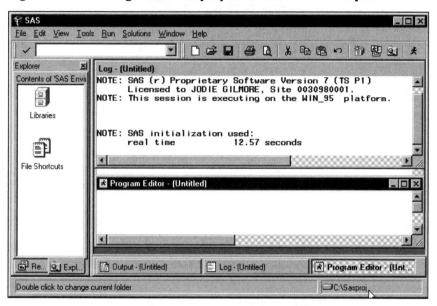

Changing the Working Folder During Your SAS Session: To change the working folder, double-click on the folder name in the lower-right corner of the SAS workspace. The Change Folder dialog box appears, similar to Figure 3.7.

Figure 3.7 Change Folder Dialog Box

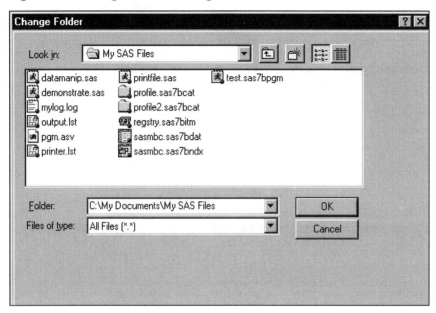

You can change the folder in a number of ways. You can type the full pathname of the folder in the **Folder** field. Or, you can use the mouse to navigate the list of folders and double-click on the folder that you want to use. To move up in the folder hierarchy, click on the icon showing a folder with an up arrow, to the right of the **Look in** field.

Once the **Folder** field contains the name of the folder you want, click on **OK**. If you change the folder more than once during a single SAS session, the **Folder** field remembers all the folders you have used. To select a previous working folder, click on the down arrow by the **Folder** field and select the correct folder. Then click on **OK**.

Note

Changing the working folder using the Change Folder dialog box is not a permanent change. The next time you invoke the SAS System, the working folder defaults to the last working folder that was permanently set.

Changing the Working Folder Permanently: To permanently change the working folder, you must do it outside of the SAS System. Follow these steps:

1. Open the Windows Explorer by right-clicking on the **Start** button and clicking on **Explore**.

2. By default, the Windows Explorer shows you the contents of the **Start Menu** folder. Double-click on **Programs** in the right half of the window, then double-click on **The SAS System** folder.

3. Right-click on **The SAS System for Windows V7,** then click on **Properties.**

4. When the Properties dialog box appears, click on the **Shortcut** tab.

5. Double-click in the **Start in** field, and type the name of the folder that you want to use as the SAS working folder. Be sure to include the full pathname of the folder.

6. Click on **OK.**

The next time you start the SAS System, the new folder is used as the working folder.

Note

This change applies only to the shortcut to the SAS System accessed from the SAS System program group. If you have created additional shortcuts to the SAS System (such as on the desktop), you must change each shortcut's properties individually.

Opening Files

 FasTip: Click on the Open icon on the SAS tool bar.

This section provides details about opening files into the Program Editor window.

Using the Open Dialog Box: To open this dialog box, click on **File** in the SAS System main menu, then click on **Open**. Figure 3.8 shows a sample Open dialog box.

Figure 3.8 Open Dialog Box

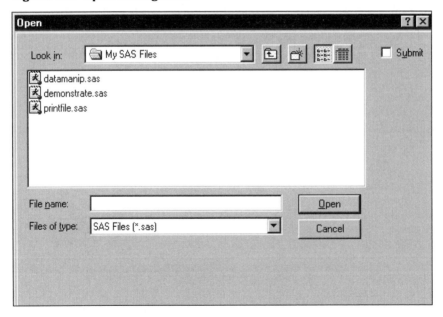

By default, the Open dialog box shows the contents of C:\My Documents\My SAS Files. You can type the name of the file that you want to open in the **File name** field. Or, use the **Look in** and folder list to navigate to the folder where the file is stored. To move up in the folder hierarchy, click on the icon showing a folder with an up arrow, to the right of the Look in field. To open a subfolder, double-click on it in the folder list.

You may want to "filter" the files listed. If a folder contains many files, you can control which extensions are listed. Click on the down arrow by the **Files of type** field. You can choose to show only files with .SAS, .LOG, .LST, or .DAT extensions, or to show all files (*.*). Click on your choice to change the value in the field.

When you have found the file you want to open, click on its name, then click on **Open**. The file is copied to the window from which you opened the dialog box (usually the Program Editor).

If you click on **Submit** in the Open dialog box before you click on **Open**, the file is immediately submitted. Use this option only with files that contain SAS code.

Using the Command Bar: If you prefer, you can issue the INCLUDE command from the Command bar to open a file into the Program Editor window. The syntax of the INCLUDE command is as follows:

INCLUDE *filename*

For example, the following command opens a file named DATAMANIP.SAS:

```
INCLUDE DATAMANIP.SAS
```

If the file is not in the working folder, you must type the full pathname of the file.

The INCLUDE command copies a file to the Program Editor but does not submit it.

Using the Most Recently Used File List: Like many Windows applications, the SAS System remembers the files you have used most recently and lists them in the **File** portion of the SAS System main menu. To see these files, click on **File**. To open a listed file, click on its name. For example, Figure 3.9 shows the **File** menu with three files listed. Clicking on **C:\My Documents\My SAS Files\datamanip.sas** opens that file in the Program Editor window.

Figure 3.9 File Menu Showing the Three Most Recently Used Files

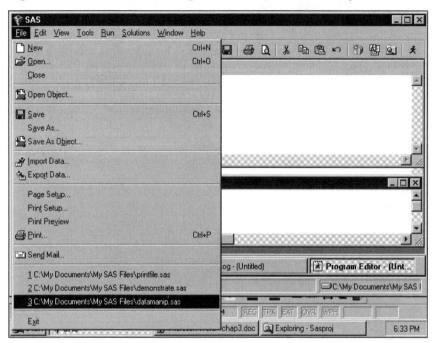

Note

If you already have a file open and click on its name again, you end up with two copies in the Program Editor window.

See "Using the General Tab" in Chapter 6 for information on customizing the recently used file list.

Saving Files

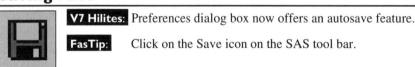

V7 Hilites: Preferences dialog box now offers an autosave feature.

FasTip: Click on the Save icon on the SAS tool bar.

Saving files works similarly to opening files. In Chapter 2, you learned a little about using the Save As dialog box to save a file. This section provides more details about saving files.

Saving an Existing File: If you have a file open in the Program Editor or other SAS window, the name of the file is listed in the window title bar. For example, in Figure 3.10, the mouse pointer is positioned in the Program Editor title bar, near the filename (datamanip.sas).

Figure 3.10 Program Editor Window Showing the Open Filename

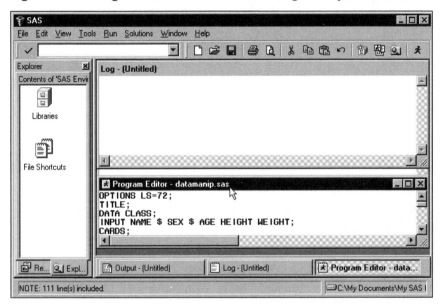

If you have made changes and want to save them to the same file, click on **File**, then click on **Save**. The file is immediately saved. If this is the first time that you have saved a file in this SAS session, the FILE STATUS dialog box illustrated in Figure 3.11 appears (see the discussion that follows the figure).

You can also use the Save As dialog box to save an existing file. Click on **File**, then click on **Save As**. When the Save As dialog box appears, double-click on the filename in the list of files, then click on **Save**. The FILE STATUS dialog box appears, as shown in Figure 3.11.

Figure 3.11 FILE STATUS Dialog Box

This dialog box tells you that the file already exists and gives you the choice of overwriting (replacing) the file or appending new data to it. Because you want to save your changes, choose **Replace**. Choose **Append** only if you are adding new data to the end of your file.

The choice you make in the FILE STATUS dialog box becomes the default for your SAS session. If you want to change the replace/append action, use the Save As dialog box to save the existing file. When you double-click on the existing filename then click on **Save**, the FILE STATUS dialog box opens.

Saving a New File: To save a previously unsaved file, click on **File**, then click on **Save As**. This opens the Save As dialog box, as shown in Figure 3.12.

Figure 3.12. Save As Dialog Box

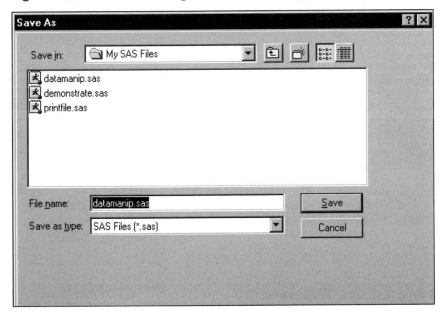

Besides typing the name of the file that you want to save in the **File name** field, you can also use the folder list field to control where the file is stored. The **Save in** field shows the current folder. If you want to save the file in a subfolder of that folder, double-click on the subfolder's name in the folder list. To move up in the folder hierarchy, click on the icon showing a folder with an up arrow, to the right of the **Save in** field.

If you specify a filename that already exists in the folder that you've chosen, you are prompted about replacing or appending the file. If you typed the wrong filename by mistake, click on **Cancel** and type a different filename.

Note

By default, the Save and Save As dialog boxes show the contents of C:\My Documents\My SAS Files.

Using the Command Bar: If you prefer, you can issue the FILE command from the Command bar. The syntax of the FILE command is as follows:

FILE *filename*

For example, the following command saves a file named DATAMANIP.SAS to the working folder:

```
FILE DATAMANIP.SAS
```

If you do not want the file saved to the working folder, you must type the full pathname of the file.

As in using the Save As dialog box, if the file already exists, the FILE STATUS dialog box asks if you want to replace or append the file.

The FILE command copies the contents of the SAS window (for example, the Program Editor) to the file but does not clear the text from the window.

Automatically Saving a File: If you'd like the SAS System to save your file automatically periodically while you work on it, follow these steps:

1. Open the Preferences dialog box by clicking on **Tools** in the SAS System main menu, then on **Options**, then on **Preferences**.

2. Click on the **Edit** tab, and select the **Autosave** option.

3. If necessary, adjust the autosave period (the default is every ten minutes).

4. Click on **OK** to save your changes.

Using a Different Text Editor

Although the SAS System provides the Program Editor, NOTEPAD, and other SAS Text Editor windows, you do not have to use them to develop your SAS code if you prefer another text editor. This is one of the major advantages of using the SAS System under Windows—the ability to share information (including text) between applications.

Earlier in this chapter, you learned to cut, copy, and paste text in the SAS System. Most other Windows applications, including text editors and word processing applications, also support cutting, copying, and pasting text. So, you can type your SAS code in the text editor you prefer to use. Then, copy the code to the Clipboard, and paste it into any SAS Text Editor window (such as the Program Editor, NOTEPAD, or SOURCE window). Examples of applications that you may prefer to use instead of the SAS Text Editor include WordPad (which is shipped with Windows), Microsoft Word, WordPerfect, and WordPro.

Transferring Formatted Text: Formatting, such as bold, underlining, or different font sizes, is not preserved when you paste text into a SAS window. The pasted text in the SAS window is plain unformatted text. (The converse is not true—text copied from the SAS System to another application retains all formatting except color, providing that the target application supports the Rich Text Format.)

Submitting Code from Another Editor: You do not even have to paste code into the SAS System—you can submit it directly from the Clipboard. See "Submitting Code Stored on the Clipboard" and "Using Drag and Drop" in Chapter 4.

Using the SAS System Viewer

V7 Hilites: Lots of new file types are now supported.

SAS System Viewer executable is now named SV.EXE.

Includes enhanced printing, code submission, data-viewing, and other features.

The SAS System Viewer enables you to

- view files created with the SAS System (such as SAS tables) without starting the SAS System—you can even use the SAS System Viewer without having the SAS System installed on your computer.

- edit and save text-based files (such as .sas and .txt files).

- submit SAS code in batch or interactive mode (see Chapter 4).

- print many different kinds of files (including SAS tables and text-based files such as SAS programs)—see Chapter 5.

Note

The SAS System Viewer is freely redistributable.

File Types Supported by the Viewer: The SAS System Viewer can show you the contents of the following types of files:

- SAS programs (.sas) and other text-based files (.dat, .cfg, .html)

- SAS tables (.sas7bdat, .sd7, and .sd2)

- SAS output (.lst)

- SAS logs (.log)

- directory information for Version 6 SAS catalogs (.sc2)—but not Version 7 SAS catalogs

- Release 6.12 FDB (.sf2), MDDB (.sm2), and JMP tables

- SAS transport files (.stx)

- comma-delimited (.csv) and space-delimited (.prw) files.

Once you have a file open in the SAS System Viewer, you can edit it (if the file is a text-based file), print it, search for text, subset your data, format your data, sort your data, and many other useful tasks. If the file is a SAS program, you can submit the code from the SAS System Viewer. Also, you can have several files open at once. Figure 3.13 shows the SAS System Viewer with two files open—a table and a SAS program.

Figure 3.13 SAS System Viewer

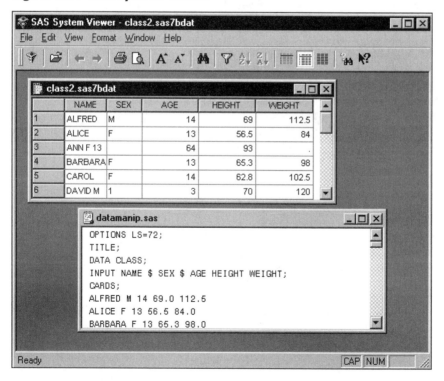

To customize your SAS System Viewer, click on **File** in the SAS System Viewer main menu, then click on **Options**.

For further information on the SAS System Viewer, start the Viewer up and click on **Help** in the Viewer menu. Now click on **Help Topics** and select a topic that interests you. For information specific to printing from the SAS System Viewer, see "Printing from the SAS System Viewer" in Chapter 5.

You can start the SAS System Viewer in several ways.

Starting the SAS System Viewer from the Desktop: To start the SAS System Viewer from the Windows desktop, follow these steps:

1.   Click on the **Start** button.

2.   Click on **Programs**→**The SAS System**→**The SAS System Viewer V7.**

This opens the SAS System Viewer but does not open any particular file. Use the SAS System Viewer's **File** menu to open the file you want to see.

Starting the SAS System Viewer from the DOS Prompt: Use the following syntax to start the SAS System Viewer from the DOS prompt:

sv *<SAS-file>* </p | /pt *printer-name>*

- *SAS-file* is the name of one of the supported types of SAS files (such as a SAS program or a SAS table). If you do not provide a filename, the SAS System Viewer starts but does not open any SAS file.

- /p prints the SAS file to the default printer.

- /pt *printer-name* prints the SAS file to the specific printer named by *printer-name*. See "Discovering What Printers Are Available" in Chapter 5 for more information. Use quotes around a printer name that contains spaces or special characters.

The /p and /pt options are mutually exclusive.

Note

Unless you have added the folder that contains the SV.EXE program to your Windows system variable PATH, you must specify the full pathname for the SV program at the DOS prompt. By default, the full pathname for the SV program is as follows:

C:\PROGRA~1\SAS\SASSYS~1\SV.EXE

The folder names in this path look odd because they contain more than eight characters, but DOS prompt commands recognize only eight-character or shorter filenames. The long names for the folders are Program Files and SAS System Viewer.

Note

The "DOS prompt" referred to in this chapter is called the "command prompt" under Windows NT. Other than this difference in terminology, all the examples and explanations are the same for both Windows 95 or Windows 98 and Windows NT users.

Using Drag and Drop with the SAS System Viewer: You can start the SAS System Viewer by dragging a file icon that represents a text-based file (such as .htm or .sas) and dropping it on an icon that represents the SAS System Viewer. The Viewer starts up and shows the contents of the file you dropped. You cannot start the SAS System Viewer by dragging and dropping SAS tables or catalogs.

If the SAS System Viewer is already open, you drag and drop both text-based files and SAS files (such as SAS tables and catalogs) to the SAS System Viewer.

Note

Drag-and-drop with the SAS System Viewer is available only from the Windows Explorer; you cannot drag and drop file icons from the SAS Explorer onto the SAS System Viewer.

Submitting SAS® Code and Generating Output

4

Introduction

V7 Hilites: The SAS Explorer offers a quick way to submit SAS code.

You can now generate HTML output in addition to the regular text-based output.

Now that you have learned how to use the Program Editor window to open a file and edit it, your next logical step is to submit the code. You learned one way in Chapter 2, using the **Submit** item in the **Run** menu. But there are many other ways to submit code. Which method you choose depends on the following:

- where your code is (it does not have to be in the Program Editor window)

- your preferences for using menus, function keys, tool bars, and the Command bar/command line.

This chapter also presents information on the following topics:

- stopping a SAS job

- managing your SAS log and output files

- generating HTML output.

Note

This chapter and the ones preceding it have focused on using the interactive features of the SAS System. The SAS System also supports batch processing, where you do not interact at all with it and no SAS session windows appear on your screen. See Chapter 9 for information on submitting batch SAS programs.

Submitting Code from the Program Editor Window

 V7 Hilites: Menu items for submitting code are now under **Run** in the SAS System main menu.

FasTip: Click on the Run icon in the SAS tool bar.

In Chapter 2, you submitted your code using the menus. This is one of the ways to submit code from the Program Editor window. Two shortcut methods are to use the tool bar and function keys:

- To submit code via the tool bar, click on the Run icon.

- To submit code via the function keys, press F3.

Note

Before you use any of these methods, be sure the Program Editor window is the active window.

Submitting a Certain Number of Lines

V7 Hilites: **Submit Top Line** is now a menu choice, and the **Submit N Lines** menu choice opens a new dialog box.

FasTip: Click on **Run→Submit Top Line** or **Submit N Lines**.

Highlight text, then press F3.

Instead of submitting a whole block of code, you can submit a certain number of lines, choosing between three methods:

- the **Submit Top Line** menu choice

- the **Submit N Lines** dialog box

- highlighting text.

Submitting a portion of your code is useful if you want to test the first few lines of a program (such as a group of FILENAME or LIBNAME statements) without running the entire program. Or perhaps the code you want to run is the top portion of an existing file. Use one of these techniques to submit only the portion of code you need. Highlighting only the code you want to submit is a handy method of submitting a section of code from the middle of a file.

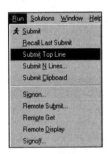

Using the Submit Top Line Menu Choice: If you want to submit only the top line of code, click on **Run** in the SAS System main menu, then on **Submit Top Line**.

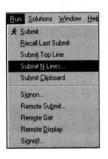

Using the Submit N Lines Dialog Box: If you want to submit more than just the top line of code, but all the code that you want to submit is at the top of your program, you can use the Submit N Lines dialog box. Click on **Run** in the SAS System main menu, then click on **Submit N Lines**. The Submit N Lines dialog box appears, as shown in Figure 4.1.

Figure 4.1   Submit N Lines Dialog Box

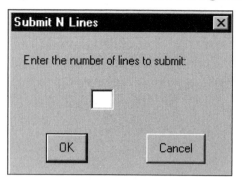

In the text entry field, enter the number of lines you want to submit, then click on **OK**.

Submitting Highlighted Text: To submit a section of code in the middle of your program, you cannot use the Submit N Lines dialog box. However, you can highlight the code, then submit the highlighted text (press F3, click on **Run→Submit**, click on the Run icon, or issue the SUBMIT command.)

Submitting Code from the Open Dialog Box

FasTip: Click on **File→Open**, then choose the filename, click on the **Submit** option, and click on **OK**.

If you know you want to submit a file (not edit it), when you open the file, click on the **Submit** option in the Open dialog box before you click on **OK**. When you do click on **OK**, the file is immediately submitted.

Submitting Code Stored on the Clipboard

FasTip: Click on **Run→Submit Clipboard**.

If you are familiar with a mainframe environment such as OS/390, the SAS System's Program Editor window was your only choice for submitting code. That is, the code you wanted to submit had to be in the Program Editor window before you could run it. Not so for Windows SAS users. Under Windows, you can develop your code using some other tool than the SAS System and submit the code without ever using the Program Editor window. For example, you prefer editing text in Word or some other word processing application, as discussed in "Using a Different Text Editor" in Chapter 3.

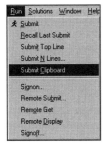

To use this technique, copy your SAS program to the Clipboard while in the other application. Now switch to your SAS session and click on **Run** in the SAS System main menu, then click on **Submit Clipboard**. The text stored on the Clipboard is submitted to the SAS System. The messages associated with your program appear in the SAS Log window, but the Program Editor window remains empty.

Using Drag and Drop

In Chapter 3, you learned how to drag and drop text. You can use this technique to submit code. You can also drag and drop file icons to submit code.

Dragging and Dropping Text: By default, when you highlight a section of text, drag it, and drop it into the Program Editor window, the text is included—but not submitted. You cannot drop text over a non-text-editing SAS window, such as the Log window.

If you use the right mouse button instead of the left mouse button to drag and drop the text, a dialog box asks whether you want to include or submit the code. To submit the code, click on **Submit** in the dialog box. This technique works only for text dragged from one SAS window to another and from applications that support right mouse button dragging.

Dragging and Dropping File Icons: When you look at the contents of a folder in the SAS Explorer, each file is represented by an icon. To submit a file that contains SAS code, open the SAS Explorer and display the folder that contains the file you want to submit. Also, make sure the other SAS window (such as the Program Editor, Log, or Output window) is visible.

Whether the text of the file is only copied to the SAS window or submitted immediately depends on where you drop the file icon:

- To submit the file immediately, drop the icon on the Log or Output window.

- To copy the text of the file to the SAS System without submitting the code, drop the icon on the Program Editor window.

Submitting Several Files at Once: If you select two or more files in the SAS Explorer and drop them on the Program Editor window, the files are submitted or included sequentially. However, you cannot predict the order in which the programs are submitted or included.

You select several files by using the Shift and Control keys when you click on the files, as explained here:

- To select a contiguous block of files in the SAS Explorer, click on the first file. Now hold the Shift key down and click on the last file.

- To select several non-contiguous files in the SAS Explorer, click on the first file. Now hold the Control key down and click on the other files.

Note

You can also drag and drop files from the Windows Explorer. See Appendix 3 for more information on the Windows Explorer.

Right-clicking on File Icons: By right-clicking on a SAS program file icon in the My Favorite Folders window, you can choose to submit the code in several different ways. Open the My Favorite Folders window (see "Using the My Favorite Folders Feature" in Chapter 2), and display the folder that contains the SAS program file that you want to submit. Right-click on the file—a menu opens as shown in Figure 4.2.

Figure 4.2 Submitting a File from the My Favorite Folders Window

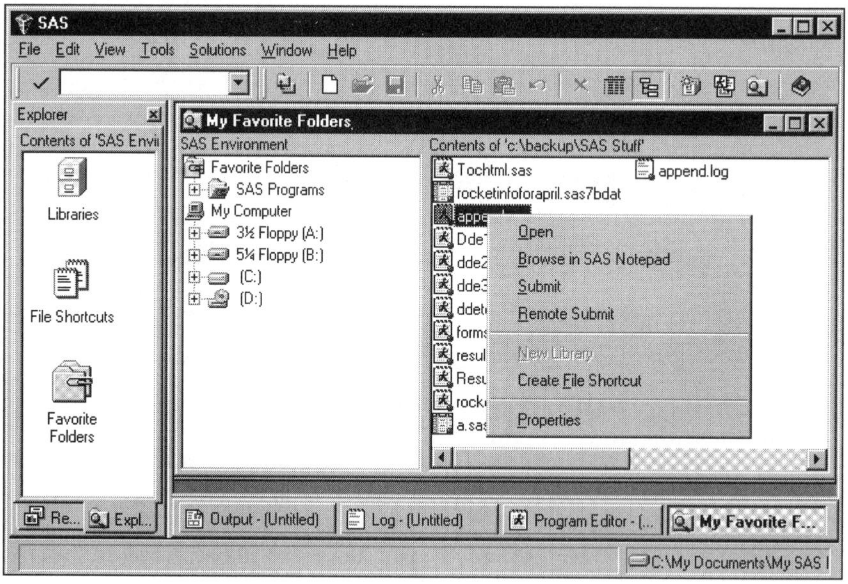

Note

> You can also customize the docked SAS Explorer window to show the My Favorite Folders folder; see "Customizing the SAS Explorer" in Chapter 6 for more information on how to do this.

You can choose one of three ways to submit your code:

- Clicking on **Open** copies the program to the Program Editor window, but does not submit the code. This is useful if you want to edit the program before submitting it.

- Clicking on **Submit** copies the code to the Program Editor window and submits the code.

- Clicking on **Remote Submit** submits the code to a remote SAS session using SAS/CONNECT software; see Chapter 12 for more information on using SAS/CONNECT software.

Note

> You can also right-click on SAS file icons in the Windows Explorer, with much the same results. An additional feature of submitting a program from the Windows Explorer is that you can also choose to submit the file in batch mode. See Appendix 3 for more information on the Windows Explorer; see Chapter 9 for information on submitting batch SAS programs.

Double-clicking on File Icons: You can double-click on files with .SAS and .SS2 extensions in the SAS Explorer. This technique includes the file into the Program Editor window—it does not submit the code.

Note

> You can also double-click on SAS file icons in the Windows Explorer, which submits the program in batch mode. See Chapter 9 for more information on using the Windows Explorer to submit batch SAS programs.

Dropping File Icons on the SAS.EXE Icon: You can drag and drop SAS program file icons on the SAS.EXE file icon. Unlike other techniques discussed in this chapter, this technique can be used only from the Windows Explorer, and it runs the program in batch mode. Therefore, this technique is not suitable for programs that require interaction (such as SAS/GRAPH procedures, PROC REPORT windows, or other interactive SAS System components).

To use this technique, follow these steps:

1. Start the Windows Explorer by right-clicking on the **Start** button, then clicking on **Explore**.

2. Click on the file you want to submit, to highlight it.

3. If necessary, open another Windows Explorer window, and display the SAS System folder, where the SAS.EXE file is stored.

    This step is not necessary if the file you want to submit is stored in the same folder as the SAS.EXE file.

    To open a second Windows Explorer window, right-click on the **Start** button, and click on **Explore**. Use the mouse to resize and move the new window as necessary.

4. Drag the program file icon over to the SAS.EXE file icon and release it. As you drag the file icon, a plus sign follows your mouse pointer. When the plus sign is over the SAS.EXE file icon, release the mouse pointer. Figure 4.3 shows how your display might look right before you release the mouse pointer.

Figure 4.3 Dropping a File on the SAS.EXE Icon

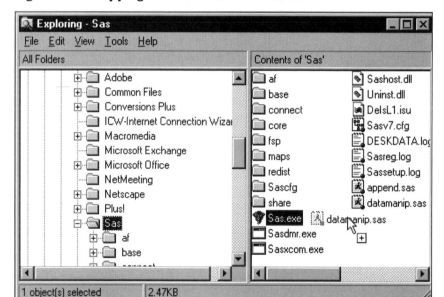

5. When you release the mouse pointer, you see a dialog box that contains the following question:

    ```
    Are you sure you want to start executable using dropped-file as
       the initial file?
    ```

    Click on **Yes** to continue; click on **No** if the executable or dropped filename is incorrect. If you click on **Yes,** the SAS System starts in batch mode and runs the file you selected. Log and list files are created as for any batch program. See "Understanding Where Batch Logs and Output Go" in Chapter 9.

Also refer to Chapter 9 for additional methods of submitting batch SAS jobs.

Note

> If the SAS System is running when you drop a file icon on the SAS.EXE icon, a second SAS session is started.

Submitting Code from the SAS System Viewer

One handy way of submitting code is from the SAS System Viewer. When you have a file that contains SAS code open in the Viewer, you can choose between submitting the code in batch mode or interactively.

 To submit a batch SAS job from the SAS System Viewer, click on the Run icon in the SAS System Viewer tool bar.

Alternatively, click on **File** in the SAS System Viewer main menu, then click on **Batch Submit**.

To submit an interactive SAS job from the SAS System Viewer, click on **File** in the SAS System Viewer main menu, then click on **Submit**. A new instance of SAS is opened (even if one is already running), and the code is submitted.

Note

> If you already have a SAS session running, your SASUSER profile will not be available to the session opened by the SAS System Viewer.

Recalling Submitted Code

V7 Hilites: **Recall Last Submit** is now located under the **Run** menu item.

FasTip: Click on **Run→Recall Last Submit**.

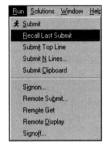

Unless you're a whiz-bang programmer, sometimes your programs contains errors. (Dang those tricky semicolons!) To recall submitted code to the Program Editor window, click on **Run** in the SAS System main menu, then click on **Recall Last Submit**. If you have submitted three blocks of code, clicking on **Recall Last Submit** three times recalls the text in the opposite order it was submitted, inserting the recalled text before whatever text is already in the Program Editor window.

(F4 is the keyboard shortcut for the **Recall Last Submit** menu choice.)

Note

Even if you have submitted text via the Clipboard, the **Submit** option in the Open dialog box, or drag and drop, the **Recall Last Submit** menu choice still recalls your programs.

Interrupting a Submit

V7 Hilites: New Attention icon on the SAS tool bar interrupts the current program.

FasTip: Click on the Attention icon on the SAS tool bar.

If you submit a long program or a program that contains an infinite loop, you may want to abort the program. You can stop a program in two ways:

- stop only the program

- cancel the entire SAS session.

Stopping a Program: To stop a SAS program, click on the Attention icon on the tool bar.

Alternatively, press CTRL-Break. The Break key may say "Pause" on it—it is usually located on the upper-right side of your keyboard.

When you click on the Attention icon or press CTRL-Break, the Tasking Manager appears. Depending on what the SAS System is busy doing, various tasks are listed in the Tasking Manager dialog box. A sample dialog box is shown in Figure 4.4.

Figure 4.4 Sample Tasking Manager Dialog Box

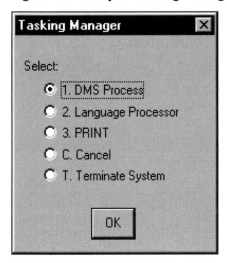

To cancel a procedure or DATA step, click on the appropriate line in the Tasking Manager dialog box, then click on **OK**. This opens the BREAK dialog box. (Figure 4.5 shows the BREAK dialog box.) If you want to end your entire SAS session, click on **Terminate SAS System** in the Tasking Manager dialog box. If you opened the Tasking Manager by mistake, click on **Cancel**. This closes the dialog box and enables your program to continue running normally.

Figure 4.5 Sample BREAK Dialog Box

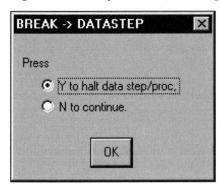

If the BREAK dialog box appears, click on **Y to halt data step/proc** to complete the program termination. If you have accessed the BREAK dialog box unintentionally, click on **N to continue**. Your program will proceed normally.

Note

It may take several seconds for the Tasking Manager or BREAK dialog box to appear—do not click on the Attention icon or press CTRL-Break more than once.

Canceling the Entire SAS Session: If your program has created problems and you think the best thing to do is to start over, cancel the entire SAS session. Click on the SAS System Close button. Any unsaved work is lost when you do this, so use it only as an emergency measure, or save your work first.

When All Else Fails...: If things are really bad, your display is locked up, and the mouse does not work, try pressing CTRL-ALT-DEL. The results differ between Windows 95 and Windows NT:

- For Windows 95, pressing CTRL-ALT-DEL once displays a list of tasks and shows you which are not responding. Click on any task that is listed as not responding, then click on **End Task**. If this has no effect, press CTRL-ALT-DEL a second time to reboot your computer.

- For Windows NT, pressing CTRL-ALT- DEL displays a dialog box. Click on the **Task Manager** button, then click on the **Applications** tab. End any task that is listed as not responding. If this has no effect, press CTRL-ALT-DEL a second time to reboot your computer.

If CTRL-ALT-DEL has no effect, you may have to turn your system off--but this is a last-ditch choice and may cause you to lose a lot of work if you have several applications open and have not saved recently. Also, Windows may request to run ScanDisk the next time you boot up.

Managing Your Log and Output Files

When you submit code, the Log window tracks the creation of tables, setting of options, procedure statements, and other items. The Output window may contain the results of your program. If you want to save the log or output of a program, click in the appropriate window to make it the active window. Then, use the Save As dialog box or the FILE command to save the file, as described in "Saving Files" in Chapter 3. Usually, log files are saved with an extension of .log and output files have an extension of .lst.

Alternatively, use the Results window to save selected portions of your output. See "Looking at the Output" in Chapter 2 for more details on the Results window.

Generating Different Kinds of Output Using the Output Delivery System (ODS)

Version 7 of the SAS System offers much more flexibility in the kinds of output you can generate. Now, as well as the regular text-based output that you could always generate, you can use the new SAS System Output Delivery System (ODS) to generate HTML output. This section gives an overview of some of the features of the ODS—see the SAS Institute documentation (online and otherwise) for the full description of the ODS.

Note

Future releases of the SAS System may support even more kinds of output, such as PostScript, PCL, and Rich Text Format.

Understanding ODS Terminology: Before you can learn to use the ODS, you need to understand some terms commonly used when talking about managing your output with the ODS. Use the list below as a reference as you read the rest of this chapter.

output object	a separate entity created by a SAS procedure, such as a table, plot, or chart. These output objects are listed in the Results window.
output object name	the name used for the output object in the Results window. See the discussion of the Results window in "Looking at the Output" in Chapter 2 for more information.
output destination	the type of formatting you want applied to the object (such as HTML).
template	a layout design for your output—such as where columns are displayed.
style	a font and color design for your output.

Telling SAS You Want HTML Output: By default, the SAS System creates regular listing output. If you'd prefer output that looks more "document ready," you may want to produce HTML output instead. You can then use the .htm files created by SAS in Word documents, on your Web site, and so on, without further formatting.

To tell the SAS System you want to generate HTML output from your code, follow these steps:

1. Open the Preferences dialog box by clicking on **Tools** in the SAS System main menu, then on **Options**, then on **Preferences**.

2. Click on the **Results** tab. This tab is shown in Figure 4.6.

Figure 4.6 Results Tab of the Preferences Dialog Box

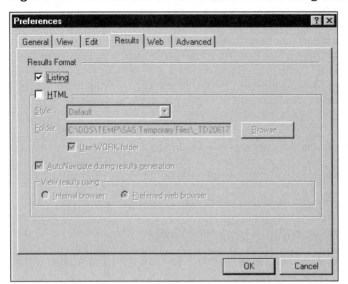

3. Select the **HTML** option and deselect the **Listing** option.

    Note

    You can select both the **Listing** and **HTML** options; in this case, the listing output goes to the Output window and the HTML output goes to the .htm file and is displayed in the Results Viewer.

4. To select a style, click on the down arrow next to the **Style** field, and click on the style you want. The style you choose affects all subsequent SAS output, until you change it again. A style affects the colors used in the display of your HTML output. The default style is called **Default**.

5. By default, the HTML output is written to a temporary .htm file in your WORK data library. The default filename is sashtm#.htm, where # starts at 0 and increments each time output is generated. (So, for example, if your code contains two PROC PRINT steps, two .htm files are created.)

    To specify a permanent file, deselect the **Use WORK Folder** choice, then click in the **Folder** field and specify the folder where you want the output stored. The filenames created in this folder are named the same as the temporary files: sashtm#.htm.

6. Decide whether you want to view the HTML output in the internal SAS browser (the default) or your preferred Web browser (such as Microsoft Internet Explorer or Netscape), and select the appropriate option.

You can control your HTML output even further by using the TEMPLATE procedure and the ODS statement; for details on the ODS statement, see "Using the Output Delivery System in Batch Mode" in Chapter 9. The TEMPLATE procedure is beyond the scope of this book; refer to the SAS online help and documentation for further details on this procedure.

Viewing the HTML Output: If you've told the SAS System that you want to view HTML output using the internal browser, click on the **Results Viewer** tab in the SAS Window Bar to see your output. Figure 4.7 shows a sample Results Viewer window with some output.

Figure 4.7 Looking at HTML Output in the Results Viewer Window

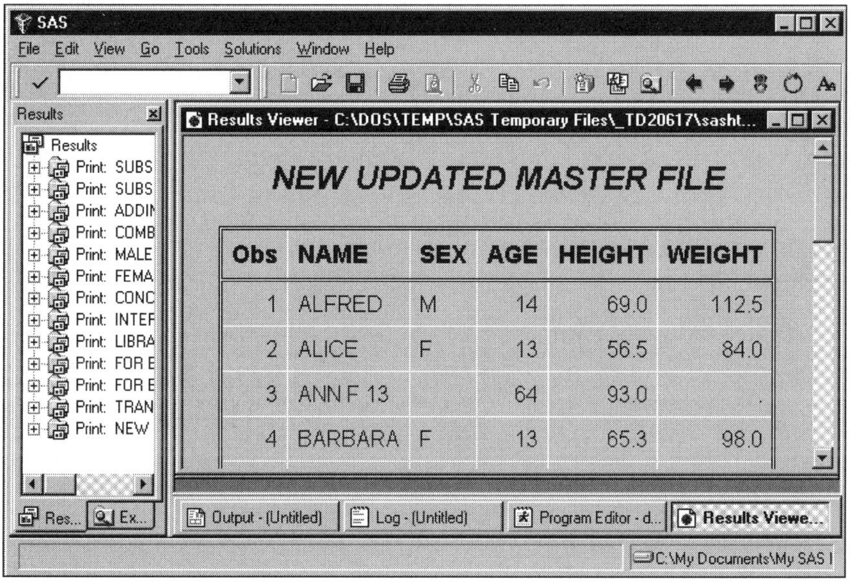

To navigate in the Results Viewer window, right-click in the window to display the popup menu. Click on **Forward** and **Back** to move to different pieces of your output. (Each procedure step that produces output is considered a separate piece.) Within each piece of output, use the scroll bar and the PageUp and PageDown keys to move the view.

If you close the Results Viewer window, you can issue the WBROWSE command from the Command bar to display already-generated HTML output, using your preferred Web browser. (There is no way to reopen the internal SAS System browser without re-running your code.) The syntax for using the WBROWSE command to display a particular HTML file is as follows:

```
WBROWSE "HTML-filename"
```

You can use your preferred Web browser to view your HTML SAS output, instead of the internal SAS System browser. If you have selected this option in the Preferences dialog box, your output appears in your Web browser automatically after you submit the code.

A final method of viewing your HTML SAS output is to use the SAS System Viewer. Simply open the Viewer, then open the HTML file you want to see. The output appears as it does in the SAS System's Results Viewer window.

You can also print your HTML SAS output—see Chapter 5 for more details.

5 Printing

Introduction

V7 Hilites: You can no longer drag and drop SAS files (such as .SAS and .LST) files onto a printer icon, as you could with Version 6. This feature may reappear in later releases of the SAS System.

If you are familiar with a mainframe environment like OS/390, you are used to printing by setting system options such as PAGESIZE and LINESIZE and issuing the PRINT command. While the system options and the command still work under Windows, you can also use dialog boxes to set the page and line size. Not only that, but the dialog boxes also enable you to choose fonts, typesizes, and other features. You can even print files such as SAS programs and SAS output without starting the SAS System, by using the SAS System Viewer.

SAS System print jobs are managed by Windows. The dialog boxes you see when printing from SAS are standard dialog boxes for selecting printer options. This chapter explains a bit about how printing works in Windows in general, then addresses printing issues specific to the SAS System.

Although the discussion in this chapter uses the Output window (because often you want to print the output from your code), the principles are the same for any SAS window (such as the Log and SOURCE windows).

Note

This chapter deals primarily with printing from a windowing session. For information on printing in batch mode, see "Printing in Batch Mode" in Chapter 9. Appendix 2, "Creating a Print File," discusses how to create files that contain printer codes. Also, except for the first two sections and the final section in this chapter, the information applies only to printing listing-formatted SAS output, not HTML SAS output. The final section describes printing HTML SAS output.

Discovering What Printers Are Available

FasTip: Click on **Start→Settings→Printers**.

Your computer may be connected to several printers—perhaps a PostScript printer, a plotter, and a network printer. To see which printers are available to your Windows applications, click on the **Start** button, then click on **Settings**, then click on **Printers**. The Printers window appears, similar to the one shown in Figure 5.1. (The Printer window displayed on your screen will be somewhat different from the figure because you will have different printers installed on your system.)

Figure 5.1 Using the Printers Window to See Which Printers Are Available

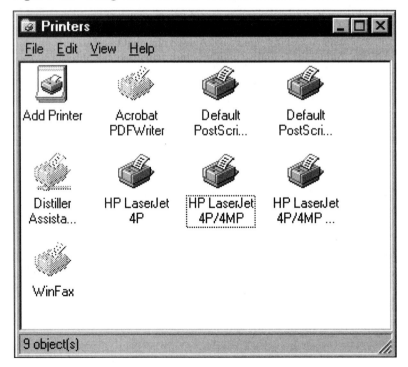

Even though you may have several printers, only one is the default printer—the printer used for a print job if you do not explicitly specify the printer. To see which printer is the default printer, click on a printer's icon, then click on **File** in the Printers window menu. If there is a check mark next to **Set As Default**, that printer is the default printer.

To change the default printer, first click on the icon in the Printers window for the printer you want to use as the default. Then click on **File** in the Printers window menu, then click on **Set As Default**.

Understanding How Windows Manages Print Jobs

By default, Windows manages all print jobs submitted from Windows applications, including from the SAS System. Windows routes the jobs to the appropriate printers, monitors the status of the printers, and controls when each job prints. In mainframe terms, this process is similar to a printer spool, except that in the PC environment, you typically have more control over the print jobs.

As print jobs accumulate, Windows creates a print queue. Use this print queue to change the order and priority of print jobs, temporarily stop printing a job (pause), resume printing a job, or delete a print job.

Listing Your Print Jobs: To list your print jobs, click on the **Start** button, click on **Settings**, then click on **Printers**. When the Printers window appears, double-click on the icon for the printer you want to access. A window similar to Figure 5.2 appears.

Figure 5.2 Listing the Jobs for a Printer

Document Name	Status	Owner	Progress	Started At
Microsoft Word - ch05-3-24-199...	Printing	jodie	23 of 47 pa...	7:52:27 AM 3/28/98
Microsoft Word - ch04-3-24-199...		jodie	12 page(s)	7:53:08 AM 3/28/98
Microsoft Word - ch03-3-24-199...		jodie	4 page(s)	7:53:40 AM 3/28/98
Microsoft Word - ch02-3-24-199...		jodie	10 page(s)	7:54:49 AM 3/28/98
Microsoft Word - ch01-3-24-199...		jodie	2 page(s)	7:55:26 AM 3/28/98

HP LaserJet 4P/4MP
Printer Document View Help

5 jobs in queue

When you send a print job from the SAS System or another Windows application, the job is listed in the appropriate printer window. From this window you can pause or rearrange the print jobs; see "Delaying Printing," "Resuming Printing," and "Changing the Order of Print Jobs" later in this chapter.

Configuring Your Printer for Use with the SAS System

V7 Hilites: The Page Setup dialog box is now directly accessible from the **File** menu.

You can now programmatically set page setup options—see Chapter 9 for details.

FasTip: Click on **File→Print Setup** or **File→Page Setup**.

You may want to configure your printer before you use it with the SAS System. For example, you may decide that you want to print a particular piece of output in landscape mode instead of the default portrait mode.

In general, you'll use the Print Setup dialog box to configure your printer, although you can also use the Print dialog box.

Selecting a Printer: Click on **File** in the SAS System main menu, then click on **Print Setup**. The Print Setup dialog box appears, similar to Figure 5.3.

Figure 5.3   Print Setup Dialog Box

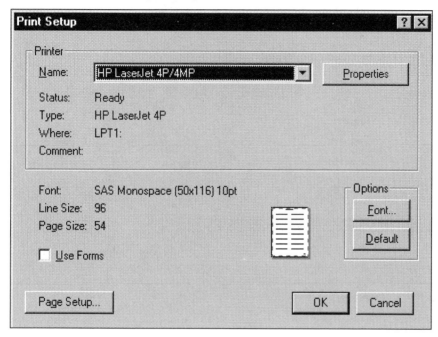

In this dialog box, use the **Printer** field to specify which printer to use (click on the down arrow to display the list of available printers). Click on **OK** to close the Print Setup dialog box.

Changing Your Page Orientation: To change the page orientation, click on **File** in the SAS System main menu, then click on **Page Setup**. The Page Setup dialog box appears, as shown in Figure 5.4.

Figure 5.4 Page Setup Dialog Box

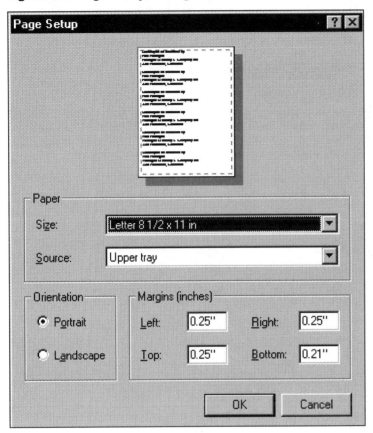

Note

You can also access the Page Setup dialog box by clicking on **Page Setup** in the Print Setup dialog box.

In the Page Setup dialog box, adjust the margins and the page orientation. To use landscape mode, click on **Landscape**. To change the various margins, either click on the up and down arrows by each value or double-click in the margin's box and type the new value. The SAS System automatically adjusts the page size and line size to fit the new margins. If you want to adjust the paper size or source, use the **Size** and **Source** fields to do so.

When you are finished, click on **OK** to close the Page Setup dialog box.

Changing Other Aspects of Your Output: If you want to change other aspects of the printer setup, explore available options for your printer by opening the Print Setup dialog box, then clicking on **Properties** in the Print Setup dialog box. When you click on this button, a printer-specific setup dialog box appears. For example, Figure 5.5 shows the printer options dialog box for the HP LaserJet 4P.

Figure 5.5 Example Printer Properties Dialog Box

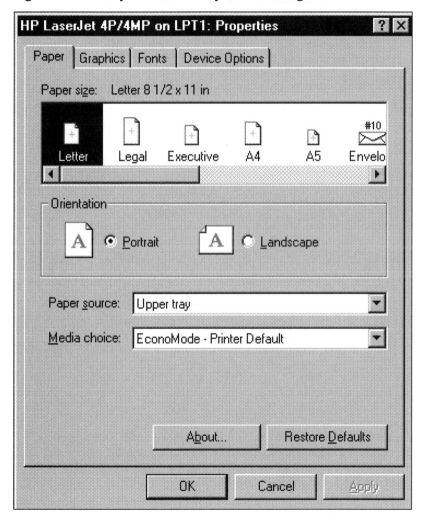

Your printer manual can help you decipher the available choices.

Click on **OK** to return to the Print Setup dialog box.

Choosing a Printer Font: Clicking on **Font** in the Print Setup dialog box opens the Font dialog box, where you can choose the font and typesize you want to use for a particular print job. Figure 5.6 shows the printer Font dialog box.

Figure 5.6 Dialog Box for Setting the Printer Font

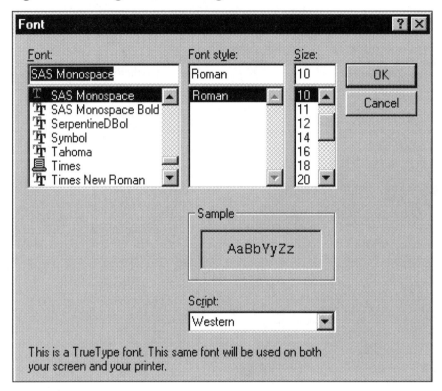

By default, the SAS System uses a 10-point SAS Monospace font for your output. To change the font, use the **Font**, **Font style**, and **Size** fields to choose a font you like (scroll if necessary).

Only monospace fonts (such as Courier and SAS Monospace) work well with SAS output. Proportional fonts (such as Times Roman and Helvetica) do not produce satisfactory results. This is because with monospace fonts each character uses the same amount of space, so columns of data align exactly. Proportional fonts use different amounts of space for different characters, so columns of data do not align correctly.

Note

The fonts the SAS System uses for output and the fonts used in SAS windows are separate. The font you choose using the **Font** button in the Print Setup dialog box does not affect the font used in SAS System windows. Use the screen Font dialog box to set the screen fonts. This dialog box is accessed through the **Tools→Options→Fonts** choice in the SAS System main menu.

Resetting Printer Options to the Default: If you have explored the various printer setup dialog boxes and made some changes that produce results you did not expect, return all printer options to their default settings by clicking on **Default** in the Print Setup dialog box.

Configuring Your Printer from the Print Dialog Box: You can configure your printer directly from the Print dialog box. Click on **File** in the SAS System main menu, then click on **Print**. When the Print dialog box appears, click on **Setup**. This opens the Print Setup dialog box, just as if you had clicked on **File→Print Setup**.

When you're finished setting print job parameters, click on **OK** until you return to the Print dialog box. Then, you can click on **Print** to print the job or on **Preview** to see how the output will look before printing. See "Previewing a Print Job" later in this chapter for instructions on previewing.

The **Properties** button in the Print dialog box also lets you set print job characteristics. Clicking on **Properties** opens a printer-specific dialog box (the same one opened by clicking on **Properties** in the Print Setup dialog box).

If the Print Setup and the printer's Properties dialog boxes contain the same parameter (such as landscape versus portrait mode), setting the parameter in one dialog box updates that parameter in the other dialog box.

Understanding How the Changes You Make Affect Your Windows Environment: The changes you make via the SAS System Print Setup and Page Setup dialog boxes are permanent. That is, they last, even if you exit the SAS System, until you change them again. However, the changes you make via the SAS System's Print Setup and Page Setup dialog boxes do not affect other Windows applications' (such as Microsoft Word) printer settings.

Printing the Contents of a SAS Window as Text

V7 Hilites: Print dialog box now offers page-range and number-of-copies options.

FasTip: Click on the Print icon on the SAS tool bar. (This bypasses the Print dialog box.)

Suppose you have submitted your SAS code, and now the Output window contains the results of your data analysis. To print the results, click on **File** in the SAS System main menu, then click on **Print** (or press CTRL-P). The Print dialog box appears, as shown in Figure 5.7.

Figure 5.7 Print Dialog Box

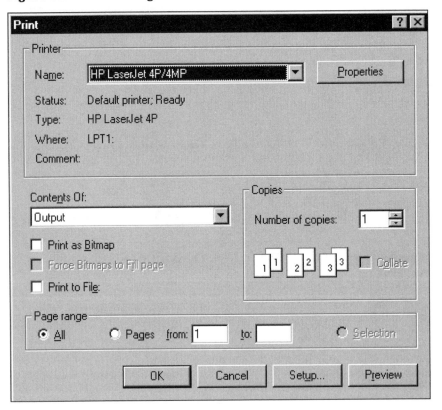

The **Contents of** field displays the title of the active window (in this case the Output window). Adjust the other option in the Print dialog box, as discussed in the following subsections. To submit the print job to the Windows print queue, click on **OK** in the Print dialog box.

Controlling How Much Information Is Printed: You can specify a page range for your print job—either click on the **All** option in the **Page range** area, or specify the beginning and ending page numbers.

Note

Remember you can also control how much output is printed by selecting individual pieces of output in the Results window.

To print only a certain portion of the information displayed in a window, first highlight that portion you want to print. Then, open the print dialog box—the **Selection** option in the **Page range** area is selected. When you click on **OK**, the highlighted portion of the window is printed.

If you want more than one copy of your output, specify the number of copies in the **Copies** area. Unless your printer supports collating, the **Collate** option is grayed out.

Configuring the Printer at the Last Minute: If you've forgotten to configure the printer for this job, click on **Setup** in the Print dialog box, which opens the Print Setup dialog box. Configure the printer, as described earlier in this chapter. Clicking on **OK** in the Print Setup dialog box returns you to the Print dialog box.

Bypassing the Print Dialog Box: If you have your print options set the way you want, you may prefer not to see the Print dialog box when you print. Clicking on the Print icon in the SAS tool bar is a quick way to print without accessing the Print dialog box.

Also, printing from the Results window bypasses the Print dialog box; before printing from the Results window, be sure your printer is configured properly.

Printing the Contents of a SAS Window as a Bitmap

FasTip: Click on **File→Print→Print as Bitmap**.

In the previous section, you printed the contents of the Output window as plain text. You can also print the whole window—including the scroll bars, maximize and minimize buttons, title bars, and so on. That is, you create a bitmap of the window.

Bitmap files are useful when you want a picture. For example, the screen dumps in this book, such as Figure 5.8, are bitmaps. If you are developing a full-screen application, you may want to print some SAS windows as bitmaps to accompany your documentation. Or, if you are teaching a class, you may want to show your students what a window looks like.

To print a window as a bitmap, click on **File** in the SAS System main menu, then on **Print**. Now click on **Print as Bitmap**. As Figure 5.8 shows, now the **Contents of** field indicates that you are going to print the Output window as a bitmap.

Figure 5.8 Print Dialog Box Ready to Print the Output Window
as a Bitmap

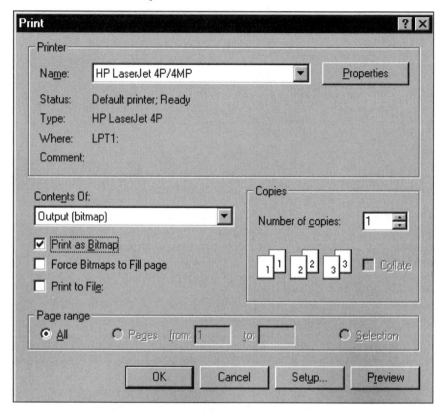

When you have the bitmap option checked, you can choose to print one of several bitmaps. Click on the down arrow by the **Contents of** field. The choices include the following:

- *active-window* (**bitmap**) - prints the active window as a bitmap

- **AWS window** (**bitmap**) - prints the whole SAS workspace as a bitmap

- **Entire screen** (**bitmap**) - prints the entire screen (including all other visible Windows applications and icons) as a bitmap

- **Clipboard** (**bitmap**) - prints whatever is stored on the Clipboard as a bitmap.

The last choice, the Clipboard, is discussed in the next section, "Printing the Contents of the Clipboard."

When you click on the bitmap option, another option appears: **Force Bitmaps to Fill page**. If you select this option, the SAS System scales the output so that it takes up the entire page.

Printing the Contents of the Clipboard

FasTip: Copy the text or graphic to the Clipboard, then click on **File**→**Print**→down arrow of **Contents of** field→**Clipboard (text)** or **Clipboard (bitmap)**.

Printing from the Clipboard is another way (besides highlighting) to print only a portion of your output.

Printing Text: Follow these steps to print text from the Clipboard:

1. Use your mouse to highlight the section of text you want to print.

2. Click on **Edit** in the SAS System main menu, then click on **Copy** (or press CTRL-C) to copy the text to the Clipboard.

3. Click on **File** in the SAS System main menu, then click on **Print** (or press CTRL-P), and click on the down arrow by the **Contents of** field. Click on **Clipboard (text)**, then click on **OK**.

The only text that is printed is the section you highlighted.

Printing Bitmaps: You can also print the Clipboard as a bitmap, to print portions of your screen that are valid bitmaps. You must be able to select and copy these bitmaps from the screen. For example, if you select and copy to the Clipboard an icon that appears in the SAS Graphics Editor window, you can then use the **Clipboard (bitmap)** option to print this icon.

To print the Clipboard as a bitmap, follow these steps:

1. Copy the appropriate image to the Clipboard.

2. Click on **File** in the SAS System main menu, then click on **Print** (or press CTRL-P), and click on the **Print as Bitmap** option.

3. Click on the down arrow by the **Contents of** field. Click on **Clipboard (bitmap)**, then click on **OK**.

You see a message that your printer is now printing the bitmap.

Previewing a Print Job

 FasTip: Click on the Preview icon on the SAS tool bar.

Before you print the contents of a window, such as the Output window, it may be helpful to see how it will appear when printed.

To preview a print job, follow these steps:

1. Make the window you want to print active by clicking in it.

2. Click on **File** in the SAS System main menu, then on **Print**, to open the Print dialog box. Use the **Setup** button to set your print job parameters. If you need help, refer to "Configuring Your Printer" earlier in this chapter.

3. Once your print job parameters are set, click on **Preview** in the Print dialog box. The Print Preview window appears, showing you your output.

    For example, Figure 5.9 shows the Print Preview window for a page of output ready to print in landscape mode.

Figure 5.9 Using the Print Preview Window

![Screenshot of the Print Preview window showing toolbar buttons Next, Previous, Zoom, Close, Help, Print, with a preview page of SAS output and status bar reading "Preview: Page 1 of 13".]

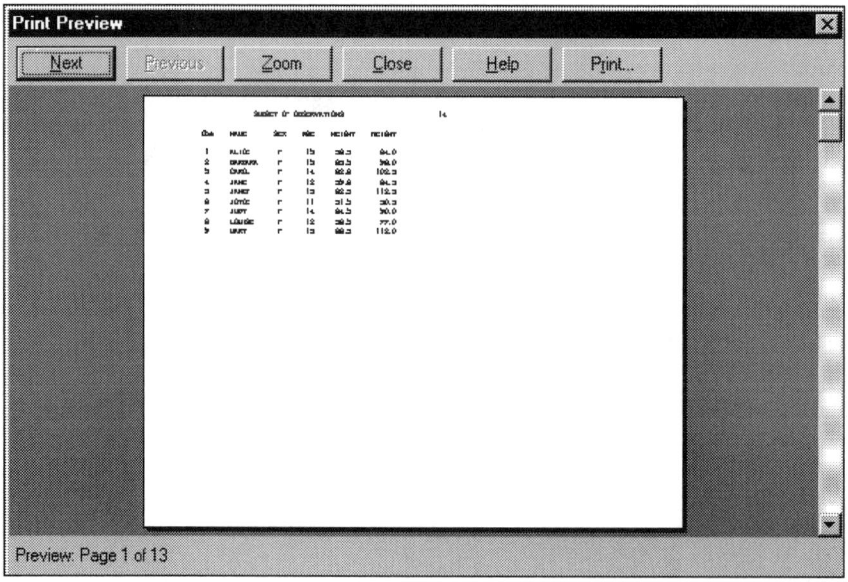

Use the PageUp and PageDown keys to scroll through multiple pages. To see the output in detail, click on **Zoom**.

4. To print your job, click on **Print** in the Print Preview window. If you decide you do not want to print, click on **Close** in the Print Preview window.

It is possible to go directly to the Print Preview window before you set your print job parameters. To do this, click on **File** in the SAS System main menu, then click on **Print Preview**. Use the **Print** button to set the print job parameters. When you click on **OK** in the Print dialog box, the output is sent to the printer.

Note

> The print preview feature is not available if you have **Use Forms** selected in the Print Setup dialog box.

Delaying Printing

FasTip: Click on the **Start** button→**Settings**→**Printers**.

Click on the icon for the printer you want to pause.

Then click on **File**→**Pause Printing** in the Printers window menu.

You may want to postpone printing all your SAS jobs and print them all at once—perhaps you want to be sure the printer contains a special type of paper, or you want to delay printing long jobs until a more convenient time. Use the Windows Printers window to delay your print jobs.

To delay the printing of a print job, follow these steps:

1. Click on the **Start**→**Settings**→**Printers**.

2. When the Printers window appears, click on the name of the printer that handles your SAS print jobs. This highlights the printer name.

3. Now click on **File** in the Printers window menu, then click on **Pause Printing**.

If you need to pause more than one printer, repeat these steps. Each printer that you have paused has a check mark next to **Pause Printing** in the **File** menu of the Printers window.

Note

Be sure to pause the printer *before* you submit your print jobs.

When you have paused the appropriate printer(s), close the Printers window by clicking on its Close button. All print jobs you submit to a paused printer (from the SAS System or any other Windows application) queue up in the printer's queue, but they do not print until you "resume" the printer. Resuming a printer is discussed in the next section.

Resuming Printing

To release the print jobs for a paused printer, follow these steps:

1. Click on the **Start→Settings→Printers**.

2. When the Printers window appears, click on the printer name you want to resume.

3. Now click on **File** in the Printers window menu, then click on **Pause Printing**.

This toggles the printer back on and erases the check mark next to the **Pause Printing** menu choice.

Changing the Order of Print Jobs

If you want to print your print jobs in a different order, use the Windows print queue to change the job order by following these steps:

1. Click on the **Start→Settings→Printers**.

2. Double-click on the icon for the printer you want to affect.

3. When the specific printer window appears, highlight the job you want to move up or down in the queue by clicking on it.

4. Use the mouse to drag the job icon up or down in the list, and drop it in the appropriate spot.

Note

You may find it helpful to pause the printer before rearranging print jobs.

Canceling a Print Job

Use the Windows print queue to delete print jobs you no longer want to print. You can delete a single print job, or you can delete all print jobs from a printer.

Canceling a Specific Print Job: To cancel a particular print job, follow these steps:

1. Click on the **Start→Settings→Printers**.

2. Double-click on the icon for the printer you want to affect.

3. When the specific printer window appears, highlight the job you want to delete by clicking on it.

4. Click on **Document** in the printer's window, then click on **Cancel Printing**.

Canceling All Print Jobs: To delete all print jobs in the Windows print queue for a particular printer, follow these steps:

1. Click on the **Start→Settings→Printers**.

2. When the Printers window appears, click on the icon for the printer you want to delete print jobs from. This highlights the printer name.

3. Now click on **File** in the Printers window menu, then click on **Purge Print Jobs**.

If you need to purge more than one printer, repeat these steps.

Using SAS Print Forms

V7 Hilites: You must turn off the HOSTPRINT system option before using SAS print forms.

FasTip: Click on **File→Print Setup→Use Forms**.

Issue the FSFORM command to create a form.

Issue the FORMNAME command to set the current form.

With some previous versions of the SAS System under other operating systems, you were required to create SAS print forms to control the margins, typeface, and other aspects of printed output. Usually, these forms are no longer necessary with the SAS System for Windows because you can now set all these aspects using the Print Setup and Page Setup dialog boxes. However, there are times when print forms are useful, even under Windows.

For example, you may have inherited some SAS print forms from a previous SAS user. Also, SAS print forms are a good way to send strings of control characters to your printer, which you cannot do with the Print Setup dialog box.

This section provides some background information on creating and editing SAS print forms. Then, it presents two examples to give you practice creating and using a SAS print form.

Note

> SAS print forms are not used when printing HTML SAS output; they apply only to the listing format of SAS output.

Telling the SAS System to Use Forms: The SAS System does not by default use SAS print forms, so you must specify that you want to use them. Open the Print Setup dialog box by clicking on **File** in the SAS System main menu, then on **Print Setup**. Now click on **Use Forms** in the Print Setup dialog box, as shown in Figure 5.10, and click on **OK**.

Figure 5.10 Print Setup Dialog Box When Using SAS Print Forms

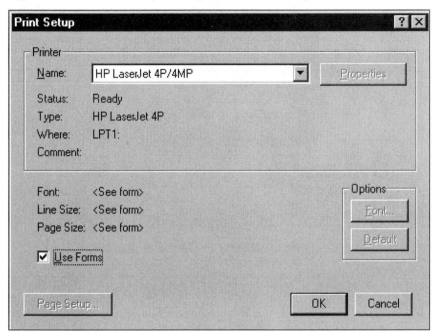

You must also turn off the HOSTPRINT system option (so Windows print spooling is suspended), by submitting the following OPTIONS statement:

```
options nohostprint;
```

Creating a SAS Print Form: To create a SAS print form, issue the FSFORM command from the Command bar. The syntax of the FSFORM command is as follows:

FSFORM *library-reference.catalog.form-name*

If you omit the library reference and catalog names, the SAS System uses the default values of SASUSER and PROFILE, respectively.

For example, to create an entry named LANDSCAPE.FORM in your SASUSER.PROFILE catalog, type

```
FSFORM LANDSCAPE
```

When you press Enter, the FORM window opens, as shown in Figure 5.11.

Figure 5.11. FORM Window – Printer Selection Screen

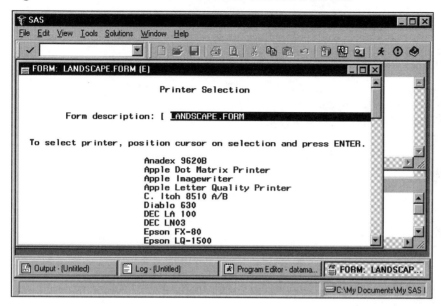

Note

You can also use the SAS Explorer to create a new form; see step 1 in Example 2 later in this section for information on how to do this.

The FORM window consists of six screens:

Printer Selection	sets the printer for the form
Text Body and Margin Information	sets the margin information
Carriage Control Information	controls page skips
WINDOWS Print File Parameters	controls the character set
Font Control Information	sets special text characters and text colors
Printer Control Language	specifies PCL codes.

This chapter focuses primarily on using the last screen, the Printer Control Language screen. The other screens are described in the SAS online help.

Selecting a Printer for Your Form: Use the Printer Selection screen to select a printer. Scroll to find the printer you want, then click on the printer name. You automatically move to the Text Body and Margin Information screen.

Note

The Printer Selection screen appears only when you create a new SAS print form. You do not see this screen when editing existing forms.

Navigating the FORM Window: To navigate through the various screens of the FORM window, click on **Tools** in the SAS System main menu. Then, depending on what you want to do, click on one of the menu choices:

- To move sequentially to the next screen, click on **Next Screen**.

- To move sequentially to the previous screen, click on **Previous Screen**.

- To move to a specific screen, such as the Printer Control Language screen, click on the screen name.

Using the Printer Control Language Screen: Creating a form requires a good understanding of your printer. You especially need to know what Printer Control Language (PCL) commands your printer supports—every printer is slightly different. The manual that accompanies your printer should contain a chapter or appendix detailing the printer's PCL details.

The Printer Control Language screen is the last screen of the FORM window. This is where you enter the printer control characters. This screen has line numbers, such as the old Program Editor window. To add and delete lines, use line commands. Type the command in the line number area and press Enter. Table 5.1 gives you the basic line commands.

Table 5.1 Command-line Commands

To	Use the following command
insert a new line after an existing line	I
insert a line above an existing line	IB
insert several lines (where # is the number of lines you want to insert)	I# or IB#
delete a line	D
move a line	M on the line to move, A or B (after or before) on the target line
copy a line	C on the line to copy, A or B (after or before) on the target line

Exiting from the FORM Window: To save your form, click on **File** in the SAS System main menu, then click on **Close**. When you are prompted whether you want to save your work, click on **Yes**. You will see a note in the log that your form was saved.

To exit the FORM window without saving your work, click on **File** in the SAS System main menu, then click on **Close**. When prompted whether you want to save your work, click on **No**. The form is not saved. Alternatively, issue the CANCEL command from the Command bar instead of clicking on **File→Close**.

Setting the Current Form: The SAS print form that is used for print jobs is determined by the current form. To set the current form, issue the FORMNAME command from the Command bar. The syntax of the FORMNAME command is as follows:

FORMNAME *library-reference.catalog.member.type*

For example, the following command sets the current form to SASUSER.PROFILE. LANDSCAPE.FORM:

```
FORMNAME SASUSER.PROFILE.LANDSCAPE
```

Displaying the Current Form: If you cannot remember which form is the current one, issue the FORMNAME command from the Command bar with no parameters. The current form name is displayed in the message area of the SAS workspace.

For example, if you set the SASUSER.PROFILE.LANDSCAPE form as the current form, then issue the FORMNAME command without any parameters, the message area contains the following text:

```
NOTE: Current print form setting is SASUSER.PROFILE.LANDSCAPE.FORM.
```

Editing an Existing Form: Use the SAS Explorer (or Active Libraries) window to display the SAS catalog in which the form you want to edit is stored. Now, double-click on the form name. The FORM window appears, but the Printer Selection screen is inaccessible when you edit a form. (If you want to change a form's printer, you must create a new form.)

Note

> You can also use the FSFORM command from the Command bar to edit an existing form.

When the FORM window appears, click on **Tools** in the SAS System main menu, then click on the name of the screen to which you want to move. When you have finished making changes, click on **File** in the SAS System main menu, then click on **Close**, and click on **Yes** when you are prompted to save the file. If you do not want to save changes, either click on **No** in the prompting dialog box, or issue the CANCEL command from the Command bar instead of clicking on **File→Close**.

Example 1 - Printing Envelopes: In this example, you create a form that prints a #10 envelope address. The address is printed in bold 12-point Antique Olive typeface (no one will have trouble reading the address!). The printer used for this example is an HP LaserJet 4P; these commands should work with most HP LaserJet printers. If you have another type of printer, such as an Epson or Apple, you need to modify the printer control commands accordingly—use your printer's manual to help you. If you want to print addresses on different-sized envelopes, you need to adjust the top and left margins to fit the envelope you're using.

Here are the steps for Example 1:

1. Create the form by issuing the following command from the Command bar:

   ```
   FSFORM SASUSER.PROFILE.ENVELOPE
   ```

2. When the Printer Selection screen appears, click on **HP LaserJet(+)**. You have to press the PageDown key to see this entry.

3. The screen that appears next is the Text Body and Margin Information screen. Do not change anything here.

4. Click on **Tools** in the SAS System main menu, then click on **Next Screen** to move to the Carriage Control Information screen.

5. On the Carriage Control Information screen, be sure YES is highlighted for **Generate Carriage Control Information**. Also, click on any selected options under **Signal Page Skips before**—when you finish, none of these options should have an asterisk in front of it.

6. Click on **Tools** in the SAS System main menu, then click on **Next Screen** to move to the WINDOWS Print File Parameters screen.

7. Do not change anything on this screen. Go to the next screen, the Font Control Information screen (**Tools→Next Screen**).

8. On the Font Control Information screen, be sure that the tilde (~) is listed in the **Character** column, that its **Number** column value is 27, and that the **Description** column reads Escape. You need the ESC character on the next screen, where you enter printer control commands. If the ~ is listed, go to the next screen. Otherwise, enter the correct information before continuing to the next screen (**Tools→Next Screen**).

9. This screen, the Printer Control Language screen, is the heart of printer forms. It is here that you send codes to the printer to set the page orientation, the font, the margins, and so on.

For the #10 envelope form, use Table 5.2 to enter the printer control codes. Type what is in the **Code** column for the given line. The **Explanation** column tells you what each code means.

The codes are case sensitive. The table uses a cursive lowercase *ℓ* to avoid confusion with the number 1. If there is room for doubt, the **Explanation** column offers further information (such as "use an uppercase O (the letter)" or "use the number 0 (zero)."

Table 5.2 PCL Commands for Envelope Example

Line	Code	Explanation
00001	PRINT INIT	Begins the section of controls that are sent to the printer before any text is sent to the printer.
00002	~&ℓ1O	Sets landscape mode. Use a number 1 (one), followed by an uppercase O (the letter).
00003	~&ℓ8E	Sets the top margin to 8 lines.
00004	~&a60L	Sets the left margin to 60 columns.
00005	~&ℓ3H	Sets the paper source to "manual envelope feed".
00006	~(8U	Sets the primary symbol set to Roman 8.
00007	~(s1P	Sets proportional spacing.
00008	~(s12V	Sets the point size to 12 points.
00009	~(s0S	Sets the type style to upright (as opposed to oblique, condensed, or shadowed). Use a zero between the s and S.
00010	~(s3B	Sets the type weight to bold.
00011	~(s4168T	Sets the typeface to Antique Olive.
00012	PRINT TERM	Begins the section of controls that are sent to the printer after all text has been sent.
00013	~9	Clears horizontal margins.
00014	~E	Resets the printer.

10. To save the form, click on **File** in the SAS System main menu, then click on **Close**. A dialog box appears, asking you if you want to save the form. Click on **Yes**.

Here is an example of the typeface that this example uses:

123 XYZ Drive
Some Town, USA 00000

Note

If you do not have access to the Antique Olive typeface, check your printer manual for the PCL code for a typeface you do have and change line 00011 in Table 5.2 accordingly.

Example 2 - Controlling Output Page by Page: If all you want to do is adjust the font and margins for your output, you might as well use the Print Setup and Page Setup dialog boxes. But forms allow you to do far more than that. With forms, you can control the output page by page. In this example, the first and third pages are printed in the default orientation (portrait). The second and last pages are printed in landscape mode; in addition, the last page is set to manual feed so that it can be printed on special paper.

As in Example 1, the printer used for this example is an HP LaserJet 4P; the commands should work with most HP LaserJet printers. If you have another type of printer, such as an Epson or Apple, you need to modify the printer control commands accordingly. Use your printer's manual to help you.

Here are the steps for Example 2:

1. Create the new form. In Example 1, you used the Command bar. You can also use the SAS Explorer to create a new form. Right-click on the **Profile** icon in the left pane of the SAS Explorer. In the popup menu, click on **New**. In the resulting New Entry dialog box, click on **Form**, then click on **OK**. This opens the FORM window.

2. Choose your printer from the Printer Selection screen as you did in Example 1.

3. Click on **Tools** in the SAS System main menu, then click on **Carriage Control**.

4. On the Carriage Control Information screen, be sure YES is highlighted for **Generate Carriage Control Information**. No option under **Signal Page Skips before** should have an asterisk next to it. (Click in the lines that do have asterisks to deselect them.)

5. Click on **Tools** in the SAS System main menu, then click on **Printer Control Language**.

6. Use Table 5.3 to enter the printer control codes on the Printer Control Language screen. Type what is in the **Code** column for the given line. The **Explanation** column tells you what each code means.

   The codes are case sensitive. The table uses a cursive lowercase ℓ to avoid confusion with the number 1. If there is room for doubt, the "Explanation" column offers further information (such as "use an uppercase O (the letter)" or "use the number 0 (zero)."

Table 5.3 PCL Commands for Page-by-Page Example

Line	Code	Explanation
00001	PAGE 2	Begins the section of controls that are sent before any text is sent for page 2 (the first landscape page).
00002	~&l1O	Sets landscape mode. Use a number 1 (one), followed by an uppercase O (letter).
00003	PAGE 3	Begins the section of controls that are sent before any text is sent for page 3.
00004	~E	Resets the printer.
00005	~9	Clears horizontal margins.
00006	PAGE 4	Begins the section of controls that are sent before any text is sent for page 4 (the landscape page).
00007	~&l1O	Sets landscape mode. Use a number 1 (one), followed by an uppercase O (letter).
00008	~&l2H	Sets the printer to manual feed.
00009	PRINT TERM	Begins the section of controls that are sent to the printer after all text has been sent.
00010	~E	Resets the printer.
00011	~9	Clears horizontal margins.

7. To save the form, click on the FORM window's Close button (this is equivalent to clicking on **File→Close**). When the dialog box prompts you to save, click on **Yes**.

Note

Creating a form from the SAS Explorer always creates a member called UNTITLED.FORM. You can rename the form once it exists.

Warning

When using the SAS Explorer to create a form, creating a second new form in the same SAS catalog without renaming the first form overwrites the first untitled form.

Printing HTML SAS Output

The ODS lets you create nicely formatted output—you can print that output as well.

Printing from the Internal SAS Browser: If you have selected the internal SAS browser on the **Results** tab of the Preferences dialog box, your output appears in the Results Viewer window. To print what appears in this window, right-click in the window, and click on **Print** in the popup menu. Figure 5.12 shows the resulting dialog box.

Figure 5.12 Print Dialog Box for Printing HTML Output

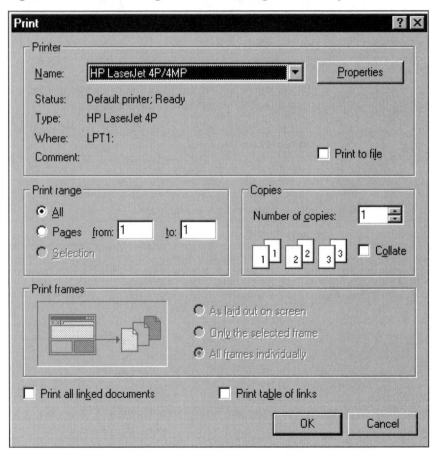

The **Printer**, **Print range**, and **Copies** areas work similarly to the corresponding areas in the regular SAS Print dialog box. For HTML output, you have a few additional options.

- If your HTML output includes frames you can choose to print the frames in one of three ways:

  - as they appear in the window

  - only the selected frame

  - one frame per page.

- If your HTML output includes links, you can choose to print all linked documents and/or print a table of links.

When you click on **OK** in the Print dialog box, the print job is submitted to the Windows print queue. When the job prints, each page includes `Page n of m` in the top right corner and the filename (or URL) in the bottom left corner of the page.

In the Results Viewer, **Print** prints only the currently displayed piece of output. For example, if your output consists of two PROC PRINT steps, and you are looking at the results of the second PROC PRINT, **Print** prints only the results of the second PROC PRINT. To print the other pieces of output, you must first navigate to them (using **Back** and **Forward** in the popup menu in the Results Viewer), then select **Print** again.

Printing from Your Preferred Web Browser: See the documentation for your Web browser for information on using it to print SAS output.

Printing from the SAS System Viewer

V7 Hilites: Enhanced printing options offer better printing features.

You can now customize your printer-specific options from the SAS System Viewer Print dialog box.

The SAS System Viewer offers a handy way of printing all your SAS files—including SAS tables and SAS programs.

Defining the Page Setup: You have a lot of control over how the SAS System Viewer presents your data. To access these features, click on **File** in the SAS System Viewer main menu, then click on **Page Setup**.

Note

The SAS System Viewer Page Setup dialog box is completely separate from the Page Setup dialog box accessed from the SAS System.

Figure 5.13 shows the SAS System Viewer Page Setup dialog box.

Figure 5.13 SAS System Viewer Page Setup Dialog Box

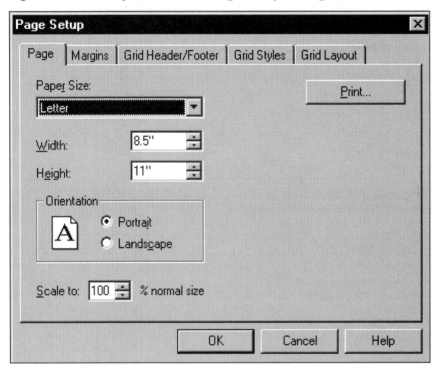

The various tabs enable you to alter settings associated with how your data is presented on the page, as described in the following list:

Page	sets paper size, orientation, and scale.
Margins	sets top, bottom, left, and right margins.
Grid Header/Footer	customizes the grid header and footer format.
Grid Styles	defines how the grid is displayed, such as using lines.
Grid Layout	controls whether rows or columns are ordered first and how the page is centered (vertically or horizontally).

When you have adjusted the settings to your satisfaction, click on **OK** in the Page Setup dialog box. The choices you have made will be reflected by all subsequent print jobs from the SAS System Viewer, until you change the settings again.

Previewing Your Print Job: If you want to see how the file will look when printed, click on **File** in the SAS System Viewer main menu, then click on **Print Preview**. Figure 5.14 shows a sample of how your screen might look:

Figure 5.14 SAS System Viewer Print Preview Feature

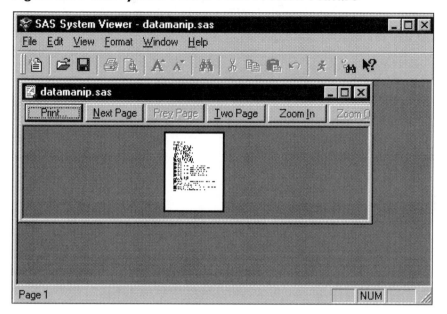

- Use the **Two Page** (toggles to **One Page**), **Zoom In** and **Zoom Out**, and **Next Page** and **Prev Page** buttons to adjust and navigate the view.

- Click on **Close** to close the print preview and return to the normal view of the file.

- Click on **Print** to open the Print dialog box (described in the next section).

Note

> If all these buttons are not visible on your display, resize the SAS System Viewer and individual windows to make them larger.

Using the SAS System Viewer Print Dialog Box: The SAS System Viewer's Print dialog box is a standard Windows Print dialog box, and works similarly to the Print dialog box in the SAS System—you can choose the printer, what pages to print, how many copies to print, and whether to print to a file.

Figure 5.15 shows the SAS System Viewer Print dialog box

Figure 5.15 SAS System Viewer Print Dialog Box

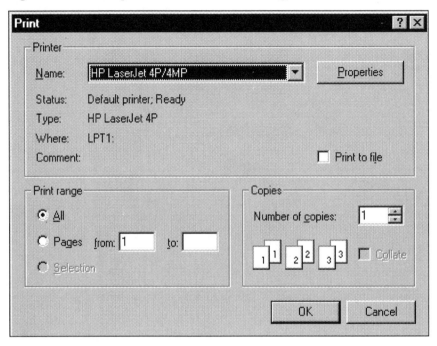

6 Adjusting Your Windows Environment

Introduction

When you install the SAS System, it uses default settings that define how your windowing environment looks. For example, these settings affect the menu bar across the top of the SAS workspace, the message area at the bottom of the SAS workspace, the scroll bars, colors, and so on. However, you can adjust your SAS windowing environment—for example, you can define new tools for the tool bar, replace the menus with command lines, or change the default colors of windows.

You make these changes in several ways. Some changes you make using the Preferences dialog box. To define new tools, you use the Customize Tools dialog box. To customize the SAS Explorer, you use the Explorer Options dialog box. Some options are set using the menus; others are set via commands issued from the Command bar.

Besides the changes discussed in this chapter, you can also make many other changes. Because this is a beginner's guide, not all possible options are discussed. For example, if you are developing a SAS/AF application, you can use SAS system options to control how the SAS workspace looks and works. Refer to your SAS reference documentation for more information.

Setting Session Preferences

V7 Hilites: Preferences dialog box offers new choices.

Many options that were controlled via the Preferences dialog box are now accessed through the Customize Tools dialog box.

FasTip: Click on **Tools→Options→Preferences**.

The Preferences dialog box controls many aspects of your windowing environment. To open this dialog box, click on **Tools** in the SAS System main menu, then on **Options**, then on **Preferences**. Figure 6.1 shows the Preferences dialog box with its default settings.

Figure 6.1 General Tab of Preferences Dialog Box

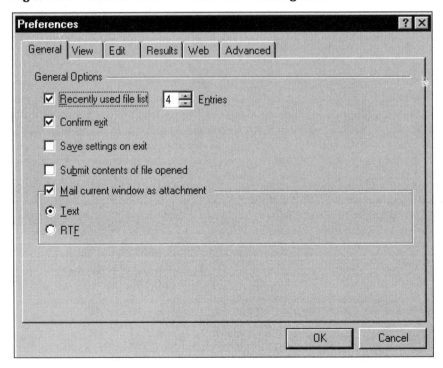

The Preferences dialog box is organized into six tabs:

General   options relating to the general use of the SAS System

View   options relating to the SAS System windowing environment

Edit   options relating to editing

Results   options relating to SAS output

Web   options relating to the Web browser used by the SAS System

Advanced   options relating to less-commonly used features of the SAS System.

This chapter mainly discusses the **General** and **View** tabs.

To move to a particular tab, click on the tab name. To change a setting, click on the option you want to change. For example, by default, on the **General** tab, the **Confirm Exit** field is checked. If you do not want the SAS System to ask you if you really want to end your SAS session, click on this option to deselect it.

Remember that options with round (radio) buttons by them are mutually exclusive—select only one; you can select one or more options that have square (check) boxes by them.

When you are finished making changes in the Preferences dialog box, click on **OK**. Your changes are saved to your SASUSER profile catalog. These changes last until you change your preferences again.

Using the General Tab: The following paragraphs explain some of the choices on the Preferences dialog box's **General** tab (shown in Figure 6.1).

- **Recently used file list** – Adjust the number up or down to display more or fewer recently used files in the SAS System's **File** menu. You can choose to display 0 to 9 files.

- **Confirm exit** – If this option is selected, a dialog box prompts you to confirm whether you really want to end your SAS session. Deselect this option if you want the SAS System to terminate without prompting for confirmation.

- **Save settings on exit** – Select this option to save the placement and attributes of all open SAS windows. Selecting this option is similar to issuing a WSAVE ALL command from the Command bar.

- **Submit contents of file opened** – Select this option if you always want to submit a file when you open it with the Open dialog box. This option has no effect on files opened by other means (such as from the recently used file list or the INCLUDE command). Selecting this option is equivalent to selecting the **Submit** option in the Open dialog box.

Using the View Tab: The following paragraphs explain several of the choices on the Preferences dialog box's **View** tab, shown in Figure 6.2.

Figure 6.2 View Tab of Preferences Dialog Box

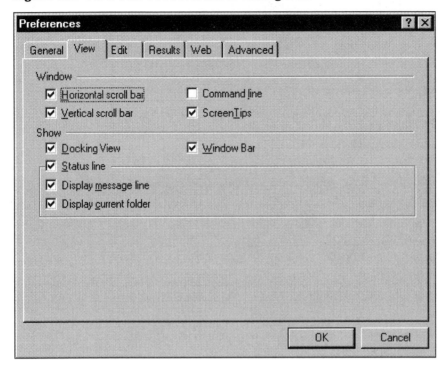

- **Window** – Use this section to turn on or off the vertical and horizontal scroll bars, the command line, and screen tips (helpful hints that appear when you place your mouse pointer over an area in the SAS workspace). The **ScreenTips** option in this area does not affect the tool tips that appear when you place your mouse pointer over tools in the SAS tool bar.

- **Show** – Use this section to control how the status line (at the bottom of the SAS workspace) appears. Turn the whole thing off, or turn off portions, such as the message area, the Window Bar, or the working folder icon.

  You can also affect how the SAS Explorer and Results windows (and other docked windows) appear by selecting or deselecting **Docking View**:

  - If **Docking View** is not selected, these windows appear anywhere inside the SAS workspace.

  - If **Docking View** is selected, these windows are "locked" to the left side of the SAS workspace.

  See "Undocking SAS Windows" later in this chapter for more information.

Customizing the Tool Bar and Command Bar

V7 Hilites: Tool switching is now the default and cannot be turned off via the Preferences or Customize Tools dialog boxes.

Switching between the Command bar/Command box and tool bar/toolbox is now accessed by right-clicking in either the Command bar or the tool bar and clicking on **Docked**.

FasTip: Click on **Tools→Customize** to change aspects of the Command bar and SAS tool bar.

You can customize how the Command bar and SAS tool bar look by using the Customize Tools dialog box. Access this dialog box by clicking on **Tools** in the SAS System main menu, then on **Customize**. Figure 6.3 shows the **Toolbars** tab of the Customize Tools dialog box.

Figure 6.3 Toolbars Tab of the Customize Tools Dialog Box

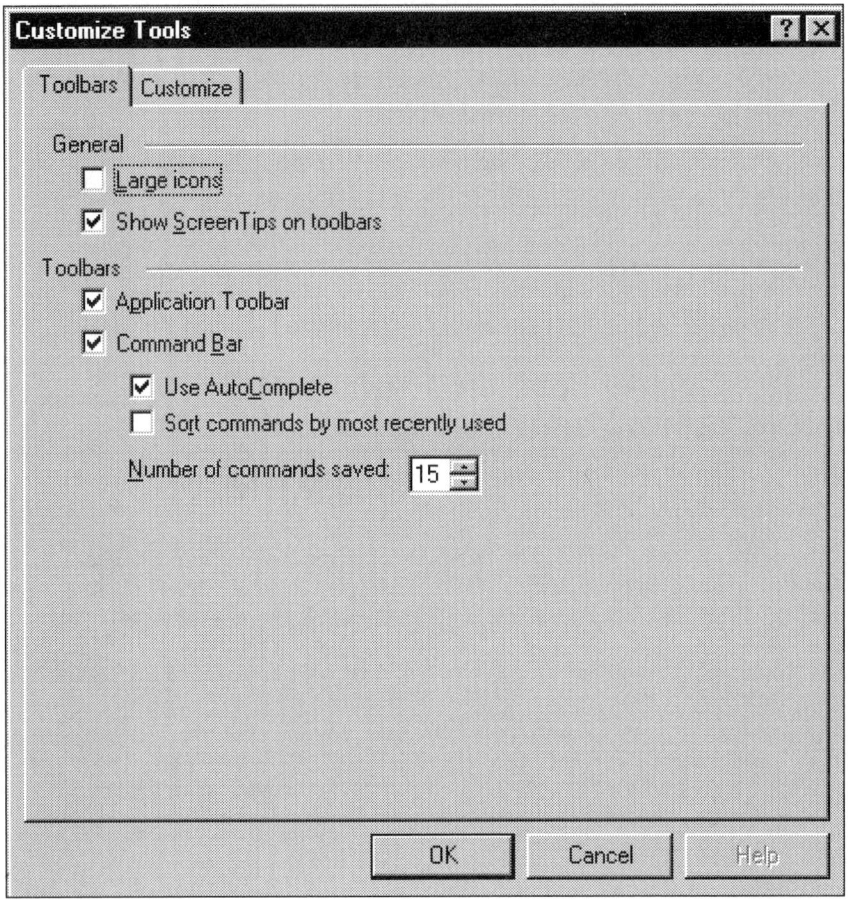

A quick way to access the Customize Toolbars dialog box is to right-click in the SAS tool bar, then click on **Customize**.

- **Large icons** – Select this option to increase the size of the tool icons in the tool bar (this option does not affect the tool box). Large tools are most helpful with high-resolution displays because on these displays, the tool bitmaps are small. If you have trouble distinguishing the tools, see if using the larger tools helps. If, when you choose this option, all the tools are no longer visible but extend off the right side of the screen, you do not have a high-resolution display, and you should not use the large tools.

- **Show ScreenTips on toolbars** – Select this option to control whether helpful hints appear when you position the mouse pointer over a tool. For example, if you place your mouse pointer over the Run icon in the SAS tool bar, the tool tip for that tool says **Submit**, as shown in Figure 6.4. (This option is independent of the **ScreenTips** option on the **View** tab of the Preferences dialog box, which affects screen tips for areas of the SAS workspace other than the tool bar.)

Figure 6.4 Tool Tips Explain What Tools Do

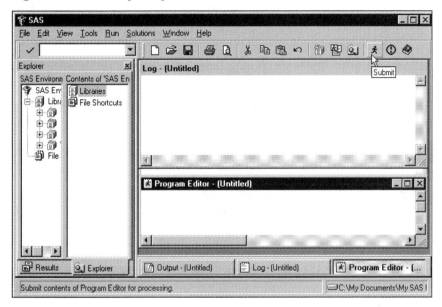

- **Application Toolbar** – This selection controls whether the SAS tool bar appears in the SAS workspace.

- **Command Bar** – This selection controls how the Command bar works. Your three choices are

  - **Use AutoComplete** – This selection activates the autocomplete feature of the Command bar. If this feature is on, the SAS System uses the first few characters of a command that you type to guess the command you want, based on commands previously issued in the SAS session.

  - **Sort commands by most recently used** – This selection changes the ordering of the list of commands remembered by the Command bar. By default, when you click on the down arrow to the right of the Command bar, the commands are listed in a most commonly used order. That is, commands you use most often are toward the top of the list, while less common commands are at the bottom of the list. Selecting this option changes the ordering algorithm used by the

Command bar, although the list does not immediately reorder itself; the list is gradually reordered as you continue to issue commands.

- **Number of commands saved** – This selection controls the number of commands listed by clicking on the down arrow in the Command bar. The default number is 15; you can adjust this number up or down to suit your needs.

The **Customize** tab of the Customize Tools dialog box is discussed in "Adding and Editing Tools on the Tool Bar" later in this chapter.

Switching between the Command Bar/Box and Tool Bar/Box: If you prefer to use a Command box or SAS toolbox (windows), which can be moved outside the SAS workspace, right-click in the check mark to the left of the Command bar or on the SAS tool bar. In the resulting popup menu, click on **Docked**. Depending on where you right-clicked, the Command bar or tool bar now becomes a separate window. Figure 6.5 shows how the SAS workspace might look if you undocked the Command bar.

Figure 6.5 SAS Session with a Command Box instead of a Command Bar

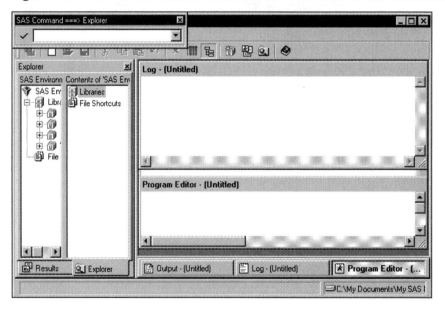

Note

The title bar of the Command box shows the active SAS window, to which commands will apply.

Turning Off the Command Bar or Tool Bar: If you do not want the SAS workspace to show the Command bar or the SAS tool bar, right-click in the tool bar and click on either **Command Bar** or **Application Toolbar**. Depending on which you clicked on, the Command bar or the SAS tool bar disappears.

To display the Command bar or SAS tool bar again, simply right-click in the SAS tool bar again and reselect the appropriate item (**Command Bar** or **Application Toolbar**).

Adding and Editing Tools on the Tool Bar

V7 Hilites: The menu path to edit tools is now **Tools→Customize**, then click on the **Customize** tab.

Tool-editing dialog box offers new features, such as a tool bar.

FasTip: Right-click in the SAS tool bar, then click on **Customize**, then click on the **Customize** tab.

Use the TOOLLOAD command to load alternative tool bars.

The tool bar across the top of the SAS workspace is a handy way to execute commands. While the default tools may be sufficient for many users, you may want to add a tool, change the icon for a tool, or otherwise edit the look and feel of the tool bar.

To begin editing the tool bar, click on **Tools** in the SAS System main menu, then on **Customize**. The Customize Tools dialog box opens. Click on the **Customize** tab, which is shown in Figure 6.6.

Figure 6.6 Customize Tab of the Customize Tools Dialog Box

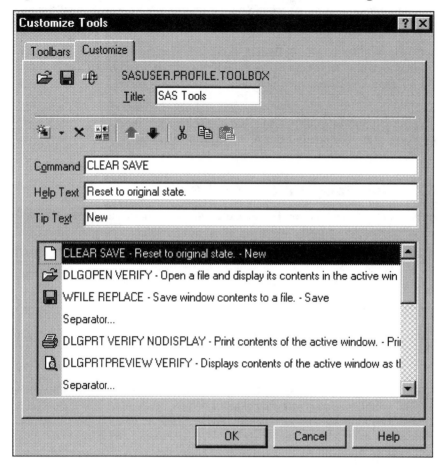

This section shows you how to

- add a tool to the tool bar

- edit an existing tool

- create an alternate tool bar

- associate a tool bar with a specific SAS window.

For information on other tasks, such as changing the order of tools, deleting tools, and so on, click on the **Help** button in the **Customize** tab of the Customize Tools dialog box.

Returning to the Default Tools: Before you begin to make changes, remember that you can always return to the default tools by clicking on the Restore Defaults icon on the **Customize** tab. When you do so, you are asked if you really want to return the definitions to their default values. Click on **Yes**, then click on **OK** to close the Customize Tools dialog box. When prompted to save your changes, click on **Yes**.

Adding a Tool: The following example illustrates adding a new tool to the default SAS tool bar. Open the CUSTOMIZE dialog box and follow along:

1. Make the Program Editor window active by clicking in it.

2. Open the Customize Tools dialog box by clicking on **Tools→Customize** in the SAS System main menu. Now click on the **Customize** tab of this dialog box.

3. Click on the down arrow next to the Add Tool icon, and click on **Blank Tool**. Tools are added before the tool that is highlighted in the list of tools.

   A blank line and blank icon appear in the list of tools.

4. Click in the **Command** field once to move your cursor, and type the SAS windowing command you want the tool to execute. If you want the tool to execute a string of commands, separate the commands with semicolons.

   For example, type the following to create a tool for submitting code stored on the Clipboard:

   ```
   GSUBMIT
   ```

5. Click in the **Help Text** field, and type the help string that appears in the SAS workspace message area when you hold your mouse pointer over the tool. For example, type:

   ```
   Submit code from the Clipboard
   ```

6. Click in the **Tip Text** field, and type the help string that appears in the tool tip (the short description that appears under the tool when you place your mouse pointer over a tool). For example, type:

   ```
   Submit Clipboard
   ```

As you type in the **Command**, **Help Text**, and **Tip Text** fields, your characters are copied to the tool definition in the list of tools.

Figure 6.7 shows how the **Customize** tab looks after you have typed all this text in.

Figure 6.7 Adding a Tool

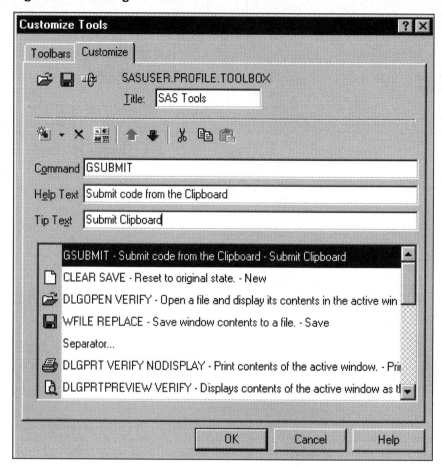

7. To pick an icon for the new tool, click on the Change Icon icon. The Bitmap
    Browser dialog box opens, as shown in Figure 6.8.

Figure 6.8 Bitmap Browser Dialog Box

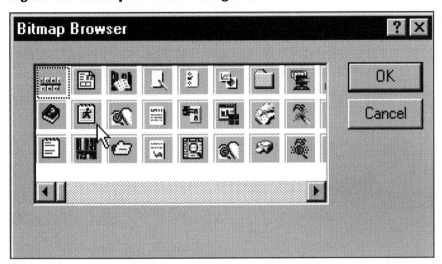

8. Click on the icon you want, then click on **OK**. The icon appears by the new tool.

    For example, because you already have a submit tool that uses the jogger icon, you may want to choose a different icon for the new tool. Click on the jogger-on-a-page icon (second icon from the left in the middle row, indicated by the mouse pointer in Figure 6.8), then click on **OK**.

9. To save your changes, click on the Save the Toolbar icon. When the Save Tools dialog box appears, click on **OK**.

Now click on **OK** in the Customize Tools dialog box. This closes the dialog box, and your new tool appears on the tool bar. Figure 6.9 shows the SAS tool bar with the mouse pointer pointing to the new tool.

Figure 6.9 Tool Bar with the New Tool Added

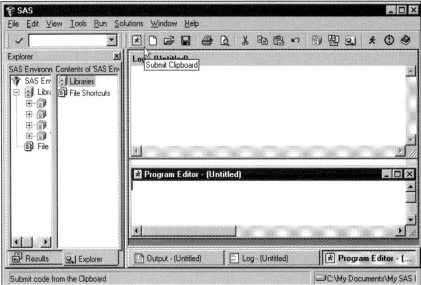

Increasing the Number of Visible Tools: The number of tools visible on the tool bar depends on the resolution of your screen. Screen resolution is expressed in vertical X horizontal "pixels" or dots. On many screens, the resolution is 640 X 480. In this case, by default only 13 tools are visible at once; when you add the GSUBMIT tool, the right-most tool disappears off the right side of the screen. If you are using a low resolution such as 640 X 480, limit each set of tools to 13 tools, and create additional tool sets as described in "Creating an Alternative Tool Bar" later in this chapter. You can also use the **Customize** tab of the Customize Tools dialog box to delete the separators between tools. If you delete all separators, you can fit 14 tools on a 640 X 480 display.

To increase the space available for tools, you can resize the Command bar by placing the mouse pointer over the vertical double-bar that appears to the right of the Command bar (the pointer turns into a double-headed arrow). Drag this bar to the left, making the Command bar smaller. This leaves more space for tools.

You can also choose to make the Command bar into a Command box (see "Switching between the Command Bar/Box and Tool Bar/Box" earlier in this chapter), which leaves more room for tools in the tool bar.

Editing an Existing Tool: You do not have to accept how the tool icons look—you can choose a different icon for a tool. For example, you may not think that the icon for the tool that opens the New Library dialog box is intuitive:

Change the icon for a tool by following steps similar to those in this example:

1. Open the Customize Tools dialog box by clicking on **Tools** in the SAS System main menu, then on **Customize**. Now click on the **Customize** tab.

2. Use the scroll bar in the list of tools to scroll down until the tool you want to change is visible. In this example, we're going to change the tool with the open file drawers and the command LIBASSIGN.

3. Click on that line in the list of tools. It is highlighted, as shown in Figure 6.10.

Figure 6.10 Customize Tools Dialog Box with New Library Tool Highlighted

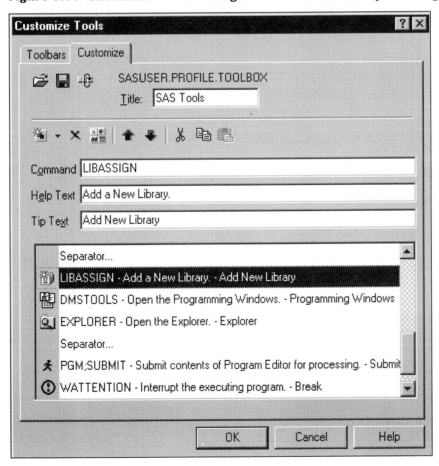

4.   Click on the Change Icon icon to display the Bitmap Browser dialog box.

Be sure you are scrolled all the way to the left in the dialog box. Click on the second icon over in the bottom row—it looks like this:

5.   Click on **OK**. The icon changes in the tool list. Click on the Save the Toolbar tool to save your changes; click on **OK** when prompted.

Similarly, edit other parts of a tool by clicking on its line in the tool list, then clicking in the **Command, Help Text,** or **Tip Text** fields and editing the contents of these fields.

Click on **OK** to close the Customize Tools dialog box.

Creating an Alternative Tool Bar: One of the most powerful aspects of the SAS System's tool bar is that you can create several tool bars and load whichever set of tools you need for a specific SAS session. For example, you can create a tool bar for each SAS/AF application you write.

This section walks you through creating a small tool bar. One tool prints and clears the Output window; the other tool saves the text of the window in RTF format. The following two sections show you how to load a specific tool bar and how to return to the original tool bar.

To create a new tool bar, follow steps similar to those in this example:

1.   Click on **Tools** in the SAS System main menu, then click on **Customize**. The Customize Tools dialog box opens; click on the **Customize** tab.

Each tool bar you create is stored as a catalog entry. The title bar of the **Customize** tab shows the catalog entry name for the tool bar you are editing (the entry type, TOOLBOX, does not appear in the title bar). The SASUSER.PROFILE.TOOLBOX entry is the default tool bar.

2. In the **Title** entry field, give your new tool bar a title. This title serves as a descriptive label for the tool bar.

    Highlight the contents of the **Title** field by marking it with the mouse. Now type your new title. For example, type:

    ```
    My Personal Tool Bar
    ```

3. To delete tools you do not want, click on the tool in the tool list, then click on the Remove Tool icon.

    Continue until all the tools and separators are gone.

4. Now add your own tools. In this example, we add two tools. Click on the down arrow next to the Add Tool icon, then click on **Blank Tool**. In the **Command** field, type:

    ```
    Output; DLGPRT; CLEAR
    ```

    In the **Help Text** field type:

    ```
    Print the Output window and clear it
    ```

    In the **Tip Text** field type:

    ```
    Print/clear Output
    ```

5. Click on the Change Icon icon to open the Bitmap Browser dialog box and choose an appropriate icon.

    For example, choose the printer icon that is approximately in the middle of the collection of icons (use the scroll bar to move to the right), on the bottom row:

6. For the second tool, click on the down arrow next to the Add Tool icon, then click on **Blank Tool**. The **Command**, **Help Text**, and **Tip Text** fields should look like this:

    ```
    WRTFSAVE "C:\Myfile.rtf"
    Save the active window text as an RTF file
    Save as RTF
    ```

7. Click on the Change Icon icon again and choose another icon. For example, choose the first icon in the bottom row:

8. Now you are ready to save your new catalog entry. Click on the Save the Toolbar icon.

The Save Tools dialog box appears, as shown in Figure 6.11.

Figure 6.11 Save Tools Dialog Box

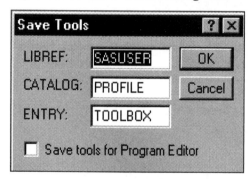

You can save the entry in any catalog. For this example, we'll store it in the SASUSER.PROFILE catalog and give it a name of MYTOOLS. Double-click in the **ENTRY** field to highlight the entry name and type MYTOOLS. Now click on **OK**. This writes the new catalog entry to the SASUSER.PROFILE catalog.

9. Notice that the title bar of the Customize Tools dialog box now says SASUSER.PROFILE.MYTOOLS. Click on **OK** to close the Customize Tools dialog box.

Loading a Specific Tool Bar: To load your new tools, use the TOOLLOAD command. The basic syntax is as follows:

TOOLLOAD *tool-set*

For example, to load the tools you created in the previous section, issue the following command from the Command bar:

```
TOOLLOAD SASUSER.PROFILE.MYTOOLS
```

Figure 6.12 shows the SAS workspace with the new tools loaded.

Figure 6.12 Using the New Tool Bar

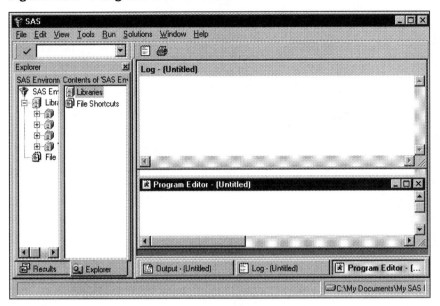

Instead of loading a tool bar manually with the TOOLLOAD command, you can associate a tool bar with a particular window and have that tool bar load automatically every time you open the window. See "Associating a Tool Bar with a Specific SAS Window" later in this chapter for more information.

You can also create a tool that invokes another tool bar—simply create a tool with the appropriate TOOLLOAD command in the **Command** field of the **Customize** tab of the Customize Tools dialog box.

Loading the Default Tool Bar: To return to the default tool bar, issue the following command from the Command bar:

```
TOOLLOAD SASUSER.PROFILE.TOOLBOX
```

Associating a Tool Bar with a Specific SAS Window: Because you perform different tasks from different windows, it may be helpful to have a tool bar for each window. Follow these steps to set the window for a tool bar:

1. Click in the window with which you want the tool bar associated (this makes the window active).

2. Open the Customize Tools dialog box by clicking on **Tools** in the SAS System main menu, then click on **Customize**; now click on the **Customize** tab.

3. Create a new tool bar, as described earlier in this chapter.

4. Click on the Save the Toolbar icon in the Customize Tools dialog box. When the Save Tools dialog box appears, enter the catalog entry information, and also click in the check box by the line that reads **Save tools for** *active-window.*

The new tool bar is saved, and when you switch to the tool bar's window, the tool bar is automatically loaded.

Customizing the SAS Explorer

In Chapter 2 you learned how to use the SAS Explorer to manage SAS files. You can customize the SAS Explorer so that it better meets your file-management needs. To customize the SAS Explorer, open the Explorer Options dialog box by clicking on **Tools** in the SAS System main menu, then on **Options**, then on **Explorer**.

Note

The **Explorer** menu choice under **Tools→Options** is available only if the SAS Explorer window is active.

Figure 6.13 shows the Explorer Options dialog box.

Figure 6.13 Explorer Options Dialog Box

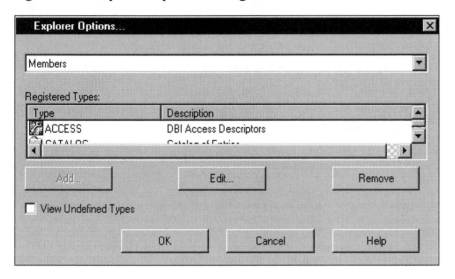

The following paragraphs get you started by explaining how to use several features of the Explorer Options dialog box.

Note

The changes you make in the Explorer Options dialog box affect the SAS Registry. The SAS Registry keeps track of file types and actions (such as Open or Print) associated with those file types. For more details on the SAS Registry, including the REGEDIT command, refer to the online SAS help.

To get help in the Explorer Options dialog box, click on the **Help** button, which brings up the "Using the Explorer Options Window" help topic.

To close the Explorer Options dialog box, click on **Close**.

Adjusting Member Types: The SAS Explorer window shows you the contents of SAS data libraries; the **Members** portion of the Explorer Options dialog box controls what types of library members are listed and what actions are associated with those member types. By default, the member types shown in Table 6.1 are listed:

Table 6.1 Default SAS Data Library Members Listed by the SAS Explorer Window

Type	Description
ACCESS	Access descriptor
CATALOG	Catalog of entries
TABLE	Data tables (previously called data sets)
FDB	Financial database
MDDB	Multi-dimensional database
PROGRAM	Compiled DATA step code
VIEW	SQL, DATA step, or database interface views

The icon shown in the **Type** column is the icon shown in the SAS Explorer window, representing that member type.

You can change and add actions associated with any of the member types by clicking on the member type in the **Type** column, then clicking on the **Edit** button. See the online help for further information.

Note

You cannot use the **Remove** button to remove any of the default member types.

Adjusting Catalog Entry Types: When you double-click on a SAS catalog in the SAS Explorer window, the window shows you the contents of the catalog, listing all the catalog entries; the **Catalog Entries** portion of the Explorer Options dialog box controls what types of catalog entries are listed and what actions are associated with those entry types.

To adjust what actions are associated with a catalog entry, begin by clicking on the down arrow that is to the right of the top field in the Explorer Options dialog box, then click on **Catalog Entries** in the resulting list. Now the **Type** column shows all the catalog entry types that are currently listed by the SAS Explorer window, along with a description of each entry type.

The icon shown in the **Type** column is the icon shown in the SAS Explorer window, representing that entry type.

You can change and add actions associated with any of the entry types by clicking on the entry type in the **Type** column, then clicking on the **Edit** button. See the online help for further information.

Note

You cannot use the **Remove** button to remove any of the default catalog entry types.

Adjusting External File Types: The My Favorite Folders window shows the contents of your computer system (such as floppy drives and your hard drive). You can customize the actions associated with various file types.

Begin by clicking on the down arrow that is to the right of the top field in the Explorer Options dialog box, then click on **Host Files** in the resulting list. Now the **Type** column shows all the external file types that are currently listed by the SAS Explorer window, along with a description of each file type.

The icon shown in the **Type** column is the icon shown in the SAS Explorer window, representing that file type.

You can change and add actions associated with any of the file types by clicking on the file type in the **Type** column, then clicking on the **Edit** button. See the online help for further information.

Note

You cannot use the **Remove** button to remove any of the default external file types.

Changing the Default SAS Explorer Contents: By default, the SAS Explorer window shows you only the **Libraries** and **File Shortcuts** icons. You can customize what is shown by default, using the Explorer Options dialog box. The other icons than can be listed by the SAS Explorer window are **Extensions** (that is, external files), **Favorite Folders**, and **Results**.

Begin by clicking on the down arrow that is to the right of the top field in the Explorer Options dialog box, then click on **Initialization** in the resulting list. Now the **Type** column shows all the possible folders that can be listed by the SAS Explorer window, while the **Description** column shows you whether that folder is listed (**On**) or not (**Off**). Folders that are listed by the SAS Explorer have a plus sign by them in the **Type** column; folders that are not listed by the SAS Explorer window have a red minus sign by them in the **Type** column.

To turn on a folder, click on its name in the **Type** column, then click on the **Add** button. The minus sign changes to a plus sign, to indicate that folder will be listed in the SAS Explorer window from now on. (If a SAS Explorer window is currently open, it is automatically refreshed.)

To turn off a folder, click on its name in the **Type** column, then click on the **Remove** button. The plus sign changes to a minus sign, to indicate that folder will not be listed in the SAS Explorer window. (If a SAS Explorer window is currently open, it is automatically refreshed.)

Undocking SAS Windows

By default, when the SAS System starts up, the SAS Explorer and Results windows open and are locked to the left side of the SAS workspace. This is called the "docking view."

You can "undock" a specific window by following these steps:

1. Make the window active by clicking in the window.

2. Click on **Window** in the SAS System main menu then on **Docked**. The check mark next to **Docked** disappears.

The window is now like other SAS windows and can be moved around inside the SAS workspace.

To undock all docked windows, open the Preferences dialog box by clicking on **Tools→Options→Preferences** in the SAS System main menu. Click on the **View** tab, and deselect **Docking View**. Now all docked windows are undocked.

Redocking Windows: Whether you've undocked a single window or all windows, you can redock individual windows by clicking on **Window** in the SAS System main menu, then click on **Docked**.

Undocking the Command Bar and Tool Bar: To undock the Command bar (which changes it to a Command box) or the tool bar (which changes it to a tool box), right-click on one of the following:

*   the check mark to the left of the Command bar

*   anywhere in the tool bar.

In the resulting popup menu, click on **Docked**. This changes the bar to a floating box, and erases the check mark next to **Docked** in the popup menu. Repeat this process to redock the Command bar or tool bar.

Changing Colors

V7 Hilites: SASCOLOR window is now located under **Tools→Options→Colors.**

FasTip: Use the SASCOLOR window (affects all SAS windows).

Issue the COLOR command (affects individual SAS windows).

Click on the **Start** button, then click on **Settings→Control Panel**, then double-click on the **Display** icon. Now click on the **Appearance** tab (affects all Windows applications).

You can customize your SAS session by changing the color of windows and window elements. For example, you may not like the default stark white background of the Program Editor, Log, and Output windows. Also, you may want titles in the Output window to appear in a certain color (default is blue) but footnotes in a different color. And you may want to adjust the color of title bars, scroll bars, and other window "decorations." Decide what you want to change, and whether you want to change the attribute

- for all windows in your SAS session

- for only a particular SAS window

- for all windows in all applications.

Deciding Which Method to Use: The three methods of changing colors and their effects in the SAS System are

- SASCOLOR window—affects all SAS windows

- COLOR command (issued from any SAS window)—affects only the SAS window from which the command is issued

- Display Properties window, from the Windows Control Panel—affects all windows in all Windows applications, including the SAS System.

Each method lets you change the colors of a variety of window attributes; sometimes there is overlap, where an attribute can be changed by more than one method. In the latter case, one method has precedence over another.

Note

> The SASCOLOR window and the COLOR command do not affect HTML output displayed in the Results Viewer window. To change the colors used to display HTML output, you must select a style on the **Results** tab of the Preferences dialog box, as described in "Telling SAS You Want HTML Output" in Chapter 4.

Understanding the Precedence of Color Specifications: The Windows Control Panel overrides all other methods of color specification. For example, even though the COLOR command supports the SCROLLBAR option, it has no effect because scroll bars are controlled by the Control Panel.

Any specifications you make with the COLOR command override options set by the SASCOLOR window.

Using the SASCOLOR Window: Use the SASCOLOR window to set colors for all SAS windows. Table 6.2 shows the window elements supported by the SASCOLOR window.

Table 6.2 Elements Supported by the SASCOLOR Window

Background	Secondary Background
Border	Secondary Border
Banner	Command
Message	Error
Warning	Note
Foreground	Label
Row Label	Informational Text
Column Label	Help Main Topic
Help Link	Help Subtopic & Syntax
Selected Area	Source
Data	Footnote
Header	Title
Byline	

Open the SASCOLOR window by clicking on **Tools** in the SAS System main menu, then click on **Options**, then click on **Colors**. Figure 6.14 shows the SASCOLOR window.

Figure 6.14 SASCOLOR Window

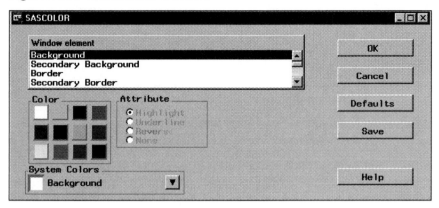

Note

You can also issue the SASCOLOR command from the Command bar to open the SASCOLOR window.

First, choose a window element by selecting one from the **Window element** list. Use the scroll bar to view the whole list. Select the element by clicking on it.

If the window element you have chosen supports attributes such as highlighting, reverse video, or underlining, these attributes are listed in the **Attribute** area. Unavailable attributes are light gray and not selectable. Click on any attribute you want the window element to have. Now choose a color from the **Color** area. To change more window elements, chose a different element, then set its attributes and color.

The **System Colors** area of the SASCOLOR window allows you to link the color of SAS window elements to colors set by the Windows Control Panel. The three choices for system colors are **Foreground**, **Background**, and **Secondary Background**. Table 6.3 shows how these choices correspond to the choices in the Display Properties window of the Control Panel (on the **Appearance** tab).

Table 6.3 How SASCOLOR Window System Colors Relate to the Control Panel Window Elements

Choice in SASCOLOR Window	Control Panel Window Element	Control Panel Window Element Attribute
Foreground	Window	Font Color
Background	Window	Item Color
Secondary Background	3D Objects	Item Color

For example, if you want selected text in SAS windows always to be the same color as the 3D Objects color set in the Control Panel, select **Selected Area** in the SASCOLOR window **Window element** list. Then, click on the down arrow to the right of the **System Colors** area and click on **Secondary Background**.

When you are finished setting colors and attributes in the SASCOLOR window, click on **OK** if you want to save your changes and close the SASCOLOR window. If you want to save your changes but leave the SASCOLOR window open, click on **Save**.

When you click on **OK** or **Save**, a catalog entry named SAS.CPARMS is created in your SASUSER.PROFILE catalog.

If you change several window elements but decide you do not like your changes, return to the default configuration by clicking on **Defaults** in the SASCOLOR window.

To get information on what the various window elements are, click on the **Help** button in the SASCOLOR window. This opens the **Using This Window** help topic for the SASCOLOR window.

Note

Although the SASCOLOR window affects all SAS windows, if you have changed a window element's color with the COLOR command and then issued a WSAVE command to save your changes, that window's element is not affected by the changes you make via the SASCOLOR window. (See "Saving Your Changes" later in this chapter for more information on WSAVE.)

Note

Currently open SAS windows do not reflect the new colors you have chosen from the SASCOLOR window until you close the windows and reopen them.

Using the COLOR Command: Use the COLOR command to set colors for a specific SAS window. You can issue the COLOR command from almost any SAS window. The basic syntax is

```
COLOR window-element color
```

where *window-element* is the name of a part of a window (like banner, note, or message) and *color* is an abbreviation for a supported color. Table 6.4 shows the window elements supported by the COLOR command, and Table 6.5 shows the supported colors and their abbreviations.

Table 6.4 Window Elements Supported by the COLOR Command

Background	Border	Banner
Command	Message	Scroll Bar
Byline	Data	Error
Footnote	Header	Mtext
Note	Numbers	Source
Text	Title	Warning

Table 6.5 Color Abbreviations Used by the COLOR Command

B	blue	R	red	G	green
C	cyan	P	pink	Y	yellow
W	white	K	black	M	magenta
A	gray	N	brown	O	orange

Note

Not all window elements listed in Table 6.4 are valid for all SAS windows. For example, the **Header** element is not valid in the Log window.

If you issue the COLOR command, then end your SAS session, the default colors return the next time you invoke the SAS System. To make the changes permanent for a window, perform one of the following actions:

- To save the colors set in just one window, issue the WSAVE command from the Command bar after the COLOR command. This saves the window's attributes to an entry in your SASUSER.PROFILE catalog, with the name *active-window*.WSAVE.

- To save the colors set in all windows (as well as all other window attributes), select **Save settings on exit** on the **General** tab of the Preferences dialog box. This is similar to issuing a WSAVE ALL command from the Command bar, and creates .WSAVE entries for all open SAS windows.

 If you've saved changes but then decide to return to the default configuration, delete the appropriate entries from your SASUSER.PROFILE catalog. These entries include all entries that have the WSAVE icon. To decide which .WSAVE entries to delete, display the contents of your PROFILE catalog in the SAS Explorer window, then click on **View→Details** in the SAS System main menu. The **Description** column explains what each entry is. (You may have to scroll or resize the right pane of the SAS Explorer window to see the **Description** column.)

Caution

Deleting entries that begin with a window name can also delete attributes other than color, such as customized key definitions.

Using the Control Panel's Display Properties Window: Use the Control Panel's Display Properties window to set colors for all windows in all Windows applications. Table 6.6 shows the window elements supported by the Display Properties window.

Table 6.6 Window Elements Supported by the Display Properties Window

3D Objects	Active Title Bar
Active Window Border	Application Background
Desktop	Inactive Title Bar
Inactive Window Border	Menu
Message Box	Selected Items
Tooltip	Window

To open the Control Panel's Display Properties window, click on the **Start** button, then click on **Settings→Control Panel**. Now double-click on the **Display** icon. The Display Properties window opens. Click on the **Appearance** tab. The window now looks like the one shown in Figure 6.15.

Figure 6.15   Appearance Tab of the Windows Display Properties Window

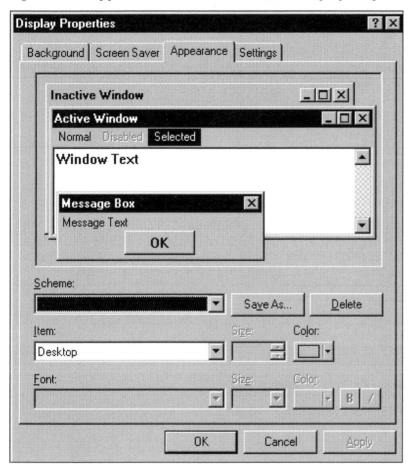

The window attributes you set on the **Appearance** tab of the Display Properties window affect all applications installed on your system. For example, if you set active title bars to be orange, the SAS System title bar is orange, and so is the title bar for Microsoft Word, Paint, and even the Control Panel.

To set the color of a particular window attribute, follow these steps:

1.   Click on the down arrow by the **Item** field, and use the scroll bar to scroll to the element you want to set. For example, about halfway down the list you see **Menu**.

2.   To select an element, click on it. The name of the element appears in the **Item** field.

3. Click on the **Color** button next to the **Item** field, then on the colored square that represents the color you want for the window element. For window elements that also contain text, you can click on the **Color** button next to the **Font** field to change the text color.

    For example, tool tips are normally light yellow with black text. If you prefer light green with magenta text, click on the light green rectangle displayed by the **Color** button next to the **Item** field. Then click on the **Color** button next to the **Font** field, and click on the magenta rectangle.

    When you click on a color, the sample window on the left side of the **Appearance** tab reflects your changes, showing the effect.

4. If you want to change other window elements, use the **Item** list to select another element, then select its color. When you are finished, click on **OK** to close the Display Properties window and save your changes.

Warning

> Be careful when you are selecting elements and colors. For example, it is possible to set both the window text and the window background to white, so that you cannot see anything. While you can fix this by going back to the Display Properties window, it is disconcerting to say the least.

If you want to see the Windows help on this topic, click on **Start→Help→Help Topics→How to→Change Windows Settings→Change How Windows Looks→Changing how items on the desktop look.**

Resizing and Organizing Windows

FasTip: Click on **Window→Tile, Cascade**, or **Resize**.

In Chapter 1, you learned how to move and resize windows using the mouse. You can also affect how windows are arranged within the SAS workspace by using the menus and commands.

Minimizing Windows: To minimize a window (that is, reduce it to an icon), click on the minimize button.

If you want all your SAS windows minimized, click on **Window** in the SAS System main menu, then click on **Minimize all windows**.

Tiling Windows: A quick way to make all open windows visible at once is to tile them. This arranges them in a mosaic pattern within the SAS workspace. To tile your windows, click on **Window** in the SAS System main menu, then on **Tile**. Figure 6.16 shows a SAS session with three tiled windows.

Figure 6.16 SAS Session with Three Tiled Windows

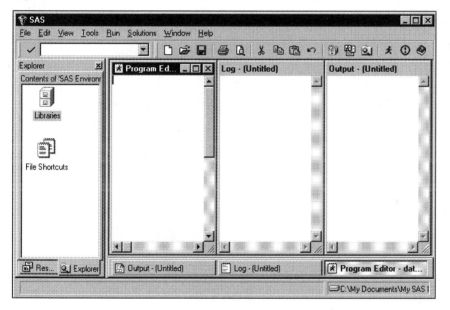

If you prefer issuing commands, issue the TILE command from the Command bar.

Note

The **Tile** menu choice does not tile docked windows.

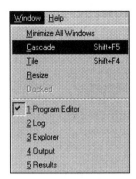

Cascading Windows: An alternative to tiling windows is to arrange them in layers, so that each window's title bar is visible. To cascade your windows, click on **Window** in the SAS System main menu, then click on **Cascade**. Figure 6.17 shows a SAS session with three cascaded windows.

Figure 6.17 SAS Session with Cascaded SAS Windows

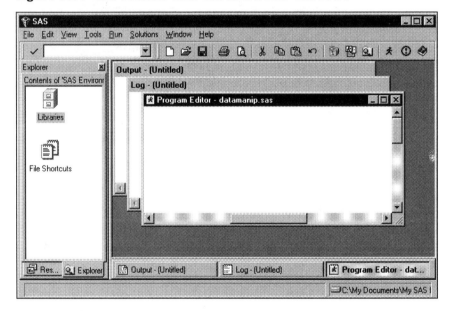

If you prefer issuing commands, issue the CASCADE command from the Command bar.

If you want a different window on top but still want the windows cascaded, first switch to the window you want, then reissue the CASCADE command. The windows are cascaded with the active window on top.

Note

The **Cascade** menu choice does not cascade docked windows.

Undoing Your Changes: If you decide you do not want your windows tiled or cascaded, return to the default arrangement by clicking on **Window** in the SAS System main menu, then on **Resize**. If you prefer issuing commands, issue the RESIZE command from the Command bar.

Note

Resize also resets other window attributes, such as size and position. It does not affect docked windows.

You can also change the default position of the SAS Explorer and Results windows by selecting or deselecting **Docked** in the **Window** menu.

Defining Function Keys

V7 Hilites: The KEYS window is now located under **Tools→Options→Keys**.

FasTip: Open the KEYS window and redefine the key definitions.

While the point-and-click features of Windows applications are a boon to many users, you may not like this approach to issuing commands. You can issue commands to the SAS System in other ways, bypassing the menus.

Three common alternatives to using the menus are

- function keys

- keyboard shortcuts

- command-line commands.

Earlier in this chapter, you learned how to use the **View** tab in the Preferences dialog box to turn on command lines. And in Chapter 1, you learned about keyboard shortcuts (such as CTRL-C for Cut) and hotkeys (the underlined letters in the menus). This section shows you how to define function keys (such as F1 or Shift-F10) and other keys (such as CTRL-H and the mouse buttons) for use with the SAS System.

Many function keys come defined with the SAS System, and you can add and change the default definitions. To see what keys have been defined, open the KEYS window by clicking on **Tools** in the SAS System main menu, then on **Options**, then on **Keys**. Figure 6.18 shows the default KEYS window.

Figure 6.18 KEYS Window

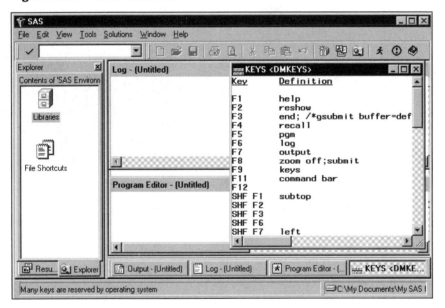

Use the scroll bars or PageUp and PageDown keys to see what keys are defined. Use Table 6.7 to understand the key name abbreviations.

Table 6.7 Abbreviations Used in the KEYS Window

Abbreviation	Key
SHF	Shift key
CTRL	Control key
ALT	Alt key
RMB	right mouse button
MMB	middle mouse button

(If you have a two-button mouse, MMB is not listed in the KEYS window.)

To define a key, type the command that you want associated with that key in the **Definition** column. To assign a string of commands to a single key, separate the commands with a semicolon (;).

Returning to the Default Key Definitions: When you close the KEYS window, the changes you've made are saved to your SASUSER.PROFILE catalog in an entry named Dmkeys. If you should ever want to go back to the default key definitions, delete the Dmkeys entry from your SASUSER.PROFILE catalog and close your SAS session. The next time you invoke the SAS System, the KEYS window lists the default function key definitions.

An alternative to deleting the Dmkeys entry is to rename it. (This prevents the SAS System from loading the definitions stored in the file.) Because the SAS System cannot find the Dmkeys entry, it uses the default key definitions. When you want to use your customized definitions again, rename the entry back to Dmkeys.

Note

Windows also defines some useful keys. Refer to Table 1.1 in Chapter 1 for a list of keys you may find helpful while working with the SAS System.

Changing the Display Font

V7 Hilites: The Font dialog box is now located under **Tools→Options→Fonts**.

Default display font size differs between low-resolution and high-resolution screens.

FasTip: Click on **Tools→Options→Fonts**.

You may not like the default font (Sasfont) used in SAS System windows. Or, you may want to change the font size (the default is 8 points for low-resolution screens and 10 points for high-resolution screens). To change the SAS System display font, click on **Tools** in the SAS System main menu, then on **Options**, then on **Fonts**. This opens the Font dialog box. Now choose the font and typesize you want to use. Figure 6.19 shows the Font dialog box.

Figure 6.19 Font Dialog Box for Changing the Display Font

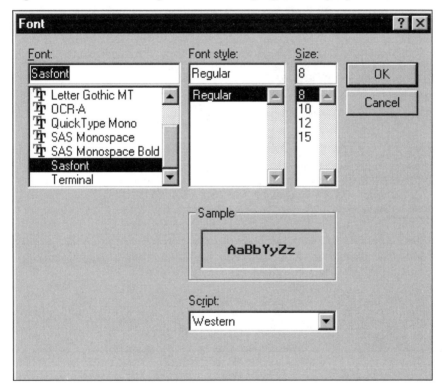

Only monospace fonts work well with the SAS System—proportional fonts do not produce satisfactory results. By default, the SAS System uses the Sasfont font in windows. Other monospace fonts that are common include Courier and IBMPCDOS.

Note

The font you choose in the Font dialog box accessed through the **Tools→Options** menu affects only the font used in SAS windows. To affect the font used for printer output, use the **Font** button in the Print Setup dialog box.

Adjusting Your Editor Options

You can adjust many aspects of the SAS Text Editor, using the Editor Options dialog box. To open this dialog box, make sure a text-editing window is active (such as the Program Editor or NOTEPAD window). Now click on **Tools** in the SAS System main menu, then on **Options**, then on **Editor**. Figure 6.20 shows the resulting dialog box.

Figure 6.20 Editor Options Dialog Box for the Program Editor Window

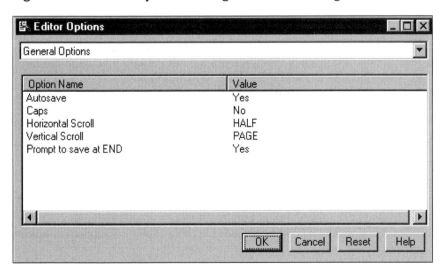

Note

There is a similar Editor Options dialog box for the Log and Output windows, as well.

To change one of the **General Options**, double-click on its name in the **Option Name** column. This opens the Modify dialog box, as shown in Figure 6.21.

**Figure 6.21 Modify Dialog Box Accessed
from the Editor Options Dialog Box**

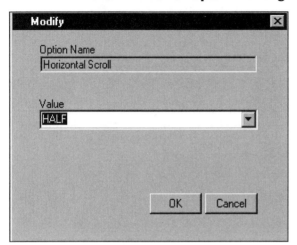

Click on the down arrow next to the **Value** field, and click on a new value. Now click on **OK** to close the Modify dialog box.

To change other options, click on the down arrow next to the top field in the Editor Options dialog box, and click on **Browse Options**. Now the **Option Name** column lists several more options. Modify these options as you did the **General Options**.

When you are finished modifying option values, click on **OK** to close the Editor Options dialog box.

Making the Program Editor Window Look Familiar

V7 Hilites: Line numbers are now turned on via the NUMS ON command.

The Preferences dialog box is organized differently.

FasTip: Issue the NUMS ON command to turn on line numbers in the Program Editor window.

Click on **Tools→Options→Preferences→View** to turn off the horizontal scrollbar, vertical scrollbar, and status line and turn on the command line.

Click on **Tools→Customize** to turn off the tool bar and Command bar.

You may have liked how the Program Editor and other windows looked in previous versions of the SAS System in mainframe environments—line numbers, a command line, no tools, status areas, or scroll bars. You can adjust the settings of various options in the SAS System to emulate the "old" look.

Activating Line Numbers: To activate line numbers in the Program Editor, issue the NUMS ON command from the Command bar.

Note

You can also turn line numbers on in other SAS Text Editor windows, such as NOTEPAD and Source.

Turning on Command Lines: Click on **Tools→Options→Preferences** in the SAS System main menu to open the Preferences dialog box. Click on the **View** tab. Select **Command line**.

Turning off the Scroll Bars and Status Area: Click on **Tools→Options→Preferences** in the SAS System main menu to open the Preferences dialog box. Click on the **View** tab. Deselect **Vertical scroll bar**, **Horizontal scroll bar**, and **Status line**.

Turning Off the Command Bar and Tool Bar: Click on **Tools→Customize** in the SAS System main menu. Deselect **Command Bar** and **Application Toolbar**.

Saving Your Changes to the Windowing Environment

After you've made changes to your SAS windowing interface, you may not want to make these changes again. You can tell the SAS System to save the changes you've made. Or, you can save the changes only to a particular window.

Saving All Your Changes: To save all the windowing interface changes you have made, follow these steps:

1. Click on **Tools** in the SAS System main menu, then on **Options**, then on **Preferences**.

2. In the Preferences dialog box, click on the **General** tab.

3. Select the **Save settings on exit** option.

4. Click on **OK**.

Following these steps is equivalent to issuing a WSAVE ALL command from the Command bar, and creates an Awswsave.WSAVE entry in your SASUSER.PROFILE catalog.

Saving Changes to a Particular Window: To save the changes you've made in a particular window, but not to other windows, follow these steps:

1.   Make the window you want to save active.

2.   Issue a WSAVE command from the Command bar.

This creates a *window-name*.WSAVE entry in your SASUSER.PROFILE catalog.

Returning to the Default Environment

If you want to undo only one change from among many, you may want to redo the command. For example, if you have used the COLOR command to change many aspects of several windows and want to save the majority of the changes, your best approach is to reissue the COLOR command for the few window aspects you want to change. Or, if you are happy with most of the settings in the Preferences dialog box but want to change one of them, open the dialog box, make your change, and click on **OK**.

If, however, you want to completely undo a set of changes, such as all color settings or all tool bar changes, use the techniques in Table 6.8. Where several actions are listed, try each of them in order—you may have to take several steps to completely return to the default settings.

Note

To see the entry types for catalog entries in the SAS Explorer window, click on **View→Details** in the SAS System main menu. You may have to scroll or resize the SAS Explorer window to see the **Type** column. You can also use the **Description** field in the SAS Explorer window to help you find specific entries.

Table 6.8 Returning to the Default Windowing Environment

Window Element	To Return to Default Settings
Keys	Delete or rename the Dmkeys entry in your SASUSER.PROFILE catalog
Tools	Open the Customize Tools dialog box, click on the **Customize** tab, and click on the Restore Defaults icon Delete all .TOOLBOX entries in your SASUSER.PROFILE catalog
Colors	Open the SASCOLOR window and click on **Defaults** Delete all .WSAVE entries in your SASUSER.PROFILE catalog Delete the SAS.CPARMS entry in your SASUSER.PROFILE catalog
Preferences	Delete the *xyz*wsave entries from your SASUSER.PROFILE catalog, where *xyz* represents the various tabs in the Preferences dialog box
Window size and position	Click on **Window** in the SAS System main menu, then click on **Resize** Delete .WSAVE entries with a window name from your SASUSER.PROFILE catalog Delete or rename the Dmsdef entry in your SASUSER.PROFILE catalog Restart your SAS session

7 Managing SAS® Files

Introduction

V7 Hilites: The Active Libraries dialog box has replaced the Libraries dialog box.

The SAS Explorer lets you rename, delete, move, and copy SAS files (such as tables and catalog members).

The SAS Explorer lets you modify the passwords associated with a SAS table.

The V604 engine is not available in Version 7; this engine may become available again in subsequent releases of the SAS System.

It is often best to manage SAS files such as SAS tables and catalogs using the SAS System's file management capabilities.

This chapter first discusses some data protection issues you should consider before deciding how to manage your SAS files. Then, it shows you how to perform the following file management tasks:

- rename and delete SAS files using the SAS Explorer window

- move and copy SAS files using the SAS Explorer window

- manage your SAS library references and file shortcuts

- manage your SAS catalogs.

Note

> The Windows Explorer, discussed in Appendix 3, is also useful for managing files. For example, you cannot rename, move, or copy SAS programs using the SAS Explorer (because files with a .SAS extension are considered by the SAS System to be host files), so you must perform this task using the Windows Explorer.

Understanding Data Protection

V7 Hilites: You can now specify SAS System data set passwords via a dialog box.

The Windows environment and the SAS System both provide data protection services—which one you choose (or you may choose to use both) depends on how you plan to access and manage your files.

Setting SAS System Passwords: The SAS System lets you assign passwords to SAS tables. These passwords control file access and are assigned using the READ=, WRITE=, and ALTER= data set options.

- READ= allows read-only access to the file.

- WRITE= allows read and write access to the file (including the ability to modify, delete, and add columns).

- ALTER= allows read and write access to the file, plus the ability to delete the file, rename columns, and create indexes.

If you do not specify the correct password with the correct option, you cannot access the file. See the SAS online help for the syntax of these data set options.

Warning

> If you forget the password, you will not be able to access your protected SAS files. Therefore, you may want to record the password in a safe place.

Warning

> If you choose to use the Windows Explorer to rename or delete SAS files, remember that SAS password protection does not prevent you from deleting files using the Windows Explorer.

With Version 7, you can modify the READ=, WRITE=, and ALTER= values from the SAS Explorer. To do so, right-click on the SAS table name, then click on **Passwords** in the popup menu. This opens the dialog box shown in Figure 7.1.

Figure 7.1 Password Dialog Box

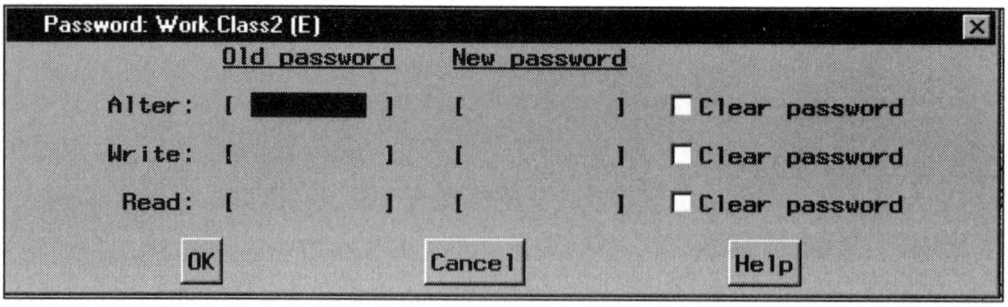

Type the old password and new password for the appropriate option, then click on **OK**. When the Password verification dialog box appears, type the new password again, and click **OK**.

To clear a password, type the old password, then select the **Clear password** option next to READ=, WRITE=, or ALTER=. Now click **OK**.

Using File Attributes: You can also use the Windows Explorer to set file attributes, which are different than SAS System passwords. Here are the steps to display a file's attributes in the Windows Explorer:

1. Open the Windows Explorer by right-clicking on the **Start** button, then clicking on **Explore**.

2. Display the folder containing the file for which you want to display attributes.

3. Right-click on the file for which you want to see attributes.

4. Click on **Properties** in the popup menu. The Properties dialog box for the file appears.

For example, Figure 7.2 shows the properties for DATAMANIP.SAS.

**Figure 7.2 Using the Windows Explorer File Properties
            Dialog Box to Set File Attributes**

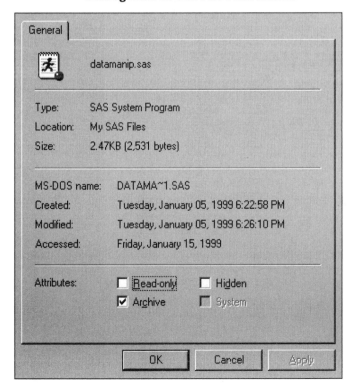

In the Properties dialog box, choose one or more of the following attributes:

• **Read-only** means users cannot write to the file, rename it, or delete it. All they can do is read it.

• **Archive** means the file is marked when it has changed since it was last backed up.

• **Hidden** means the file is not listed by default in the Windows Explorer's folder listings.

• **System** means the file is a Windows system file. You probably will not use this option with your SAS files.

Turn file attributes on and off by clicking in their respective check boxes.

If you want to see hidden files in the Windows Explorer folder listing, click on **View** in the Windows Explorer menu, then click on **Options**. In the Options dialog box, click by the **Show all files** option. Now all hidden files are listed in the folder listings, allowing you to select them and change their attributes if you want.

Warning

Hidden files are usually hidden for a purpose—they are rarely files that you need to manage in any way. You do not need to change the properties of a hidden file.

Note

Windows also provides other file-protection devices, such as lists of authorized users. Use the following help path to learn more: **Start→Help→How To→Safeguard Your Work→ Controlling access to a folder or printer**

Understanding SAS System Data Protection and Windows File Protection: Setting passwords in the SAS System does not affect file access outside the SAS System. For example, if you use the READ= data set option to mark a table read-only, you can still delete it using the Windows Explorer. Therefore, if you depend on SAS System data protection, you should perform all your file management from within the SAS System using the SAS Explorer window, the COPY procedure, and other SAS System file management features.

On the other hand, file attributes set with the Properties dialog box do affect the SAS System. For example, if you mark the program DATAMANIP.SAS as read-only using the Properties dialog box and then try to save it from the Program Editor window, you receive the following error in your SAS log: Insufficient authorization.

Similarly, if you have marked a file as hidden, it is not listed in the SAS System dialog boxes (for example, Open and Save As).

Renaming SAS Files

V7 Hilites: Use the SAS Explorer or Active Libraries window to rename SAS files.

FasTip: Right-click on the SAS filename in the SAS Explorer window, and click on **Rename**.

You can choose to rename SAS files from the SAS Explorer, or use the Active Libraries window.

Warning

Be careful when you rename files—some files, such as the SASUSER.PROFILE catalog, must have a particular name in order to work. In general, it is safe to rename catalogs and other files you have created; do not rename files created automatically by the SAS System.

Using the SAS Explorer to Rename SAS Files: To use the SAS Explorer to rename SAS files, follow these steps:

1. Double-click on the SAS data library you want to see the contents of.

2. Continue to drill down to the SAS file you want to rename (double-clicking on a catalog name if necessary).

3. Right-click on the file you want to rename, then click on **Rename** in the popup menu. A dialog box appears, as shown in Figure 7.3.

Figure 7.3 Rename Dialog Box for Renaming SAS Files from the SAS Explorer

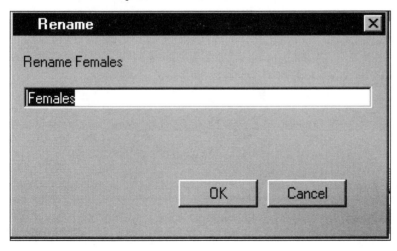

4. Type the new name in the text entry field, then click on **OK**.

Note

Remember that Version 7 of the SAS System supports long names—you are no longer limited to eight characters.

Using the Active Libraries Window to Rename SAS Files: You can also rename SAS files from the Active Libraries window. To open this window, issue the LIBNAME command from the Command bar. Figure 7.4 shows a sample Active Libraries window.

Figure 7.4 Active Libraries Window

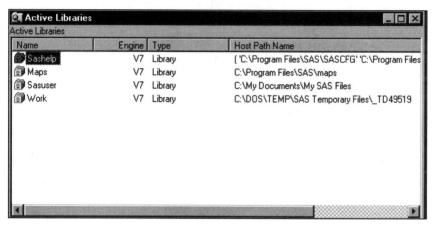

Navigate in this window as you would in the SAS Explorer window (without the tree view) until the file you want to rename is displayed. Now right-click on the filename, then click on **Rename** in the popup menu. Type the new name in the text entry field, then click on **OK**.

Note

You may need to resize or even close the docked windows in your SAS session to see the entire Active Libraries window. Even then, you will probably have to scroll to see the **Modified** field on the far right side of the window, unless you are using a high-resolution display.

Deleting SAS Files

V7 Hilites: Use the SAS Explorer or Active Libraries window to delete SAS files.

FasTip: Right-click on the SAS filename in the SAS Explorer window, and click on **Delete**.

You can choose to delete SAS files from the SAS Explorer, or use the Active Libraries window.

Warning

> Be careful when you delete files; some files, such as the SASUSER.PROFILE catalog, are necessary for the SAS System to work properly. In general, it is safe to delete catalogs and other files you have created; do not delete files created automatically by the SAS System.

Note

> If you try to delete a file that is protected by the ALTER= data set option, you are prompted to enter the correct password before the file is deleted.

Using the SAS Explorer to Delete SAS Files: To use the SAS Explorer window to delete SAS files, follow these steps:

1. Double-click on the SAS data library you want to see the contents of.

2. Continue to drill down to the SAS file you want to rename (double-clicking on a catalog name if necessary).

3. Right-click on the file you want to delete, then click on **Delete** in the popup menu.

4. When prompted whether you are sure you want to delete the file, click on **OK**.

Using the Active Libraries Window to Delete SAS Files: You can also delete SAS files from the Active Libraries window. To open this window, issue the LIBNAME command from the Command bar. Refer to Figure 7.4 for a sample Active Libraries window.

Navigate in this window as you would in the SAS Explorer window until the file you want to rename is displayed. Now right-click on the filename, then click on **Delete** in the popup menu. When prompted whether you are sure you want to delete the file, click on **OK**.

Warning

> Files deleted via the SAS Explorer window or other methods within the SAS System are not sent to the Windows Recycle Bin, and therefore cannot be easily recovered. To recover such files, you must have a third-party file restoration utility, such as Norton Utilities.

Moving and Copying SAS Files Using the SAS Explorer

V7 Hilites: Use the SAS Explorer to move and copy SAS files.

The SAS System provides the COPY procedure, and it works the same under Windows as it does under any other operating system. But if you prefer the object-oriented method of moving and copying files, use the SAS Explorer to move and copy files from one folder to another.

Warning

Moving files from one folder to another involves deleting a file from the original folder. If you have protected your SAS tables with the ALTER= data set option (which prevents you from deleting the file without providing the password), you must specify the password to move these tables.

Moving Files with Drag and Drop: To move a file using the drag and drop technique in the SAS Explorer, follow these steps:

1. Navigate until the file you want to move is displayed in the right pane of the SAS Explorer.

2. Use the right mouse button (not the left mouse button) to drag the file into the left pane and drop the file on the SAS data library or catalog you want to copy the file to.

3. When the popup menu appears, click on **Move**. The file is moved to the new folder.

Note

If the file is protected with the ALTER= data set option, you are prompted to enter the correct password before the file is moved.

Copying Files Using Drag and Drop: To copy a file using the drag and drop technique in the SAS Explorer, follow these steps:

1. Navigate until the file you want to copy is displayed in the right pane of the SAS Explorer.

2. Use the right mouse button (not the left mouse button) to drag the file into the left pane and drop the file on the SAS data library or catalog you want to copy the file to.

3. When the popup menu appears, click on **Copy**. The file is copied to the new folder.

Copying Files Using the Popup Menus: To copy a file using the popup menus in the SAS Explorer, follow these steps:

1. Navigate until the file you want to copy is displayed in the right pane of the SAS Explorer.

2. Right-click on the file you want to copy. Click on one of the following popup menu items:

   • **Copy** if you want to copy the file to a different SAS data library. Go to steps 3 and then 4.

   • **Duplicate** if you want to create a copy of the file in the same SAS data library. Go to steps 5 and then 6.

3. If you clicked on **Copy**, now navigate in the SAS Explorer until the contents of the target SAS data library or catalog are displayed in the right pane.

4. Right-click in the right pane, and click on **Paste**. The SAS file is now copied to the target SAS data library, and you are finished (do not continue with steps 5 and 6).

5. If you clicked on **Duplicate**, a dialog box appears, as shown in Figure 7.5.

Figure 7.5 Duplicate Dialog Box for Duplicating SAS Files from the SAS Explorer

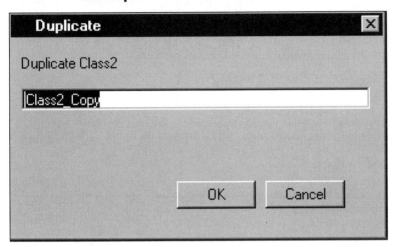

6. Type the new name for the duplicate SAS file in the Duplicate dialog box, then click on **OK**. The new SAS file appears in the right pane of the SAS Explorer.

Selecting More than One File to Move or Copy: You can move or copy more than one file from the original folder to the target folder. To do so, use your Shift and Control keys in combination with your left mouse button to select multiple files, as described here:

- To select several contiguous files, click on the first filename, hold the Shift key down, and click on the last filename.

- To select several files that are separated by files you do not want to select, click on the first filename, hold down the Control key, and click on the subsequent filenames.

Note

If you select more than one file and then choose **Duplicate**, a Duplicate dialog box appears for each SAS file you selected. Enter the new name and click **OK** to progress to the next dialog box.

Managing SAS Data Libraries

V7 Hilites: The LIBNAME command now opens the Active Libraries window.

The Add New Library icon opens the New Library dialog box; the icon has also changed.

FasTip: Use the SAS Explorer to list the active SAS data libraries, or issue the LIBNAME command to see a similar active library references list.

Click on the Add New Library icon on the SAS tool bar to create a new library reference.

SAS data libraries are central to using the SAS System. The SAS System offers several easy ways to manage SAS data libraries.

Listing Active Library References: If you have assigned many library references during a SAS session, it is often difficult to remember which library reference points to which folder.

You can view active library references in two ways:

- Double-click on the **Libraries** icon in the SAS Explorer window—this displays all currently defined library references.

- Use the Active Libraries window to display a list of currently assigned library references. To open the Active Libraries window, issue the LIBNAME command from the Command bar.

To see the members of a particular library, double-click on the library reference (in either the SAS Explorer or Active Libraries window).

Chapter 2 goes into detail on how to use the SAS Explorer. If you want to see the engine and physical pathname associated with each library reference listed in the SAS Explorer, click on **View→Details**.

Figure 7.4 earlier in this chapter shows a sample Active Libraries window. Like the detailed SAS Explorer view, the Active Libraries window shows you which SAS engine is associated with each library and the library's physical pathname.

Note

You may need to resize or even close the docked windows in your SAS session to see the entire Active Libraries window. Even then, you will probably have to scroll to see the **Modified** field on the far right side of the window, unless you are using a high-resolution display.

Viewing the Contents of a SAS Data Library: To view the contents of a particular data library, double-click on its name in the SAS Explorer or Active Libraries window.

Creating a New Library Reference: To create a new library reference, click on the Add New Library icon on the SAS tool bar.

Alternatively, you can right-click on the **Libraries** icon in the SAS Explorer, then click on **New** in the popup menu. In either case, the New Library dialog box opens, as shown in Figure 7.6.

Figure 7.6 New Library Dialog Box

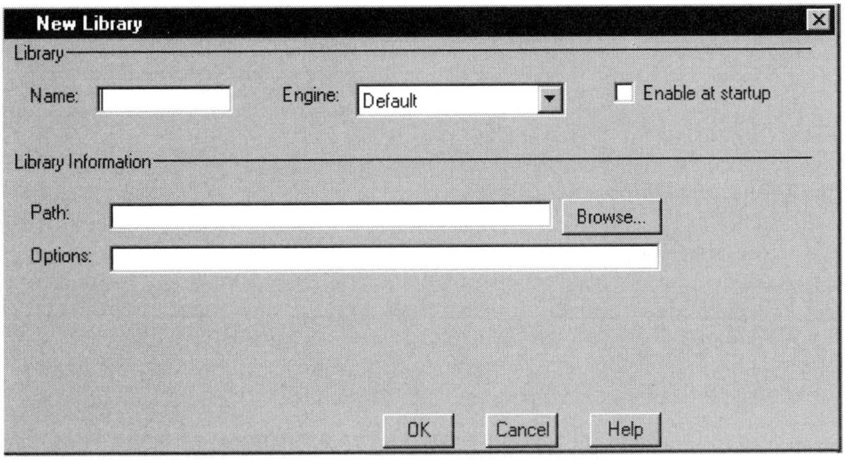

This dialog box is like a point-and-click LIBNAME statement.

Type the new library reference in the **Name** field. Use the **Browse** button to find the folder you want to associate with the library reference. When you have found the folder you want, click on **OK**. This copies the folder name to the **Path** field in the New Library dialog box. Alternatively, you can type the folder name directly into the **Path** field. Choose the engine you want to associate with the library reference by clicking on the down arrow next to the **Engine** field and clicking on the correct engine name. (The default engine is V7.)

Note

Version 7 does not include the V604 engine; this engine may be available in subsequent releases of the SAS System.

Type any options you want to associate with the library reference in the **Options** field. The options you can enter depend on which engine you select for the library. For example, to create a read-only Version 7 SAS data library, you can specify the following in the **Options** field:

```
ACCESS=READONLY
```

When you have filled in all the fields, click on **OK**. This creates the new library reference.

Creating a Concatenated SAS Data Library: To create a library reference that points to a concatenation of folders, click in the **Path** field in the New Library dialog box and enter a quoted list of folders contained inside parentheses. For example, if you want the library reference to point to both the folders C:\BACKUP and C:\Old Files, enter the following in the **Path** field:

```
('c:\backup' 'c:\old files')
```

Assigning Library References Automatically: If you select the **Enable at startup** check box in the New Library dialog box, a library definition is stored in your SASUSER.PROFILE catalog. The library reference is available as soon as you start your SAS session—no LIBNAME statement or other action is necessary.

Deleting a Library Reference: To delete a library reference, display the library reference in either the SAS Explorer or the Active Libraries window. Right-click on the library reference you want to delete, then click on **Delete** in the popup menu. When prompted if you really want to delete the library reference, click on **OK**. (Remember, this deletes the library reference, which is a pointer to the folder, but this does not delete the actual folder.)

Note

You cannot modify the properties of an existing data library (such as its name or engine). To change a data library's properties, you must create a new library reference with the desired properties, then delete the old library reference.

Managing File Shortcuts

V7 Hilites: The FILENAME command now opens the Active File Shortcuts window.

FasTip: Double-click on the **File Shortcuts** icon in the SAS Explorer window, or issue the FILENAME command.

Chapter 2 showed you how to create a file shortcut (called a fileref in Version 6 of the SAS System), using the SAS Explorer. However, once you create several file shortcuts, it can be hard to remember which shortcut points to what file.

You can display the active file shortcuts in two ways:

- Double-click on the **File Shortcuts** icon in the SAS Explorer window.

- Open the Active File Shortcuts window by issuing the FILENAME command.

Chapter 2 goes into detail about the SAS Explorer window. If you want to see details, such as the physical pathname associated with each file shortcut listed in the SAS Explorer, click on **View→Details**.

Figure 7.7 shows a sample Active File Shortcuts window.

Figure 7.7 Active File Shortcuts Window

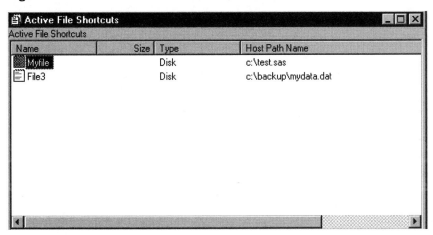

The Active File Shortcuts window lists each file shortcut, the physical file the file shortcut points to, and other attributes as appropriate (such as file size and file type). You may have to scroll right in the window to see all the information.

Managing SAS Catalogs

V7 Hilites: The CATALOG command now opens the Active Libraries window.

While you can manage your catalogs programmatically with the CATALOG procedure, you may find it easier to use the SAS Explorer and Active Libraries windows to rename, move, copy, and delete SAS catalog entries.

If the entry is an executable entry, such as NOTEPAD.SOURCE or a BUILD entry, double-clicking on an entry opens that entry. This is the same as pointing at the entry name, right-clicking to activate the popup menu, and clicking on **Open**. Other possible actions, depending on the type of entry you are pointing at, include **Rename**, **Delete**, and **Copy**.

Warning

Be careful renaming catalog entries—some entries have required names (such as SAS.CPARMS). In general, it is safe to rename entries you have created but not entries created automatically by the SAS System. Also, exercise care when deleting entries. For example, if you delete the entry GENWSAVE.WSAVE, you lose all the general preferences you have set via the Preferences dialog box.

Customizing Your Start-up Files and SAS® System Options

Introduction

V7 Hilites: The default name of the SAS configuration file is now SASV7.CFG.

There is a new SAS System Options window, which includes a Find Option feature.

Under every operating system, the SAS System uses two start-up files: the configuration file and the autoexec file. This chapter explains how these two files work under Windows and how to modify them. Much of the information is similar to other operating systems, so you should become adept quickly at using these files under Windows.

As a reminder, here are the differences between the configuration and autoexec files:

- The configuration file sets SAS system options. These options control various aspects of the SAS System, such as the size of the SAS workspace, printer options, and more. When you install the SAS System, a default configuration file named SASV7.CFG is created in the SAS folder.

- The autoexec file executes SAS programming statements immediately after the SAS System starts. The default name for the autoexec file is AUTOEXEC.SAS. No autoexec file is created at SAS System installation—if you want one, you must create it yourself.

Under Windows, you can also specify SAS system options in the **Target** field of the Properties dialog box for the SAS System icon. The system options you specify in the **Target** field are used in addition to the system options in the configuration file. Later in this chapter, "Altering the Properties of the SAS System Icon" provides more information about this technique.

If you want to alter the value of a SAS system option while SAS is running, use the SAS System Options window, as described in "Customizing Your SAS System Options" later in this chapter.

Note

> This and subsequent chapters cover complex tasks that require many steps and considerations; therefore, these chapters do not contain many FasTips.

Editing Your Start-up Files—An Overview

To edit your configuration file or autoexec file, you need to use a text editor that saves the file as plain text. (If you use a word processing application, be sure to save the file as a plain ASCII text file without formatting codes.) Here are two text editors to choose from:

*   Windows Notepad editor

*   SAS Text Editor window, such as the Program Editor or the NOTEPAD window.

Note

> If you use a SAS window to edit your start-up files, you must restart the SAS System to see the effects of your changes.

This section shows you the basics of using the Windows Notepad editor. If you use the SAS System to edit the SAS start-up files, then see Chapter 3 for information on using the SAS Text Editor.

Warning

> When editing your start-up files, be sure to use an editor that creates plain ASCII files so that no special formatting codes are inserted into the files. If you decide to use an editor other than the ones listed here, be sure to save the file as ASCII text.

Overview of Using the Windows Notepad Editor: To open a file in the Windows Notepad editor, click on the **Start** button, then click on **Programs**, then click on **Accessories**. Finally, click on **Notepad**.

If you are creating a new file, simply start typing. To edit an existing file, click on **File** in the Notepad menu, then click on **Open**. Type either `C:\Program Files\SAS\SASV7.CFG` or `C:\Program Files\SAS\AUTOEXEC.SAS` in the **File name** field, and click on **Open**. The file is copied to the Notepad window.

Use your cursor arrow keys and the PageUp and PageDown keys to move to where you want to make your changes. When you have finished editing the file, click on **File** in the Notepad menu, then click on **Save**. (If the file has not been saved before, give the file a name in the Save As dialog box and then click on **Save**.) To close the Notepad editor, click on Notepad's Close button.

Making Changes to the SAS Configuration File

Although the default configuration file that is created when the SAS System is installed may be sufficient for some users, you may need to add or modify option specifications.

There are many required system options in the default configuration file. Unless you are certain of your changes, do not edit the existing option specifications. When you add options, you should not add them in the portion of the file that the SAS System INSTALL utility controls. Figure 8.1 shows the SASV7.CFG file open in the Notepad editor; add your options above the boxed comment.

Figure 8.1 SASV7.CFG File Open in the Windows Notepad Editor

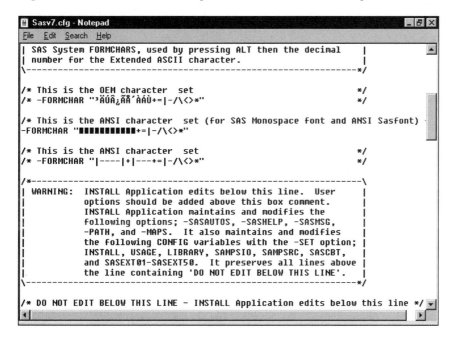

After opening the configuration file in the editor of your choice, use the scroll bars or the PageDown key to scroll to the boxed comment shown in Figure 8.1. Click on the blank line right above the box and press Enter twice. Now type your new option specifications. Precede each option with a hyphen (dash).

There are two kinds of system options—the on/off kind and the kind that take some value. For example, the SPLASH option is an on/off option. It controls whether the SAS System logo and copyright information appear when the SAS System initializes. To suppress the logo (also called the splash screen), specify NOSPLASH.

The FONT option is an example of a system option that takes a value. It controls the screen font that the SAS System uses. Here is how these two options might look if you add them to your configuration file:

```
-NOSPLASH

-FONT 'Sasfont' 12
```

Some options can take both the on/off and value forms. The PRINT option is an example of this kind of option. Notice that for options that take values, you do not use an equal sign—use only a space between the option name and its value.

Discovering Which System Options Are Available: To find out which system options are available under Windows, follow this help path:

Help→SAS System Help→Using SAS with Your Operating System→Using SAS under Windows→SAS System Options under Windows→SAS System Options under Windows

The list of operating-system-specific options is displayed. To see the syntax and description of an option, click on its name.

For example, Figure 8.2 shows the help that is available for the FONT option.

Figure 8.2 Example Help Window for SAS System Options

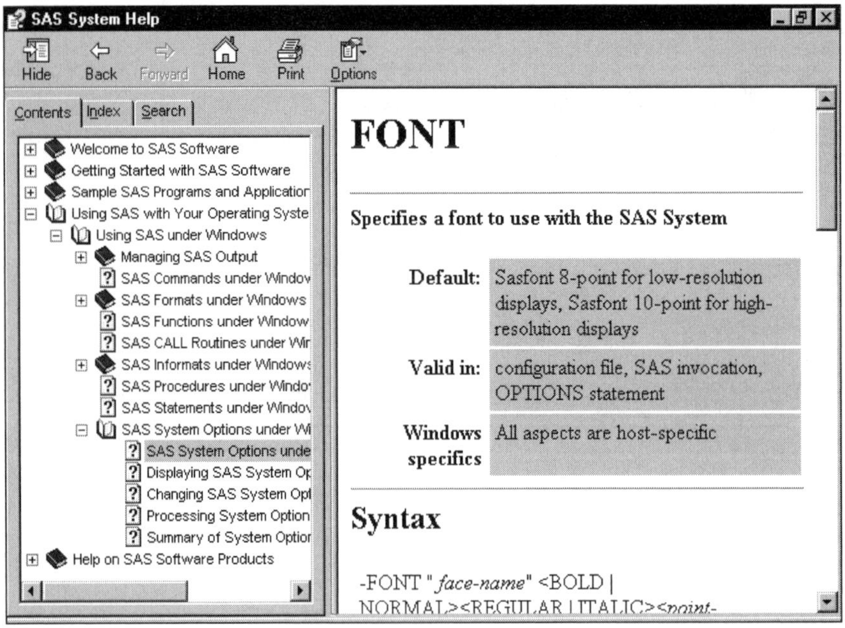

Creating and Editing the Autoexec File

The autoexec file contains SAS programming statements that are executed before your SAS session begins. Use the autoexec file to customize and automate your SAS session. Here are some ways to use your autoexec file:

* set SAS system options with the OPTIONS statement

* issue windowing commands with the DM statement

* define SAS library references and file shortcuts with the LIBNAME and FILENAME statements

* perform data processing with DATA and PROC statements

* invoke SAS/AF applications with the AF statement.

For example, suppose your reports need a special line size, and you find yourself creating the same library reference every time you invoke the SAS System. Suppose you also need to see all your open windows at once. Your AUTOEXEC.SAS file might look like this:

```
options linesize=50;
libname currdata 'c:\saledata\current';
dm 'tile';
```

When your SAS session initializes, the line size is set to 50, the CURRDATA library reference is created, and the Log, Program Editor, and Output windows are tiled.

No AUTOEXEC.SAS file is created when the SAS System is installed, so you must create it yourself. If you use the Windows Notepad editor, open the editor, and begin typing.

To save the file, click on **File** in the Notepad editor menu, then click on **Save As**. Type C:\PROGRAM FILES\SAS\AUTOEXEC.SAS in the **File name** field, and click on **Save**. To close the editor, click on its Close button.

If you or someone else have already created an autoexec file, edit it using the same techniques as described for the configuration file.

Note

Remember to end each statement with a semicolon. There is no size limitation on the autoexec file—it can contain as many SAS programming statements as you want.

Some system options are not valid in the OPTIONS statement, and therefore you cannot specify them in the autoexec file. The autoexec file cannot contain system options that affect the SAS System initialization (such as ALTLOG or SPLASH). If you look up an option in the SAS online help and the **Syntax** section lists only the format preceded by a hyphen, then that option is not valid in the autoexec file. If the syntax lists both the hyphen form and the OPTIONS statement form, then you can use that option in the autoexec file.

Altering the Properties of the SAS System Icon

When you click on an icon to start an application, Windows uses properties to control how that application behaves. For example, for the SAS System, properties can specify which folder to use as the working folder, which system options to use at invocation, and whether the application begins as a normal-sized, maximized, or minimized window.

To change the system options used in the SAS command that starts the SAS System, use the Properties dialog box. To access this dialog box, follow these steps:

1. Open the Windows Explorer by right-clicking on the **Start** button, then click on **Explore**.

2. By default, Windows shows you the contents of the Start Menu folder. Double-click on the Programs folder in the right half of the window.

3. Double-click on The SAS System folder.

4. Right-click on the **SAS System for Windows V7** icon, then click on **Properties**.

5. Click on the **Shortcut** tab.

6. Click in the **Target** field, and use the Backspace and Delete keys to delete any system options you do not want to use; type any new system options after the SAS.EXE. Remember that each system option begins with a hyphen.

7. When you have finished editing the **Target** field, click on **OK**. The next time you click on the SAS System icon to start the SAS System, the new system options will be in effect.

Note

This change applies only to the SAS System shortcut that is accessed from the SAS System program group. If you have created additional shortcuts to the SAS System (such as on the desktop), you must change each shortcut's properties individually.

Using the Run Dialog Box to Specify SAS System Options

You can use the Run dialog box to specify SAS System options, instead of editing your SAS configuration file or the properties of the SAS System icon. This technique is useful when you need the options only occasionally.

To open the Run dialog box, click on the **Start** button, then click on **Run**.

Type `C:\Program Files\SAS\SAS.EXE` in the **Open** field, followed by whichever system options you want to use for that session. For example, if you do not want to see the SAS logo when the SAS System starts up, type the following in the **Open** field:

```
c:\program files\sas\sas.exe -nosplash
```

Click on **OK** to start the SAS System.

The system options that you add to the **Open** field in the Run dialog box are used in conjunction with the options in the SAS configuration file (that is, they do not replace the configuration file).

Because the **Open** field can contain up to 255 characters, you can specify many system options. If you need more space than this, put the options in your configuration file instead.

Understanding the Precedence of System Options

System options can appear in several places, so it is important to know which specifications take precedence:

- An OPTIONS statement in the autoexec file has the last word and overrides options that are specified in either the SAS configuration file or the Run dialog box.

- The Run dialog box overrides options that are specified in the SAS configuration file.

For example, if the same option is specified in the SAS configuration file and in the **Open** field of the Run dialog box, the value in the dialog box takes precedence. Or, if the same option is specified in the SAS configuration file and in an OPTIONS statement in the autoexec file, the value in the autoexec file is used.

Accommodating Multiple Users

Sometimes several people use the same PC, and each person may have a different concept of what the SAS session should look like, what it should do, and so on. The same problem arises when people on a network use a single copy of the SAS System.

The answer to this problem lies in setting up configuration and autoexec files for each user. Alternatively, create SAS System shortcuts for each user. The following sections discuss how to use each approach.

Creating Start-up Files for Each User: Suppose three people use the same PC—Nancy, Kurt, and Paulo. Nancy creates sales reports with PROC REPORT, and Kurt uses SAS/GRAPH to produce monthly sales charts. Paulo, a summer intern, does not know much about the SAS System, but he is responsible for using a SAS/AF application to enter weekly sales data into the tables that Nancy and Kurt use. These three users have distinct needs, yet, they must share the same software. Separate SAS System start-up files help them use the SAS System efficiently.

Although the default name of the SAS configuration file is SASV7.CFG and the autoexec file is named AUTOEXEC.SAS, these files can have any name, as long as you tell the SAS System where to find them. Here are the steps for creating start-up files for each user:

1. Use the Windows Explorer to copy the original SASV7.CFG file, which is located in the SAS folder, to three new files in the same folder.

   a) Open the Windows Explorer by right-clicking on the **Start** button, then clicking on **Explore**.

   b) Navigate to the SAS folder, and highlight the original SASV7.CFG. (If you need help using the Windows Explorer, refer to Appendix 3.)

   c) Click on **Edit→Copy** in the Windows Explorer menu.

   d) Click on **Edit→Paste**. A file named "Copy of SASV7.CFG" appears in the folder listing.

   e) Rename this file to NANCY.CFG.

   f) Repeat steps d and e twice to create KURT.CFG and PAULO.CFG.

2. Have each user edit his or her personal configuration files and save them.

3. Have each user create a file that contains the SAS programming statements they want to have executed each time the SAS System initializes, and save these files with names like AUTONANCY.SAS, AUTOKURT.SAS, and AUTOPAULO.SAS.

   Continuing with the above example, here is what each file might contain:

   AUTONANCY.SAS

```
libname sales 'c:\products\saleinfo\qtr4';
libname expense 'c:\products\expinfo\qtr4';
proc report;
... report-generating statements
```

   AUTOKURT.SAS

```
libname sales 'c:\products\saleinfo\qtr4';
proc gplot;
... chart-generating statements
```

   AUTOPAULO.SAS

```
libname apps 'c:\products\sasapps';
af apps.product.entry.menu;
```

Now each user has his or her own version of the SAS configuration and autoexec files. All that remains is to tell the SAS System which files to use. When Nancy, Kurt, or Paulo invokes the SAS System, he or she must open the Run dialog box and type the following in the **Open** field:

```
c:\Program Files\sas\sas.exe -CONFIG C:\Program Files\SAS\xyz.CFG
   -AUTOEXEC C:\Program Files\SAS\AUTOxyz.SAS
```

where *xyz* is the user's name (NANCY, KURT, or PAULO). If the options are already typed, use the cursor arrow keys to position the cursor where the changes need to be made, and type the new name (use the Backspace key, if necessary, to erase extra characters). Click on **OK** to start the SAS System. The appropriate start-up files are used.

Creating Copies of the SAS System Icon: Using the Run dialog box to change the options for an application every time you want to use it can be cumbersome. Another approach is to create copies of the SAS System icon, each having its own properties. Each user can double-click on the SAS System icon that he or she needs.

A drawback to this approach is that displaying several icons uses system resources. If your Windows desktop is rather cluttered, you may run out of system resources if you add too many more icons.

When you create a copy of a program icon, it is called a shortcut. To create customized SAS System shortcuts, follow these steps:

1. Open the Windows Explorer by right-clicking on the **Start** button, then click on **Explore**.

2. By default, the Windows Explorer shows you the contents of the Start Menu folder. Double-click on the Programs folder in the right half of the window.

3. Double-click on The SAS System folder.

4. Right-click on the **SAS System for Windows V7** icon, then click on **Create Shortcut**. An icon named **Copy of the SAS System for Windows V7** appears. Rename this icon to something descriptive, such as **Nancy's SAS System**.

5. Right-click on the new icon, and click on **Properties**. The Properties dialog box appears, as shown in Figure 8.3.

Figure 8.3 Properties Dialog Box for the New SAS System Shortcut

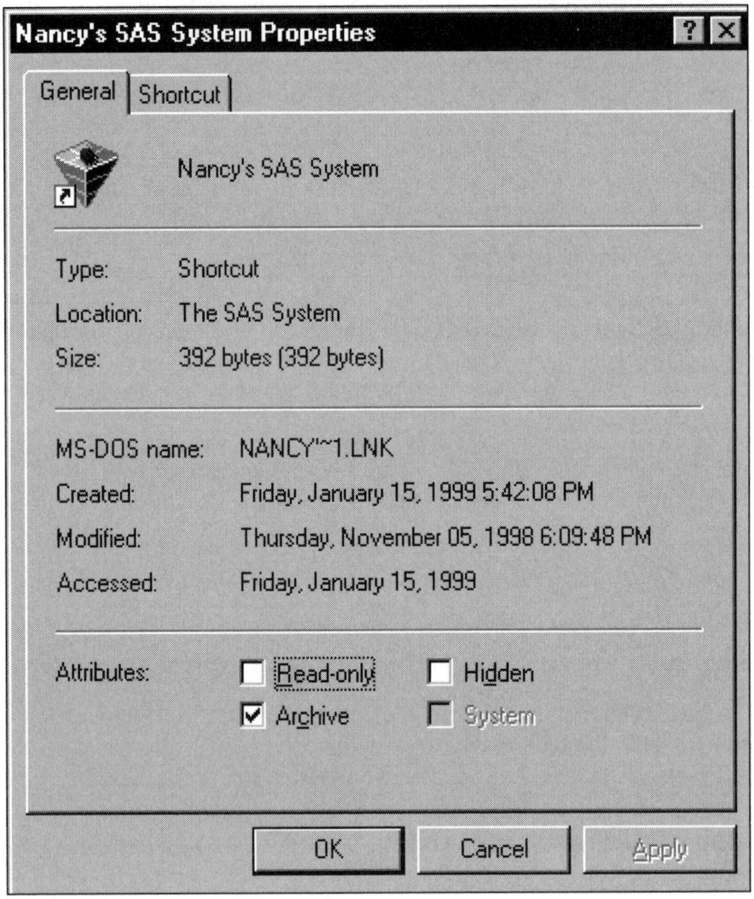

6.   Click on the **Shortcut** tab.

7.   In the **Target** field, edit the SAS system options to suit the individual user, then click on **OK**.

Create as many shortcuts as you need. Figure 8.4 shows how the SAS System program group might look after you have added Nancy's copy of the SAS System icon.

Figure 8.4 SAS System Program Group with the New SAS System Shortcut

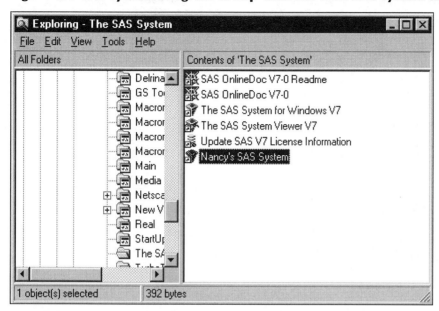

Relocating Shortcuts: Shortcuts can be moved from their folders to more convenient places. For example, you may want to have the shortcut icons on the desktop so that you can start the SAS System without having to click on the **Start** button.

To move a shortcut to the desktop, open the Windows Explorer and display the folder that contains the shortcut. Click once on the shortcut you want to move, to highlight it. Now use the mouse to drag the shortcut out of the Windows Explorer and onto the desktop. (Resize other applications if necessary, so that you can see the desktop.) Release the mouse button when the shortcut is where you want it. Figure 8.5 shows how the Windows desktop might look after the **Nancy's SAS System** shortcut has been dragged onto the desktop. Double-clicking on the shortcut starts the SAS System.

Figure 8.5 Windows Desktop with the New SAS System Shortcut

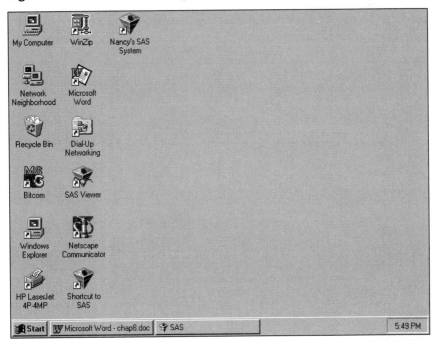

Note

If you need help using the Windows Explorer, refer to Appendix 3.

Customizing SAS System Options

V7 Hilites: The new SAS System Options window lets you edit the values of many SAS System options.

FasTip: Click on **Tools→Options→System** to open the SAS System Options window.

You can adjust the value of many SAS System options using the SAS System Options window. You can use this window to change any option you can change with the OPTIONS statement. (That is, you cannot edit a system option that is valid only at start-up, such as LOG or SPLASH.)

To open the SAS System Options window, click on **Tools** in the SAS System main menu, then on **Options**, then on **System**. Figure 8.6 shows the SAS System Options window.

Figure 8.6 SAS System Options Window

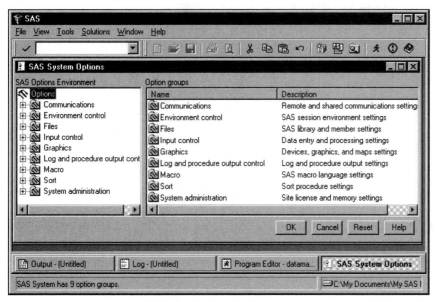

This window works like the SAS Explorer window. Double-click on group names in the left pane to expand the group; click on a subgroup to see the contents of the subgroup. The option names and their values are shown in the right pane of the window.

To edit the value of an option, double-click on the option name in the right pane of the window. This opens the Modify Value dialog box. Figure 8.7 shows a sample Modify Value dialog box (in this case, for the ENGINE option).

Figure 8.7 Modify Value Dialog Box for Changing SAS System Option Values

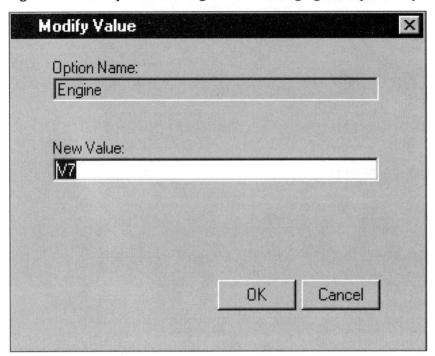

Type the new value in the **New Value** field or select a value from the drop-down list, then click on **OK**. The SAS System Options window now shows the updated value.

Note

Changes that are made in the SAS System Options window affect only the current SAS session; to change the value of a SAS System option permanently, edit your SAS configuration file.

Finding a Particular System Option: Sometimes it is hard to remember which group of options a particular option is stored in. To find an option quickly, right-click in the left pane of the SAS System Options window, then click on **Find Option** in the popup menu. This opens the Find Option dialog box. Type in the name of the option you want to find, then click on **OK**.

Note

For options that have names such as SPLASH and NOSPLASH, search for the "on" name.

Undoing Your Changes: The SAS System Options window allows you to undo your changes in two ways:

* You can cancel all changes that you have made in the SAS System Options window by clicking on **Reset**—but you must do this before you close the window. This resets the option values to the values they had when you first opened the SAS System Options window.

* You can reset a particular option to its default value (the value that it had when you installed SAS) by right-clicking on the option in the SAS System Options window, then clicking on **Set to Default**.

216

⑨ Using Batch Mode

Introduction

V7 Hilites: The new Output Delivery System (ODS) enables you to create HTML-coded SAS output.

New printing options let you programmatically control margins, font, and so on.

While Windows is considered a point-and-click operating system, it does support batch execution of the SAS System. If you are more familiar with a mainframe operating system such as OS/390 or CMS, the Windows definition of batch is not quite the same as the mainframe definition, at least at the technical level. But for practical purposes, think of them as the same: batch execution under Windows means that you do not see any SAS windows, and the SAS programs you submit run without input from you.

The methods for starting a batch job are numerous. Here are some of the more common methods:

- right-clicking on a SAS program file icon in the Windows Explorer

- dropping a SAS program file icon onto the SAS.EXE file icon (from the Windows Explorer)

- clicking on the **SAS System for Windows V7** icon in the Windows **Programs** menu

- using the Run dialog box from the **Start** button

- double-clicking on a SAS program file icon in the Windows Explorer

- submitting the job from the SAS System Viewer

- starting the SAS job from a DOS prompt.

Which method you use to submit your SAS batch jobs depends on several factors, including how often you submit batch jobs, whether you submit the same program over and over or run lots of different jobs, and, of course, personal preferences.

This chapter first helps you decide when to use batch mode. Then it shows you how to use each of the methods.

At the end of the chapter, you learn how to print from a batch job, use the Output Delivery System in batch mode, control where the logs and output are stored, combine using batch and windowing sessions in one job, and submit more than one batch job at a time. Finally, you learn how to interrupt a batch job.

Note

The "DOS prompt" referred to in this chapter is called the "command prompt" under Windows NT. Other than this difference in terminology, all the examples and explanations are the same for both Windows 95 and Windows NT users.

Understanding How Batch Mode Works

When you submit a batch job, you do not interact with the SAS System. When you submit the job, by default you see the SAS System logo appear, followed by the BATCH SAS window, which tells you what program is running and where the log and output files are being stored.

Several system options affect SAS batch processing, including the following:

- NOSPLASH suppresses the SAS logo and copyright screen when the job starts

- ICON minimizes the BATCH SAS window when the job starts.

You can add these and other system options to your SAS configuration file, as described in Chapter 8.

Deciding When to Use Batch Mode

Batch mode helps save system resources by not using windows, tool icons, scroll bars, and so on. If your programs can run without user input, they may run faster and use fewer system resources in batch mode. Another approach to using batch mode is to split your job in two—run the intensive data creation, analysis, sorting, and so on part in batch mode, then run a windowing session, using the SAS files created by the first job, after all the crunch work is finished. Either way, you use the "expensive"(in terms of system resources) windows only when needed.

Right-Clicking on a File in the Windows Explorer

Perhaps the easiest way to submit a SAS file in batch mode is to use the Windows Explorer. To submit a batch job in this manner, follow these steps:

1. Open the Windows Explorer by right-clicking on the **Start** button, then clicking on **Explore**.

2. Display the folder that contains the SAS program you want to submit.

3. Right-click on this file, then click on **Batch Submit** in the popup menu.

Note

If you need more information on the Windows Explorer, refer to Appendix 3.

Dropping a File on the SAS.EXE Icon in the Windows Explorer

Another easy way to submit batch SAS jobs is to drag and drop SAS program icons onto the SAS.EXE file icon in the Windows Explorer. To use this method, follow these steps:

1. Open the Windows Explorer by right-clicking on the **Start** button, then clicking on **Explore**.

2. Display the C:\Program Files\SAS folder so that the SAS.EXE file icon is visible.

3. If your SAS program is not stored in the same folder as the SAS.EXE file, open another Windows Explorer window (right-click on the **Start** button and click on **Explore**).

   In this second Windows Explorer window, display the folder that contains the SAS program file you want to submit.

4. Use the mouse to drag the file icon you want to submit, and drop it on the SAS.EXE icon. For step-by-step instructions, refer to "Dropping File Icons on the SAS.EXE Icon" in Chapter 4.

Note

You cannot drop multiple files on the SAS.EXE icon. See "Submitting Multiple Batch SAS Programs" later in this chapter for information on submitting more than one batch file at a time.

Clicking on the SAS System Icon in the Start Menu

By default, clicking on the **SAS System for Windows V7** icon in the **SAS System** program group begins a SAS windowing session. However, you can add the filename for the SAS program you want to run to the **Target** field of the SAS System's Properties dialog box. Then when you click on the **SAS System for Windows V7** icon, the SAS System runs in batch mode. Because you have to edit the Properties dialog box to run a different program, this method is good for SAS users who run the same batch job over and over.

To use this method, follow these steps:

1. Open the Windows Explorer by right-clicking on the **Start** button, then clicking on **Explore**.

2. By default, the Windows Explorer shows you the contents of the Start Menu folder. Double-click on the Programs folder in the right half of the window, then double-click on The SAS System folder.

3. Right-click on the **SAS System for Windows V7** icon, then click on **Properties**.

4. When the Properties dialog box appears, click on the **Shortcut** tab.

5. Click in the **Target** field, right after the SAS.EXE. Add a space, then type the name of the SAS program you want to submit. For example, Figure 9.1 shows the Properties dialog box that has a program named C:\My Documents\My SAS Files\DATAMANIP.SAS added to the **Target** field.

    Be sure that the program name is right after the SAS.EXE and before any system options (these start with hyphens).

Figure 9.1 Adding the Program Name to the Target Field

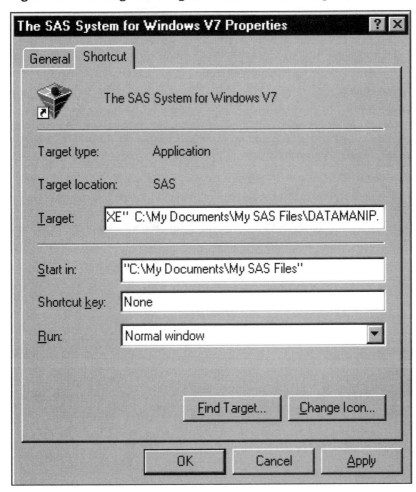

6. Click on **OK** to close the Properties dialog box. Now when you click on the **SAS System for Windows V7** icon, the DATAMANIP.SAS program is submitted in batch mode.

Note

The program name is not a system option, so it does not need a hyphen, as long as it immediately follows the SAS.EXE portion of the **Target** field contents. If you want to place the program name elsewhere, after some system options, use the SYSIN system option to specify the program name.

Note

These changes apply only to the shortcut to the SAS System accessed from the **SAS System** program group. If you have created other shortcuts (such as a shortcut to SAS on the desktop), you must change each shortcut's properties individually.

Creating Additional SAS System Shortcuts: Suppose you want to run both windowing and batch jobs. Or, you run three or four different batch jobs, but you still want to start the SAS System in batch mode by clicking on the **SAS System for Windows V7** icon. If this is the case, add additional SAS System shortcuts to the **SAS System** program group.

To add another SAS System shortcut to the **SAS System** program group, follow these steps:

1. Open the Windows Explorer by right-clicking on the **Start** button, then clicking on **Explore**.

2. By default, the Windows Explorer shows you the contents of the Start Menu folder—double-click on the Programs folder in the right half of the window, then double-click on **The SAS System**.

3. Right-click on **The SAS System for Windows V7**, then click on **Create Shortcut**. An icon appears named **SAS System for Windows V7 (2)**. Rename this icon to something descriptive, such as **Run the DATAMANIP Program in Batch Mode**. (See Appendix 3 for information on how to rename a file in the Windows Explorer.)

4. Right-click on the new icon, and click on **Properties**.

5. Click on the **Shortcut** tab.

6. In the **Target** field, add the program name after the SAS.EXE portion of the field.

7. Click on **OK**.

Repeat these steps to create additional shortcuts, giving each a descriptive name and adding the appropriate filename to the **Target** field contents.

A drawback of this approach is that each icon takes up system resources. Adding several SAS System shortcuts to your program group can cause system resource problems in the following situations:

- you are running a PC with minimal RAM (Random Access Memory). For best results, your PC should have at least 16M of RAM.

- you run a lot of applications simultaneously.

- you have a lot of icons on your screen.

If you try this method but get error messages about system memory, shut down all other open applications and try again. If the error messages persist, you should probably try a different approach to running your batch jobs.

Starting Your Batch Job from the Run Dialog Box

The Run dialog box enables you to run any program without having to click on an icon. Follow these steps to use this method:

1. Click on the **Start** button, then click on **Run**. The Run dialog box appears, as shown in Figure 9.2

Figure 9.2 Run Dialog Box

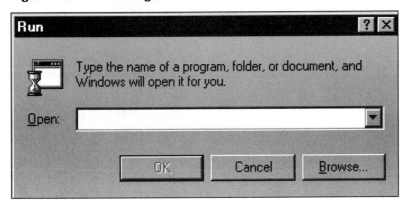

2. Type the following in the **Open** field:

    ```
    C:\SAS-folder\SAS.EXE your-SAS-program
    ```

    For example, if your SAS.EXE file is stored in the C:\Program Files\SAS folder, and the SAS program you want to submit is C:\My Documents\My SAS Files\DATAMANIP.SAS, type the following:

    ```
    C:\Program Files\SAS\SAS.EXE C:\My Documents\My SAS Files\DATAMANIP.SAS
    ```

    Add any necessary system options after the program name.

3. Click on **OK**. The program is submitted in batch mode.

Double-clicking on a File Icon in the Windows Explorer

By default, when you double-click on a SAS program file with an extension of .SAS, .SAS7BPGM, or .SS2 in the Windows Explorer, the SAS System starts in windowing mode. However, you can change the default action so that double-clicking on a SAS program file submits the program in batch mode.

To change the default double-click action for .SAS, .SAS7BPGM, and .SS2 files, follow these steps:

1. Open the Windows Explorer by right-clicking on the **Start** button, then clicking on **Explore**.

2. Click on **View** in the Windows Explorer menu, then click on **Options**.

3. When the Options dialog box appears, click on the **File Types** tab.

4. Scroll through the list of **Registered file types** until you see the entry **SAS System Program**, as shown in Figure 9.3.

Figure 9.3   Finding the SAS System Program Entry in the Registered File Types Field

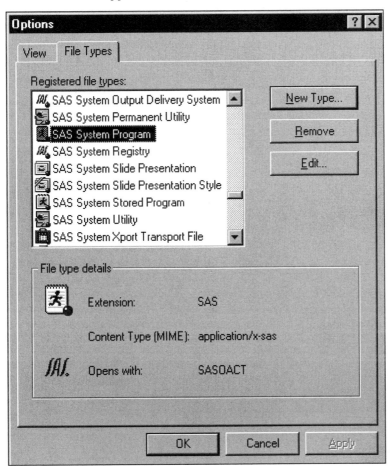

5.   Click once on **SAS System Program**, then click on **Edit**.

6.   The Edit File Type dialog box appears. In the **Actions** area, click on **Batch Submit**, then click on **Set Default**.

7.   If you want to add system options to your batch job, click on **Edit** in the Edit File Type dialog box. If you do not want to change the system options, skip to step 9.

8.   When you click on **Edit** in the Edit File Type dialog box, another dialog box opens, titled "Editing action for type: SAS System Program". In the field labeled **Application used to perform action**, click at the end of the text and add the system options you want (for

example, LINESIZE, MACRO, and so on). When you've finished adding system options, click on **OK**. This returns you to the Edit File Type dialog box.

9. Click on **Close** in the Edit File Type dialog box. This returns you to the Options dialog box.

10. Click on **Close** in the Options dialog box.

The next time you double-click on a SAS program file icon in the Windows Explorer, the program is submitted in batch mode.

Note

Follow similar steps to change the default action for SAS System stored programs (files with an extension of .SAS7BPGM, .SS7, or .SS2).

Should you ever want to return to the original default action, follow the same steps, except choose the **Open** action instead of **Batch Submit** in step 6.

Note

If you've already started a SAS session by double-clicking on a SAS program file icon, and then double-click on another, the same SAS session is used for the second file. However, if the first SAS session was started in another manner (for example, clicking on the SAS System icon or double-clicking on the SAS.EXE file icon), double-clicking on a SAS program file icon starts a second SAS session.

Starting Your Batch Job from the SAS System Viewer

If you are editing SAS code in the SAS System Viewer, you can submit the code in a batch job. To do so, follow these steps:

1. Use the SAS System Viewer to open the file you want to submit, and edit the code if necessary.

2. Click on **File** in the SAS System Viewer main menu, then click on **Batch Submit**.

Starting Your Batch Job from the DOS Prompt

Although Windows 95 and Windows NT do not require the DOS operating system like previous versions of Windows, they do support the DOS prompt for compatibility reasons. If you want to invoke SAS from a DOS prompt, you can.

First, open a DOS window from Windows by clicking on the **Start** button, then on **Programs**, then on **MS-DOS Prompt**. Now type the following command at the DOS prompt:

```
C:\SAS-folder\SAS.EXE batch-program.SAS -CONFIG C:\SAS-folder\SASV7.CFG
```

This command must be all on one line when you type it in.

Here is an explanation of the various parts of this command:

- C:*SAS-folder*\SAS.EXE starts the SAS System.

- *batch-program*.SAS is the name of the SAS program you want to submit.

- specifying the CONFIG system option enables the SAS System to find your SAS configuration file. Add any other system options after the CONFIG option.

Note

> If you do not specify the batch program name immediately after the SAS.EXE portion of the command, you must use the SYSIN system option.

The DOS window you started the SAS System from is "frozen"; that is, you cannot issue any other DOS commands from this DOS window until you close your SAS session. However, you can start other DOS windows (using the **Start** button).

Note

> Under Windows NT, the "DOS prompt" is called the "command prompt."

Printing in Batch Mode

V7 Hilites: New system options let you control various aspects of a print job, such as paper size, orientation, and font.

The SYSPRINT option no longer takes a port name and no longer controls whether the Windows print spooling is used.

The SYSPRINTFONT option now supports italic and bold specifications.

The HOSTPRINT option controls whether output is routed through the Windows print queue.

When you print in batch mode, you do not have access to the Print and Print Setup dialog boxes. However, you can accomplish many of the same things using system options and the PRINTTO procedure. The following list explains some of the most useful techniques for printing in batch mode:

- Use the SYSPRINT and SYSPRINTFONT system options to define the default printer and printer font.

- Use various system options to set the number of copies, page orientation, paper size and source, and margins.

- Use the PRINTTO procedure to route the log and procedure output to a printer.

- Use the FILENAME statement and PRINTER keyword to define a file shortcut that points to a printer. Then, use a FILE statement and that file shortcut to send DATA step output to a printer.

Understanding Printer Names: Every printer installed on your system has a unique name. For example, an HP LaserJet 4P printer may have the following name:

```
HP LaserJet 4P/4MP
```

To find your printers names, look in the SAS Print dialog box or in the Control Panel's Printers window. Familiarize yourself with the name of each printer you use, as you need this information when printing in batch mode.

Setting the Default Printer: Use the SYSPRINT system option to set the default printer. The simplest form of the SYSPRINT option is as follows:

SYSPRINT "*printer-name*"

For example, to set the default printer to "HP LaserJet 4P/4MP", specify the following SYSPRINT option in the OPTIONS statement:

```
options sysprint="HP LaserJet 4P/4MP";
```

For more information on the SYSPRINT system option, refer to the SAS online help: **Help→SAS System Help→Using SAS with Your Operating System→Using SAS under Windows→SAS System Options under Windows→SAS System Options under Windows** then scroll the topic window (both down and to the right) to find the SYSPRINT option.

Setting the Default Printer Font: If you do not want to use the default typeface in your batch output, use the SYSPRINTFONT system option.

The simplest form of the SYSPRINTFONT option is as follows:

SYSPRINTFONT '*font-name*' <*point-size*>

For example, if you want to use the Courier New font in 14 point, specify the following OPTIONS statement:

```
options sysprintfont="Courier New" 14;
```

Typeface names are case sensitive; type the font name exactly as it appears in the list of fonts. (Use the SAS Font dialog box to list available fonts.) Remember that only monospace fonts work well with the SAS System—proportional fonts result in misaligned output.

You can also use the SYSPRINTFONT option to control the weight and style of the font. For example, to specify a 14-point italic bold SAS Monospace font, specify the following:

```
options sysprintfont="Courier New" bold italic 14;
```

Caution

Once you set the SYSPRINTFONT option, that font and point size is used from then on (in all subsequent batch and interactive SAS sessions), until you set the option again.

To return to the default font and point size, specify the following in your SAS configuration file:

```
-sysprintfont 'SAS Monospace' normal regular 8
```

Alternatively, submit an OPTIONS statement to reset the SYSPRINTFONT option.

Note

If you are using a high-resolution display, specify a point size of 10 when returning to the default font.

For more information on the SYSPRINTFONT system option, refer to the SAS online help: **Help→SAS System Help→Using SAS with Your Operating System→Using SAS under Windows→SAS System Options under Windows→SAS System Options under Windows** then scroll the topic window (both down and to the right) to find the SYSPRINTFONT option.

Note

Not all fonts support italic or bold. For example, the SAS Monospace font does not support italic.

Setting Other Print Job Parameters: With Version 7, several new system options are available that let you set the same print job parameters in batch mode that you can set in the Print Setup and Print dialog boxes. Use Table 9.1 to familiarize yourself with the various new system options.

Table 9.1 System Options for Controlling Print Job Parameters in Batch Mode

Option Name	Quick Summary of Use	Easy Syntax
BOTTOMMARGIN	Sets the bottom margin, in inches	BOTTOMMARGIN=*n*
COLLATE	Turns collation on or off (by default, collation is off)	COLLATE|NOCOLLATE
COPIES	Sets the number of copies printed	COPIES=*n*
DUPLEX	Turns duplexing on or off (see also the online help for the BINDING option)	DUPLEX|NODUPLEX
LEFTMARGIN	Sets the left margin, in inches	LEFTMARGIN=*n*
ORIENTATION	Sets the page orientation (the default is portrait)	ORIENTATION=PORTRAIT|LANDSCAPE
PAPERDEST	Sets the printer bin to receive output	PAPERDEST=*printer-bin-name*
PAPERSIZE	Sets the paper size (default is LETTER)	PAPERSIZE=*paper-size-name*
PAPERSOURCE	Sets the printer bin that supplies paper to the printer	PAPERSOURCE=*printer-bin-name*
PAPERTYPE	Sets the paper type (such as PLAIN)	PAPERTYPE=*paper-type-name*
RIGHTMARGIN	Sets the right margin, in inches	RIGHTMARGIN=*n*
TOPMARGIN	Sets the top margin, in inches	TOPMARGIN=*n*

Two examples are included in this section, to get you started using these new options.

The following OPTIONS statement sets the top margin to 2 inches (for example, to accommodate a letterhead), the left and right margins to .5 inches, and the number of copies to print to five:

```
options topmargin=2 rightmargin=.5 leftmargin=.5 copies=5;
```

The following OPTIONS statement sets the page orientation to landscape and specifies that the paper is to be legal sized and that it comes from the bottom printer paper bin:

```
options orientation=landscape papersize=legal papersource=bottom;
```

For further information on each option, refer to the SAS online help:
Help→SAS System Help→Help on SAS Software Products→Base SAS Software→Using Base SAS Software→Setting System Options→SAS System Options reference then click on the appropriate option name.

Note

When you change the value for the TOPMARGIN, BOTTOMMARGIN, LEFTMARGIN, and RIGHTMARGIN system options, the PAGESIZE and LINESIZE system options are automatically recalculated by the SAS System.

Controlling Whether You Use Windows Print Spooling: The HOSTPRINT option controls whether SAS print jobs are sent to the Windows print queue. Specifying NOHOSTPRINT bypasses the Windows print queue.

When you bypass print spooling, you do not always get automatic page feeds. If your output is only one page, you may have to press the Off-line key on your printer, then the FormFeed key, then the Off-line key again to cause the page to eject. You may also have to follow this procedure to get the last page of a multipage print job. Usually, if Windows is spooling your print jobs, page feeds are automatic.

Sending the Log and Procedure Output to the Printer: The PRINTTO procedure enables you to route the SAS log and procedure output to a file shortcut. By setting up a file shortcut that points to the printer, you can direct your log and procedure output to the printer. Follow these steps:

1. Set up a file shortcut that points to the default printer:

    ```
    filename myprint printer;
    ```

2. Use the PRINTTO procedure to send the procedure output or the SAS log to the MYPRINT file shortcut:

    ```
    proc printto print=myprint;   sends the procedure output to the printer.
    run;
    ```

    ```
    proc printto log=myprint;     sends the SAS log to the printer.
    run;
    ```

3. Submit your code.

4. Submit an empty PROC PRINTTO step, which closes the printer file:

    ```
    proc printto;
    run;
    ```

Note

> You cannot send both the procedure output and the log to the printer at the same time. If you want to print both the log and procedure output, send them to separate files, then print the files.

Sending DATA Step Output to the Printer: If you want to send DATA step output directly to the printer, follow these steps:

1. Set up a file shortcut that points to the default printer:

   ```
   filename myfile printer;
   ```

2. Submit your DATA step, including a FILE statement that uses the file shortcut you have defined. For example, the following DATA step prints "This is a test":

   ```
   data _null_;
   file myfile;
       put 'This is a test';
   run;
   ```

3. Submit your program.

Using the Output Delivery System in Batch Mode

In Version 7 of the SAS System, you can use the Output Delivery System (ODS) to create other formats of SAS output besides the standard SAS listing file. For example, if you want to place the SAS output on the World Wide Web, you may want to generate HTML-coded output. You can do this, even if you are running your programs in batch mode. This section assumes you have read the description of the ODS in Chapter 4, which explains some of the terms used in the following discussion. Also, this section does not illustrate every feature of the ODS—it simply gets you started. For further information, see the online help and ODS documentation.

The main part of the ODS that you will use is the ODS statement, which enables you to set output destination attributes and select or exclude individual output objects. Although not covered by this beginner's book, you can also use the TEMPLATE procedure, which enables you to specify the formatting attributes for an output object (such as cell formats and headers, column ordering, colors and fonts, and so on).

The following sections, which discuss using the ODS to generate HTML-coded output, assume that you are familiar with HTML. If you are not, you should obtain an HTML user's guide before continuing.

Note

> You can use the ODS statement and TEMPLATE procedure in windowing as well as batch mode.

Using the ODS Statement to Generate HTML Output: To select HTML as your output destination, use the following ODS statements. The first ODS statement closes the Listing output destination (the Output window); the second opens the HTML output destination and specifies a file where the HTML output is stored:

```
ODS LISTING CLOSE;
ODS HTML FILE = 'filename.html';
```

Submit this statement before the rest of your job.

Note

> Although output is written to the HTML file as you submit code, you cannot view the output until you close the HTML output destination, as described in the next section.

Closing the HTML Output Destination: Unless you specify otherwise, after you use the ODS statement to select the HTML output destination, all subsequent output is written to that destination. To close the HTML output destination, use the following ODS statement:

```
ODS HTML CLOSE;
```

Example of HTML Output: Figure 9.4 shows what the HTML output looks like when you submit the following simple batch program:

```
ods listing close;
ods html file = 'c:\myhtml.htm';

data test;
   x=1;
   y=2;
run;

proc print;
run;

ods html close;
```

Figure 9.4 Displaying the HTML Results from Your Batch File

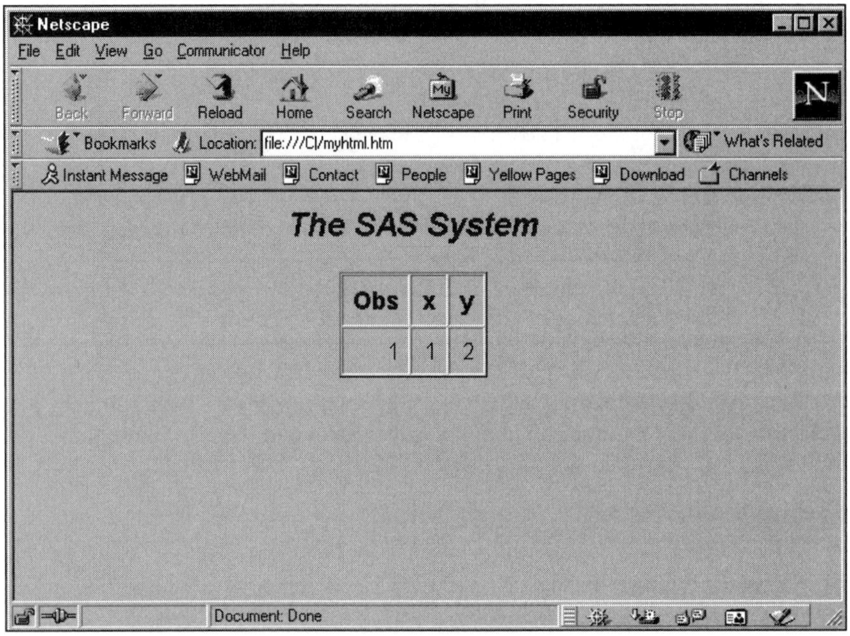

(In this figure, the output is displayed in the Netscape Web browser; you can use any browser of your choice to view your SAS generated HTML output.)

Generating a Table of Contents: If your code generates a lot of output, you may find a table of contents useful. Use the following ODS statement to generate a table of contents and display that table of contents in a frame:

```
ODS HTML PATH = "HTML-folder"(URL=NONE)
         FRAME = "frame-file.html"
          BODY = "filename.html"
      CONTENTS = "contents-file.html";
```

When you display the resulting files, the table of contents is linked to the body of the output, so if you click on an entry in the table of contents, you jump to the corresponding output object in the body of the output.

Note

> The syntax given for creating a table of contents is actually one of several methods; this particular method is guaranteed to work with all Web browsers.

Example of Creating a Table of Contents: Figure 9.5 shows the results when you submit the following code:

```
ods listing close;
ods html path = "C:\"(url=none)
         frame = "frame.htm"
          body = "body.htm"
      contents = "toc.htm";
data test;
   x=1;
   y=2;
run;

proc print;
run;


data test2;
   w=5;
   z=7;
run;


proc print;
run;


ods html close;
```

Figure 9.5 Sample HTML Table of Contents

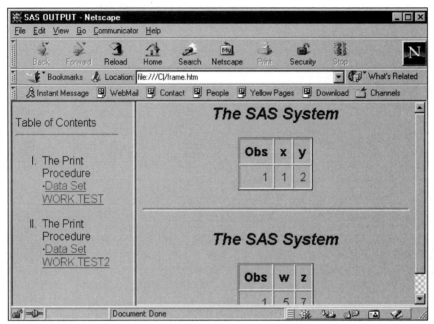

Controlling which Output Objects Are Included in Your Output: If your SAS program generates more output than you need, you can use the ODS statement to select individual output objects from your output.

The first step is to discover the names of the various output objects generated by your program. Use the TRACE OUTPUT option in the ODS statement to display all the output object names. (These names are displayed in the SAS log.)

```
ODS TRACE OUTPUT / LABEL;
```

For example, if you submit this statement before the following code, the SAS log will contain
the results shown in Figure 9.6. (In the figure, the SAS log is displayed using the Windows
Notepad editor.)

```
data test;
    do i = 1 to 150;
        group = (i > 50);
        x = normal(123);
        y1 = uniform(123);
        y2 = uniform(567);
        output;
    end;
run;


proc means;
by group;
    title 'Means Step';
run;
```

Figure 9.6 SAS Log Displaying the Results of the ODS TRACE Statement

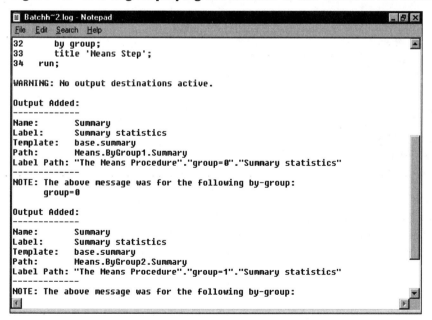

Note

No output destinations were specified because we were only interested in seeing the output
object names.

Now that you know the output object names, you can select individual output objects by specifying their names in the ODS statement, as follows:

```
ODS SELECT name-1 name-2 ... name-n;
```

To exclude output objects, use the following ODS statement:

```
ODS EXCLUDE name-1 name-2 ... name-n;
```

Note

> If the output object names are not unique, you can use the output object's label path in the ODS EXCLUDE and ODS SELECT statements.

For example, to select only the Group 1 statistics, submit the following code. Note the ODS SELECT statement just before the PROC MEANS step. Also, ODS HTML statements have been added to tell the SAS System where to store the output.

```
ods html body='c:\body2.htm';

data test;
    do i = 1 to 150;
        group = (i > 50);
        x = normal(123);
        y1 = uniform(123);
        y2 = uniform(567);
        output;
    end;
run;

ods select "The Means Procedure"."group=1"."Summary
           statistics";

proc means;
    by group;
    title 'Means Step';
run;
ods html close;
```

Submitting Multiple Batch SAS Programs

In windowing mode, you submit several programs at once by dragging and dropping the file icons onto the LOG window. There is no correspondingly easy way to submit multiple batch files—but it is possible.

The basic approach is to create a "dummy" SAS program that contains %INCLUDE statements for each program you want to submit. Then submit the dummy file as a batch job.

If your dummy program contains only %INCLUDE statements, however, the logs and output from all the files are written to big concatenated log and output files. In addition, the logs do not show the included statements. Therefore, it is usually best to add some other options and statements to control how the logs and output are created and stored. These options and statements can be defined in either the dummy file or in the individual SAS programs that you include.

Here is an example dummy file that includes two programs and controls the logs and output. The SOURCE2 system option, specified in the OPTIONS statement, causes the included lines to be listed in the log. The PRINTTO procedure lets you control where the logs and output are stored.

```
      /* Lists the included program */
      /* code in the log. */
   options source2;
      /* Sends log & output to */
      /* PROG1.LOG and PROG1.LST. */
   proc printto log='prog1.log'
       print='prog1.lst' new;
      /* Includes the PROG1.SAS */
      /* program. */
   %include 'prog1.sas';
      /* Resets the page number */
      /* for the output file. */
   options pageno=1;
      /* Sends log and output */
      /* to PROG2.LOG and PROG2.LST. */
   proc printto log='prog2.log'
      print='prog2.lst' new;
      /* Includes the PROG2.SAS */
      /* program. */
   %include 'prog2.sas';
```

The BATCH SAS window does not reflect the PROC PRINTTO information. For example, if your dummy file is named MYBATCH.SAS, the BATCH SAS window indicates that the log and output files are being written to MYBATCH.LOG and MYBATCH.LST. However, the MYBATCH.LST file is never created, and the MYBATCH.LOG file contains only an abbreviated log. The real logs are in the PROG1.LOG and PROG2.LOG files, as specified in your program.

Understanding Where Batch Logs and Output Go

When you submit a batch SAS job, by default the log and output files are stored in the SAS working folder. Normally, this is the folder that contains the SAS.EXE file. The log and output files have the same filename as the SAS program, with different extensions. The log file has an extension of .LOG, and the output file has an extension of .LST.

For example, if the SAS program you submit is C:\MYPROG.SAS, the log file is C:\MYPROG.LOG and the output file is C:\MYPROG.LST.

Accept these default filenames and locations, or add system options to either the **Target** field in the Properties dialog box or to the SAS configuration file to control where the log and output files are stored. The PRINTTO procedure is also useful when routing the log and output files elsewhere.

Note

> Although the SAS System as a general rule accepts long filenames, the batch log and output filenames are truncated to eight characters. For example, if you submit a file named BATCHHTML.SAS, the log file is named BATCHH~1.LOG and the listing is named BATCHH~1.LST. For more information on truncated filenames, see "Understanding Truncated Filenames" in Chapter 1.

Exceptions to the Rule: When you drop a program file icon onto the SAS.EXE icon in the Windows Explorer, the log and output files are created on the desktop for Windows 95. The full pathname for these files is C:\WINDOWS\DESKTOP*filename*.LOG and C:\WINDOWS\DESKTOP*filename*.LST.

Note

> The Desktop folder is not displayed as a folder in the Windows Explorer. To open this folder in the Windows Explorer, display the contents of the Windows folder, then double-click on the Desktop.grp icon.

For Windows NT, the log and output files are created in the WINNT folder.

Creating Two Copies of the Log and Output: To create copies of the log and output files, use the ALTLOG and ALTPRINT system options. This technique creates two copies of the log and output files—one in the default place and one in the place you specify. For example, add the following options to your SAS configuration file:

```
-ALTLOG C:\SASLOGS
-ALTPRINT C:\SASOUT
```

These options tell the SAS System to place one copy of the log and output files in the SAS working folder and one copy in the folders C:\SASLOGS and C:\SASOUT, respectively. The filenames are the same as the SAS program filename, with extensions of .LOG and .LST.

Creating Only One Copy of the Log and Output: If you want only one copy of your log and output files, use the LOG and PRINT system options. For example, adding the following options to your SAS configuration file causes the batch logs and output to be stored in the specified folders:

```
-LOG C:\SASLOGS
-PRINT C:\SASOUT
```

In this case, no copies of the log and output are stored in the SAS working folder.

Combining Windowing and Batch Modes

There may be times when the choice between batch mode and a windowing session is a hard one to call—you like to edit your code using the Program Editor, but you like submitting your code in batch. Or, the majority of your program is noninteractive, but you'd really like to view the data with the FSVIEW procedure.

One of the nice features of using the SAS System under Windows is that it allows you this flexibility. The next two sections describe two methods you can use to mix and match windowing and batch sessions.

Submitting Batch Jobs from a Windowing Session: Because Windows 95 and Windows NT support multiple SAS sessions, you can edit your programs using a windowing session and then submit the finalized code in a separate batch job. Here the basic steps for this approach:

1. Start a SAS session. Open your file into the Program Editor window, and edit it.

2. When the code is finalized, save it.

3. Submit an X statement:

```
x 'c:\program files\sas\sas.exe saved-code';
```

In the X statement, *saved-code* is the full pathname of the file that contains the program you saved. This X statement starts a separate SAS session, running in batch mode. When the batch job is finished, you can examine the log and output from the batch job using your windowing session.

Calling a Windowing Session from a Batch Job: Sometimes, you want to do the opposite of the previous scenario—that is, start a windowing session from a batch job. This is possible in certain situations. For example, suppose your program first does a lot of number crunching and statistics generating—no windows needed for that. So you save system resources by starting your program in batch mode. But you want to see your data in tabular form, using PROC FSVIEW. When your program calls PROC FSVIEW, it switches to windowing mode.

While you can look at your data and scroll through it, you cannot issue any windowing commands. When you close the FSVIEW window, your program returns to batch mode.

Interrupting a Batch Job

To stop a batch SAS job, make the BATCH SAS window active and click on **Cancel**.

Alternatively, press CTRL-Break. Make sure the BATCH SAS window or the SAS icon (representing the minimized batch job) is active. It may take a few seconds for the BREAK dialog box to appear; do not press CTRL-Break more than once.

Of course, if something goes terribly wrong and your display is frozen, try pressing CTRL-ALT-DEL to end the batch SAS task or to reboot, as described in "Canceling the Entire SAS Session" in Chapter 4. If the worst has happened, turn off your computer. However, this technique can result in lost or corrupted data, so use it only when absolutely necessary.

Introduction

V7 Hilites: There is no MS-DOS Session icon on the default SAS tool bar.

> The REGISTER SAS system option adds program names to the **Tools** menu instead of to the **File** menu.

Sometimes you may want to issue DOS commands or start another Windows application without leaving your SAS session. To do so, use the X statement from the Program Editor window or the X command from the Command bar. The following sections describe the details of using each technique, as well as some SAS system options that affect DOS commands you issue from your SAS session. This chapter also discusses how to add an application name to the SAS System **Tools** menu.

Note

The "MS-DOS prompt" referred to in this chapter is called the "command prompt" under Windows NT. Other than this difference in terminology, all the examples and explanations are the same for both Windows 95 and Windows NT users.

Understanding How DOS Commands Are Executed by the SAS System

Unless you specify a folder with your DOS command, the command is executed in the SAS working folder. This is usually the folder in which the SAS.EXE file is stored, unless you have changed the working folder with the Change Folder dialog box.

For example, if you submit the DOS command DIR which lists all the files in a folder, you see the contents of the SAS working folder. If you want to see the contents of the root folder C:, you must specify that folder in the command: DIR C:\. Remember, to change the working folder, click on the working folder icon in the lower-right corner of the SAS workspace. For more details, see "Changing the SAS Working Folder" in Chapter 3.

Using the X Statement and X Command

The X statement is a SAS programming statement and can be submitted in any SAS program under Windows. The X command is a windowing command that serves the same purpose as the X statement.

You can use the X statement and X command to issue DOS commands and to start other Windows applications. The following discussion uses the X statement in the examples; however, the syntax and examples are identical for the X command (except that windowing commands are not followed by a semicolon).

The syntax of the X statement to issue a DOS command is as follows:

X '*DOS-command*';

If the DOS command contains no spaces, you can omit the single quotes. Here is an example that tells DOS to display the contents of the C:\My Documents\My SAS Files folder:

```
x 'dir c:\My Documents\My SAS Files';
```

Sometimes, you may want to start a Windows application (such as Microsoft Word) without leaving your SAS session. (An example of when this is useful is in the discussion of Dynamic Data Exchange in Chapter 11.)

To start a Windows application, use the following syntax:

X '*Windows-executable*';

Here is an example that starts Microsoft Word:

```
x 'c:\winword\winword.exe';
```

When you submit the X statement, the screen displays the results of the DOS command (such as a folder listing), and you are prompted to press any key to return to your SAS session. If the X statement invokes another Windows application, that application appears on top of your SAS session, ready for input.

Using the X Statement and X Command with No Parameters: You can execute the X statement or X command without any parameters. That is, submit

```
X;
```

When you submit this statement, a full-screen DOS session is started. You can work as long as you like in the DOS session, issuing DOS commands. To return to your SAS session, type EXIT at the DOS prompt and press Enter.

While the default behavior is to start a full-screen DOS session, you can change the DOS session to a windowed session (one that does not take up the whole display) by pressing ALT-Enter. Pressing ALT-Enter again toggles the session back to full-screen.

The default folder for the DOS session is the SAS working folder. Use the DOS CD (change folder) command to switch to another folder.

Note

> By default, you cannot use your SAS session until you close the DOS session. However, you can use ALT-ESC, ALT-TAB, or CTRL-ESC to return to Windows to work in other applications while the DOS session that you started from your SAS session is still active. To return to the DOS session, click on the **MS-DOS Prompt** button in the Windows Taskbar.

Controlling How the X Statement and X Command Work

V7 Hilites: New XCMD system option controls whether you can use the X command and statement in your SAS session.

New XMIN system option controls whether an application started by the X command or statement is minimized.

These SAS system options affect how the X statement and X command work: XCMD, XWAIT, XSYNC, and XMIN.

Enabling the X Command and X Statement: The XCMD system option must be in effect before you can use the X command or X statement in your SAS session. If NOXCMD is in effect and you issue an X command or submit an X statement, you receive the following warning in your SAS log:

```
Shell escape is not valid in this SAS session.
```

The XCMD option is valid only at invocation of the SAS System. Therefore, you must specify it, for example, in your SAS configuration file, as a parameter of the **Target** field of the Properties dialog box for the SAS System icon, or as a parameter in the Run dialog box.

Making a DOS Session Automatically Return to Your SAS Session: The XWAIT option controls whether you have to press a key to return to your SAS session when you issue a DOS command from your SAS session.

By default, if you execute a DOS command via the X statement or command, you have to press a key to return to your SAS session. If you do not want to press a key, that is, you want the command to execute and then immediately return you to your SAS session, set this option to NOXWAIT.

To set the XWAIT option, issue an OPTIONS statement from the Program Editor window. Here is a sample OPTIONS statement:

```
options noxwait;
```

Note

> You can also change the setting for the XWAIT option using the SAS System Options window. See "Customizing SAS System Options" in Chapter 8.

If NOXWAIT is in effect, any time you execute a DOS command using the X statement or command, you do not have to press a key to return to your SAS session. The DOS screen still appears but flashes by fairly quickly. If you want to read the results of your DOS command, do not specify NOXWAIT.

Note

> Setting the XWAIT system option with the OPTIONS statement or the SAS System Options window affects only the current SAS session. If you want to permanently set the XWAIT system option, edit your SAS configuration file, as described in Chapter 8.

Starting an Autonomous DOS Session or Application: The XSYNC option controls whether you can use your SAS session while the DOS session or other Windows application is active. By default, you cannot do anything in your SAS session until you type EXIT at the DOS prompt or close the Windows application that you started with the X statement or command. If you want to be able to use your SAS session while the DOS session or Windows application is still active, set this option to NOXSYNC.

Note

> If your SAS program needs the results of an X statement or command before continuing, do not use NOXSYNC; if you do, your program continues to run before the results of the X statement or command are available. This may generate error messages or incorrect results.

To set the XSYNC option, issue an OPTIONS statement from the Program Editor window. Here is a sample OPTIONS statement:

```
options noxsync;
```

Note

> You can also change the setting for the XSYNC option using the SAS System Options window. See "Customizing SAS System Options" in Chapter 8.

If NOXSYNC is in effect, any time you execute a DOS command or start another Windows application using the X statement or command, your SAS session is still active.

Note

Setting the XSYNC system option with the OPTIONS statement or the SAS System Options window affects only the current SAS session. If you want to set the XSYNC system option permanently, edit your SAS configuration file, as described in Chapter 8.

Minimizing the Applications that You Start with the X Command and X Statement:
The XMIN system option controls how the applications that you start with the X command and X statement appear when they start up. By default, the XMIN system option is off, and an application starts up in its default active state (for example, Word starts up as a non-maximized window). If you prefer the applications to start up as minimized (visible only in the Windows Taskbar), specify XMIN at SAS invocation (for example, in your SAS configuration file, in the **Target** field of the Properties dialog box for the SAS System icon, or in the Run dialog box).

Adding Applications to the SAS Tools Menu

V7 Hilites: The REGISTER system option now adds applications to the **Tools** menu, not to the **File** menu.

If you find yourself consistently needing to start another Windows application (such as Microsoft Word or Lotus 1-2-3) from your SAS session, you may want to add the application's name to the **Tools** menu in the SAS System so that all you have to do is click on **Tools** and then on the application's name to start it.

To add an application to the **Tools** menu, use the REGISTER system option in your SAS configuration file. (See Chapter 8 for information on editing the SAS configuration file.) The syntax of the REGISTER system option is as follows:

REGISTER '*menu-text*' '*command*' < '*working-folder*'>

- *menu-text* is the text you want displayed in the **Tools** menu.

- *command* is the DOS command that starts the application.

- *working-folder* is optional and specifies a working folder for the application. (Some applications require a working folder specification, others do not; read your application documentation for more information.)

For example, to start Microsoft Word, you might add the following to your SAS configuration file:

```
-REGISTER 'Microsoft Word' 'C:\WINWORD\WINWORD.EXE'
```

Figure 10.1 shows the resulting **Tools** menu.

Figure 10.1   Adding an Application Name to the Tools Menu

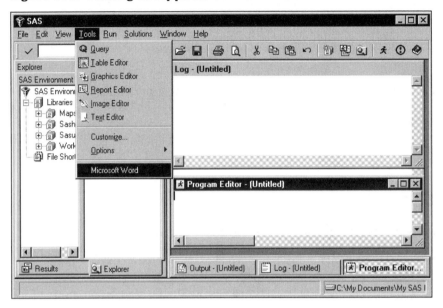

You can add up to eight applications to the SAS System **Tools** menu.

Sharing Data between Your SAS® Session and Other Windows Applications

11

Introduction

One of the biggest advantages of working under Windows is that many different applications can share data. For example, you can transfer PROC TABULATE output to a Microsoft Word file or bring spreadsheet data into a SAS table.

There are many ways of sharing data between the SAS System and other Windows applications; this chapter demonstrates the fundamental aspects of data sharing using four methods:

- cut-and-paste

- SAS Import/Export Wizard

- Dynamic Data Exchange (DDE)

- Object Linking and Embedding (OLE).

More information is available in some of the books listed in the "Welcome to Version 7 of the SAS System for Windows" section at the beginning of this book. The discussions and examples in this chapter use the following software:

- Excel

- Microsoft Word97 for Windows

- Microsoft Paint

- Corel Gallery 2

- Visio 5.

Data sharing works with many software packages. So, if you do not have the software used in the examples, you can still use the examples as a starting point, but you may not be able to use them exactly as written.

Deciding Which Method to Use

Each data sharing technique discussed in this chapter has its advantages and disadvantages, times when it is useful and times when it is not. To begin, here are some brief definitions of each technique:

- Cut-and-paste lets you use the Windows Clipboard to transfer data between two applications. It preserves rich text formatting (RTF); you can use this method to transfer text and graphics. This is a manual method, in that you must mark and copy the object in the source application, then paste the object into the target application. Cut-and-paste is a static method—after the data is pasted in, any changes in the original file do not affect the pasted copy.

- The SAS Import/Export Wizard helps you import files (such as a spreadsheet) into the SAS System or export a SAS table to another format (such as a database or comma-delimited file). Like cut-and-paste, the data transfer is not dynamic (if the original data change, the change is not reflected in the imported or exported copy).

- Dynamic Data Exchange (DDE) lets Windows applications programmatically share text-based data (for example, between the SAS System and a spreadsheet). For the SAS System, this method usually uses the FILENAME statement and DATA steps. This method is fairly automatic, and you can create a dynamic link between the SAS System and the other application.

- Object Linking and Embedding (OLE) lets Windows applications share "objects," which are a combination of data (including graphics, sound files, videos, and so on) and the functionality needed to work with that data. The examples in this chapter use OLE with SAS/AF software FRAME entries. SAS/EIS software also supports OLE.

Consider the following when choosing a data-sharing method:

- All Windows applications support cut-and-paste.

- The SAS Import/Export Wizard supports many file types, including comma-delimited files, tab-delimited files, or user-formatted files.

- For you to use either DDE or OLE, both applications—the "sender" and "receiver" (or, in computer terms, the server and the client)—must support the data sharing method.

When designing your data sharing applications, check your other applications' documentation to see if they support the data-sharing technique you want to use. Also, use Table 11.1 to choose a method that meets your needs.

Table 11.1 Summary of Data-sharing Methods

Method	Supports Textual Data	Supports Graphics	Can Be Dynamic
cut-and-paste	X	X	
Import/Export Wizard		X	
DDE	X		X
OLE	X	X	X

Using Cut-and-Paste

Cut-and-paste is probably the simplest data sharing method.

To copy text or graphics, mark the text or graphic in the source application (such as Microsoft Word or Excel). Click on **Edit**, then click on **Copy** in the source application's menu (if you want to delete the text or graphic from the source application, use **Cut** instead of **Copy**). This transfers the data to the Windows Clipboard.

Now click in the SAS window into which you want to paste the text or graphic (such as the Program Editor, SOURCE, or GRAPH window). Click on **Edit** in the SAS System main menu, then on **Paste** (or press CTRL-V).

Of course, you can also cut or copy text and graphics in the SAS System, and paste them into other applications.

Note

In order to paste graphics into the SAS System (such as into the GRAPH window or into a Graphic entry in a SAS/AF application), you must have access to SAS/GRAPH software.

When cutting and pasting text, RTF attributes (such as font, type size, and highlighting attributes such as underlining) are preserved when you copy from the SAS System to another application, provided the target application supports RTF. When you copy text from another application to the SAS System, such formatting is lost.

Note

You can paste text only into SAS windows that support text input, such as the Program Editor, NOTEPAD, and SOURCE windows.

For more information on cutting and pasting, as well as drag and drop (which is another method of cutting and pasting), see Chapter 3.

Using the SAS Import/Export Wizard

FasTip: Select **File→Import** or **File→Export**.

The SAS Import/Export Wizard is a handy method of converting data from one format to another. For example, using the Import Wizard, you can bring a tab-delimited set of data from a Word document into the SAS System as a SAS table. Or, using the Export Wizard, you can convert a SAS table into an Excel spreadsheet or a PC File Formats file (a database file).

To access the Import/Export Wizard, click on **File** in the SAS System main menu, then on **Import Data** or **Export Data**. The Import/Export Wizard is also available from other portions of the SAS System, such as the SQL Query window and SAS/ASSIST software.

Note

To use the Import/Export Wizard with database files, you must license SAS/ACCESS software.

Suppose you have a set of data about vegetables in a file where the data are separated by commas:

```
Vegetable,Germination,Zone
corn,1 week,all
eggplant,2 weeks,7 and above
beans,4 days,all
carrots,10 days,all
```

To convert this data into a SAS table using the Import Wizard, follow these steps:

1. Click on **File** in the SAS System main menu, then on **Import Data**. The Import Wizard appears, as shown in Figure 11.1.

Figure 11.1 Import Wizard – Import Data Screen

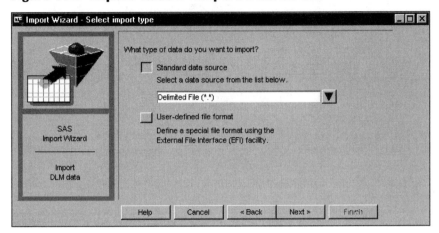

Note

Depending on your screen size and resolution, you may have to close all docked windows and maximize the SAS workspace to see all of the Import Wizard dialog box.

2. Because your file is comma-delimited, click on the down arrow next to the **Standard data source** field, and click on **Comma Separated Values (*.csv)**. Now click on **Next**, to display Figure 11.2.

Figure 11.2 Import Wizard – Select File Screen

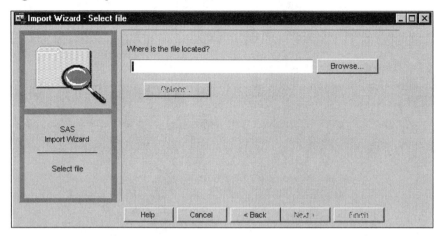

3. Type the name of the file in the text-entry field. For example, the filename might be C:\VEG.CSV.

    After you type the filename into the text-entry field, you can click on the **Options** button to set the import options. Figure 11.3 shows a sample Delimited File Options dialog box.

Figure 11.3 Delimited File Options Dialog Box for the Import Wizard

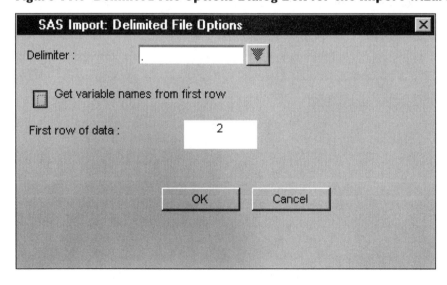

After you've set the options, click on **OK**, then click on **Next** in the Select file screen to progress to Figure 11.4.

Figure 11.4 Import Wizard – SAS Destination Screen

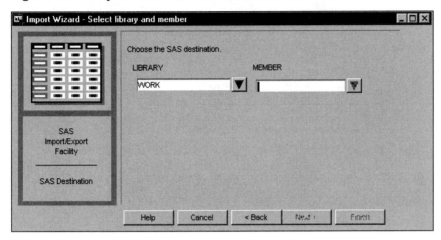

4. Click on the down arrow next to the **LIBRARY** field, and click on the SAS data library that you want to store the new SAS table in. Then, type the name of the new member in the **MEMBER** field. For example, you might select SASUSER as the data library, and give the table a member name of VEGGIES.

5. After you've selected the library and member name, click on **Finish**. The new table is created.

   You might want to scan the SAS log after the Import Wizard is finished, to see if the table creation went as you expected. Also, you may want to print the table to see if it was created properly. For example, Figure 11.5 shows the PROC PRINT output for the table created in this example.

Figure 11.5 PROC PRINT Output for the New SAS Table

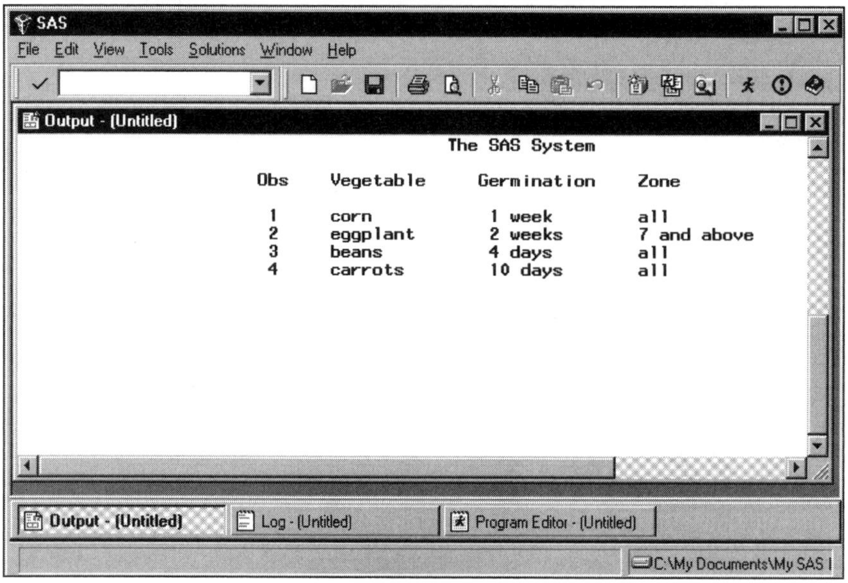

The SAS Export Wizard works similarly to the Import Wizard—simply follow the instructions on the screen, and use the **Help** button if you need help on a particular screen.

Understanding Dynamic Data Exchange (DDE)

V7 Hilites: The **DDE Triplet** menu choice is no longer available.

Using DDE with the SAS System requires a FILENAME statement that sets up a file shortcut for the specific data that you want to transfer (either from the SAS System to the other application or from the other application to the SAS System). For DDE, the syntax of the FILENAME statement is as follows:

FILENAME *file-shortcut* DDE '*DDE-triplet*|CLIPBOARD' <*DDE-options*>;

Here is an explanation of the components of this form of the FILENAME statement:

- *file-shortcut* can be any valid file shortcut for the SAS System.

- DDE is a required keyword that tells the SAS System you are using DDE.

- *DDE-triplet* or CLIPBOARD tells the SAS System exactly which data you want to transfer. Think of the DDE triplet as the ID for the data. Each unique set of data has a unique ID.

- *DDE-options* are one or more options that control how the data exchange is handled. For example, the NOTAB option is useful when you want to transfer data that does not contain tabs between values.

Specifying the DDE Triplet: When you specify CLIPBOARD in the FILENAME statement, the SAS System looks at the data stored in the Clipboard and determines the DDE triplet for you. The only thing that you have to do is to copy the data you want to transfer to the Clipboard. To do this, highlight the data in the other Windows application, click on **Edit** in the application's menu, then click on **Copy**. Now return to your SAS session to submit the FILENAME statement.

But sometimes the SAS System cannot find the DDE triplet using the Clipboard; in these cases (for example, with Microsoft Word), you must specify the DDE triplet directly.

To specify the DDE triplet directly, you must know three things about the application that you are writing data to or reading data from:

- the name of the executable file for the application

- the name of the file that you want to access (worksheet, document, and so on)

- how to refer to the access point in the file (rows/columns, bookmarks, and so on).

This information is separated by special characters, as follows:

executable-file\data-file!access-point

The executable file is always followed by a vertical bar, and the name of the data file is always followed by an exclamation point.

Here are three examples of DDE triplets and an explanation of each:

- `123w|august.wk4!a:a1..a:f5`

    `123w` is the name of the Lotus 1-2-3 executable file.
    `august.wk4` is the name of the Lotus 1-2-3 file that you want to access.
    `a:a1..a:f5` refers to worksheet A and the row/column range A1 through F5.

- `winword|august.doc!bookmk1`

  `winword` is the name of the Microsoft Word executable file.
  `august.doc` is the name of the Word document that you want to access.
  `bookmk1` is the name of the bookmark in the Word file that marks the place in the document that you want to access.

- `excel|sheet1!r5c1:r27c3`

  `excel` is the name of the Excel executable file.
  `sheet1` refers to the Excel file that contains the data that you want to access.
  `r5c1:r27c3` refers to rows 5 to 27, columns 1 to 3.

If you want to use DDE with another application, you must figure out how files are named and how you reference the exact place in the file you want to access. But after you determine how one type of DDE triplet is formed (for example, for spreadsheets or word processing documents), you can almost guess the triplet for another application of the same type.

DDE Example I—Reading Data from Microsoft Word: Here is an example of reading data from Microsoft Word using DDE. The online help and SAS Institute documentation contain many other examples. For DDE to work between the SAS System and Microsoft Word, you must define bookmarks in your Word document at each place where you want to read or write data. Then, you submit a FILENAME statement for each bookmark. Also, Word must be running and the document must be open when you access it via DDE from your SAS session.

This example uses a Word document named AUGUST.DOC. It contains data about a company's billing for August. In the document, a bookmark named NUMBER marks the invoice number, and a bookmark named CLIENT marks the client's name. The SAS program reads the information at each of these bookmarks and prints them in the OUTPUT window.

Here is the code for this example:

```
   /* Define the file shortcuts for the two bookmarks. */
   /* The NOTAB option is necessary so the */
   /* SAS System does not expect tabs */
   /* between columns. */
filename number dde 'winword|august.doc!number'
        notab;
filename client dde 'winword|august.doc!client'
        notab;
   /* Associate the library reference INVOICE with */
   /* the folder C:\SAS\INVOICES. */
libname invoice 'c:\sas\invoices';
   /* Create the table INVOICE.AUGUST, */
   /* read the information at the two */
   /* bookmarks, and store the data in columns. */
```

```
data invoice.august;
   /* Set the column length to an */
   /* arbitrary number. */
length invnum $45 invclnt $45;
   /* Get ready to read the first bookmark. */
    infile number;
      /* Read the invoice number as a */
      /* character column. */
    input invnum $;
      /* Get ready to read the second bookmark. */
      /* Because the data include spaces, use some */
      /* other arbitrary character as the */
      /* delimiter. */
    infile client dlm='@';
      /* Read the client as a character column. */
    input invclnt $;
run;
   /* Print the output. */
proc print;
run;
```

DDE Example 2—Opening and Closing a Word Document: Because you must have all of the documents open before submitting your DDE code, you may want to have your SAS program open the documents for you. You accomplish this using the special keyword SYSTEM in the DDE triplet, which enables you to send commands to another application.

In this example, the null DATA step sends the appropriate File-Open command to Word. Word must be running before you submit this code.

```
filename cmds dde 'winword|system';
data _null_;
   file cmds;
   put '[FileOpen.Name="c:\invoices\august.doc"]';
run;
```

(This example does not start Word itself—see the next example for how to do that.)

When your program is finished, you may want to close the document and close Word. The following code accomplishes this (assuming that the file shortcut CMDS is still active):

```
data _null_;
   file cmds;
       /* Close the active Word document. */
   put '[FileClose]';
   put '[FileExit]'; /* Close Word. */
run;
```

If you have more than one file open, you can use a DO loop to close all the files, then close Word.

The syntax of the commands is totally application dependent. For example, Excel has different commands to open a file than Word does. A good way to determine the commands that your application accepts is to use the application's macro recorder. For example, to determine Word's file-open command, turn on the macro recorder and open a file. Then look at the text of the macro that you generated. Usually, commands sent via DDE are enclosed in square brackets.

Note

If you are using DDE with Microsoft Word, remember that DDE works only with Word Basic—it does not work with Visual Basic. Newer versions of Word use Visual Basic when you record macros; this macro syntax will not work with DDE. Because Word Basic is also not included in the online help in newer versions of Word, you may need to obtain a copy of the *Word Developer's Kit, 3rd Edition* to help you with Word Basic syntax.

DDE Example 3—Starting Word from Your SAS Session: In Example 2, you had to start Word manually, before you submitted your SAS program. Your SAS program can start an application by using the X statement. The X statement is not part of DDE but it is useful in DDE programs. For example, the following statement starts Word:

```
x 'c:\winword\winword.exe';
```

Before using the X statement to start another Windows application, submit an OPTIONS statement to specify NOXSYNC. Otherwise, your SAS session is unusable until you close the other Windows application. Also, because it takes awhile for the other Windows application to start up, you may want to submit a null DATA step and the SLEEP function after the X statement to pause your SAS program long enough for the application to get ready.

The following code sets the NOXSYNC option, starts Word, and pauses the SAS System for 15 seconds:

```
options noxsync;
x 'c:\winword\winword.exe';
data _null_;
   x=sleep(15);
run;
```

Refer to Chapter 10 for more information on using the X statement.

Understanding Object Linking and Embedding (OLE)

V7 Hilites: The BUILD command and PROC BUILD now invoke the SAS Explorer window, from which you can create your FRAMEs.

The BUILD command syntax has changed.

The BUILD: DISPLAY window has a new interface.

The SAS Explorer window offers a quick way to build and run SAS/AF applications.

Like DDE, Object Linking and Embedding (OLE) is a way of sharing data between Windows applications. But OLE is more flexible and powerful than DDE. While this chapter does not explain or illustrate all aspects of using OLE with the SAS System, it does provide enough information to get you started.

Note

> OLE is not simple to use. By the time you understand OLE and have followed the examples, you will no longer be a "Windows neophyte."

Using OLE with the SAS System requires SAS/AF or SAS/EIS software. However, after you've created the application, it can be run by users who do not have SAS/AF or SAS/EIS software installed. This chapter illustrates creating a SAS/AF application; the procedures are similar for creating SAS/EIS applications.

With OLE, you store "objects" in your SAS/AF application. Each object represents not only data but also how to work with that data. For example, if you place a Word document in your SAS/AF application, the SAS/AF application does not store the text—it stores information about the Word document and about how to retrieve that document. With OLE, you can share anything that is "data" in its widest sense: graphics, sound files, text files, video clips, spreadsheets, and so on.

In OLE parlance, your SAS/AF application is the client (or "container") application—it stores the object. The application that created the object is called the OLE server.

Understanding Linked Objects: "Linking" refers to creating a dynamic connection between an object in your SAS/AF application and that object's OLE server.

An example helps demonstrate this. Suppose you want to display a Microsoft Word text file in your SAS/AF application. You could cut and paste the text into the application. But that is a one-way process—if you change the text in your SAS/AF application after you cut and paste the text, the changes are not reflected in the original Word document. Or, if you edit the original file, the changes are not visible in the SAS/AF application.

But if you use OLE to link the text file to your application, you can edit the file by clicking on its image in your SAS/AF application, or you can edit the file by bringing up Word and editing the file from there. In either case, the changes are visible on the other end of the link.

In technical terms, the Word file is a "linked object," and the location and size of the object is stored with your SAS/AF application. (This information is called metadata and is like a map.) The actual data (the text) is not stored in the SAS/AF application.

Understanding Embedded Objects: "Embedding" an object differs from linking, in that the connection between an embedded object and the object's OLE server is not dynamic. You can edit the object only from your SAS/AF application. If you change the original file, the changes are not visible in the SAS/AF application. With embedding, both the object and its data are stored with the SAS/AF application.

Embedded objects come in two types: static and nonstatic.

* Static objects appear in the SAS/AF application, but you cannot edit them. These objects are useful in applications where you are providing information that you do not want people to change (for example, a picture).

* Nonstatic objects can be edited by the SAS/AF application user, usually by double-clicking on the object's representation in the FRAME entry. This type of object is useful in applications where you want the user to either be able to edit the object or at least have access to the application that created the object.

Understanding OLE Verbs: Every OLE object (except static embedded objects, which are really pictures) supports one or more actions, called OLE verbs. For example, a Word OLE object supports the Edit verb, while a sound file supports two verbs: Play and Edit. These verbs are defined by the OLE server application. There is always a default verb for an object—to activate the object with the default verb, you double-click on the object's icon in your SAS/AF application.

Understanding Visual versus Open Editing: Another OLE concept you need to understand is "visual editing" versus "open editing." Visual editing is available only with applications that support OLE 2.0. Visual editing means that when you edit an OLE object in your SAS/AF application, you edit that object from the SAS window—another window does not need to open. All the tools from the application that created the OLE object are available to you in the SAS window (menus, tool bars, and so on) Only the **File** and **Window** menus are maintained by the client application (in this case, the SAS/AF application).

Open editing means that when you edit an OLE object, the object's server is launched in its own window instead of sharing the client's window.

Adding OLE Objects to Your SAS/AF Application—An Overview: The first step to using OLE in your SAS/AF applications is to create a SAS catalog. Then, within this catalog, create entries—in particular, FRAME entries to hold OLE objects. Next, add OLE objects to the FRAME entry. Remember, to create FRAMEs, you must have SAS/AF software.

The following two examples walk you through creating two SAS/AF applications using OLE. The examples assume that you know a little bit about SAS/AF software, but you do not need to be an expert.

Note

There are two levels of OLE—OLE 1.0 and OLE 2.0. The SAS System supports both levels— other applications you may be using may support only OLE 1.0 (check your application's documentation). If this is the case, you may be able to use only a subset of the OLE capabilities of the SAS System. Both of these examples use only features supported by OLE 1.0. More complicated examples illustrating OLE 2.0 features are included in SAS Institute documentation.

Note

OLE takes up a lot of system resources and RAM. It is possible to run out of RAM when loading large pictures and files. If you are using OLE extensively, you should probably have at least 16M of RAM; the more RAM the better.

Example 1—Using Embedded Objects: You teach driver's education, and you are creating an online study application for students. The application displays road signs and their meanings. The students look at each screen to learn the sign, then progress to the next screen. This example uses embedded objects.

1. To begin, use the BUILD command to create a new SAS catalog and invoke the SAS Explorer window. You can use any existing SAS data library; this example uses the SASUSER library and creates a catalog named TRAFFIC. Here is the command:

    ```
    BUILD SASUSER.TRAFFIC
    ```

Note

With Version 7, you no longer specify CATALOG= in the BUILD command.

A new SAS Explorer window appears with the new catalog highlighted, as shown in Figure 11.6.

Figure 11.6 Results of the BUILD Command

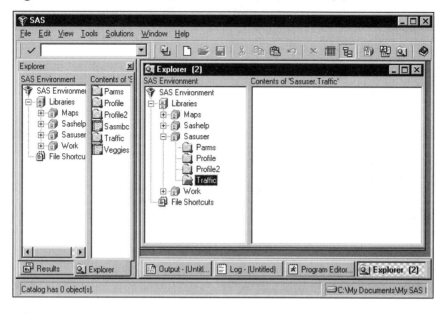

2. Right-click on the TRAFFIC catalog, and click on **New** in the resulting popup menu. This opens the New Entry dialog box, as shown in Figure 11.7.

Figure 11.7 New Entry Dialog Box

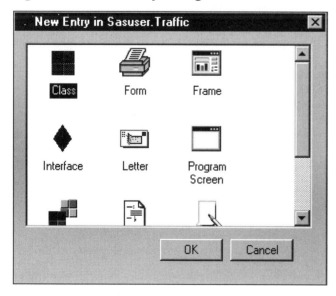

3. Double-click on **Frame** in the New Entry dialog box. This opens the BUILD: DISPLAY window for an untitled FRAME, as well as the Components window, as shown in Figure 11.8.

Figure 11.8 BUILD: DISPLAY and Components Windows

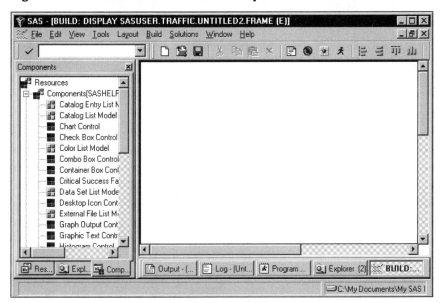

Note that in Figure 11.8, the BUILD: DISPLAY window has been maximized.

4. Place the picture of the road sign in the Clipboard. Do this by opening your graphics package, opening the sign's file, then copying it to the Clipboard. (This is usually done by clicking on **Edit**, then clicking on **Copy** in the graphics package's main menu.) After the Clipboard contains the sign's image, you're ready to paste it into the FRAME entry.

5. In the Components window, scroll to the bottom of the list and click on the plus sign next to **Version 6 objects**. The list should look similar to Figure 11.9.

Figure 11.9 Expanded Version 6 Objects Components List

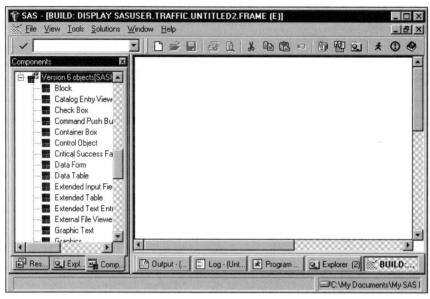

6.   Scroll through the **Version 6 Objects** list until you see **OLE - Paste Special**. Click on this
     line, then drag the component into the BUILD: DISPLAY window. When you release the
     mouse button, the Paste Special dialog box appears, as shown in Figure 11.10.

Figure 11.10 Paste Special Dialog Box

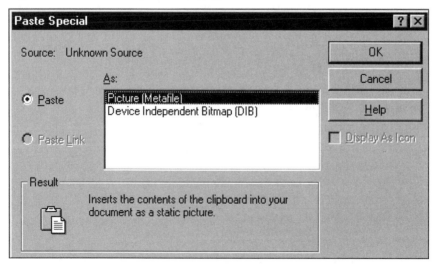

7. To create an embedded object, make sure the **Paste** option is selected, not **Paste Link**. In Figure 11.10, the **Paste Link** option is grayed out because the source of the graphic (Corel Gallery 2, version 2.0 in this case) does not support OLE.

    Choose the format of the graphic in the **As** field. In Figure 11.10, the **Picture (Metafile)** format is chosen. If you plan to share your SAS/AF application across computer systems (such as Windows and OS/2), you may want to choose the **Device Independent Bitmap** format.

8. After the options are set to your satisfaction, click on **OK**. The sign appears in the FRAME, as shown in Figure 11.11.

Figure 11.11 The Sign Object in the BUILD: DISPLAY Window

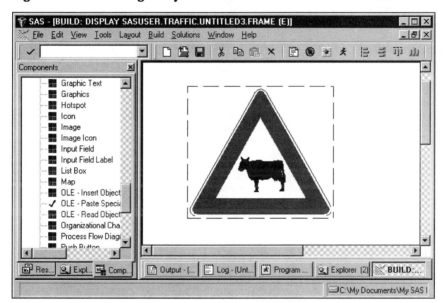

Don't worry if the sign is not exactly where you want it in the window—you can move it (see step 9). Also, the object is given a default name, which you can change (see step 10).

Depending on your graphic's source, you may see another dialog box before the graphic appears in the BUILD: DISPLAY window. For example, Corel Gallery displays a Paste Graphic dialog box that enables you to set the size of the graphic. Some graphics packages do not display this type of dialog box.

9. If the sign is not the right size or in the right place, resize it and move it. Click once inside the region to select it. Now place the mouse pointer over the corners or sides and resize it as you would a window. When the mouse pointer is over a corner, it turns into a four-headed arrow. When the mouse pointer is over a vertical or horizontal resize area, it turns into a two-headed

arrow. To move the graphic, place the mouse pointer over a side where the pointer turns into a hand. Now drag the region to where you want it.

10. If you do not want to use the default name for the object, you can rename it. Right-click on the object, then click on **Object Attributes** in the resulting popup menu. The OLE – Paste Special Attributes dialog box appears, as shown in Figure 11.12.

Figure 11.12 OLE – Paste Special Attributes Dialog Box

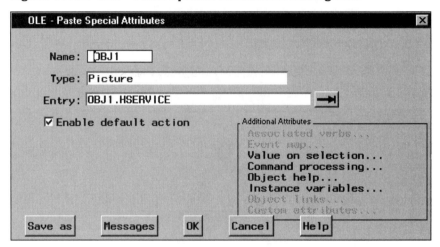

11. To change the object's name, edit the **Entry** field, which currently reads **OBJ1.HSERVICE**. Use the arrow and Backspace keys to delete the OBJ1 part of the name, and type in the name of the object that you want to use, such as SIGN1. Do not change the entry type (.HSERVICE). When you are finished, click on **OK**.

Note

> You may have to make the Components window smaller so that you can see the entire OLE – Paste Special dialog box.

12. To describe the sign, you need to create an object that displays text. There are several ways to do this, but one way is to paste in a text object, created from a graphics program such as Microsoft Paint.

To open the Paint application, click on the **Start** button, then click on **Programs**, then click on **Accessories**, then click on **Paint**.

Type the sign's description, and mark the text. Now copy it to the Clipboard. If you have never used Paint before, use the **Help** menu in the Paint window to learn how to type and mark text.

13. Now return to the BUILD: DISPLAY window, and drag another **OLE - Paste Special** component into the BUILD: DISPLAY window. In the Paste Special dialog box, choose **Paste**, and click on the **Picture (MetaFile)** object type. Now click on **OK**.

14. Rename the object if you want, using the OLE - Paste Special Attributes dialog box, then click on **OK**. The text appears in the object; if it is not positioned correctly, move and resize it to your satisfaction. Figure 11.13 shows how your screen should look after you have added the sign's description.

Figure 11.13 The First Sign and Its Description

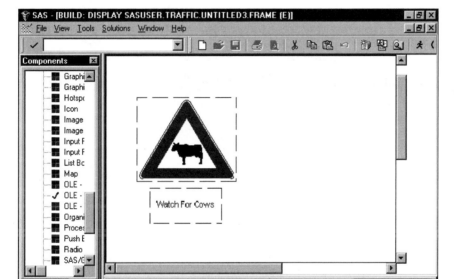

This method of inserting a text object ensures a static object—that is, one that cannot be edited by users of your SAS/AF application (you do not want people changing the sign's description).

15. You must save your work before the OLE objects become permanent parts of your FRAME entry. To save your work, click on **File** in the SAS System main menu, then click on **Save**. The Save As dialog box appears, as shown in Figure 11.14.

Figure 11.14 Save As Dialog Box for Saving Catalog Entries

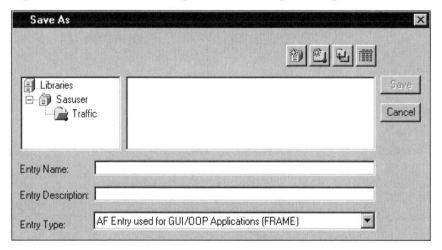

Enter an entry name, such as SIGNS, in the **Entry Name** field, and an entry description, such as Traffic Signs, in the **Entry Description** field. Now click on **Save**.

16. For some signs, you may need to provide more information than the small description can hold. For these signs, add a "Text Document" icon. First, create the text file that contains the detailed information about the sign. Create this file with a word processing program that supports OLE, such as Microsoft Word, Windows Notepad, or the Windows WordPad editor. Save the file.

17. Now return to the BUILD: DISPLAY window. Drag an **OLE - Insert Object** component into the BUILD: DISPLAY window. The Insert Object dialog box appears, as shown in Figure 11.15.

Figure 11.15 Insert Object Dialog Box

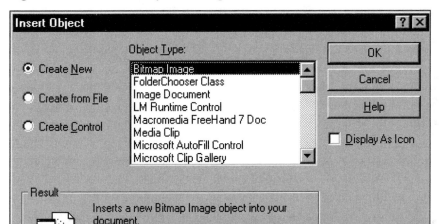

18. Click on **Create from File**, and type the full pathname of the text file in the **File** field. Also click on **Display As Icon** so that the entire text does not appear in the FRAME entry. When you click on this option, the default icon for the file you've selected appears, as does a **Change Icon** button. For this example, we'll use the default icon; it is possible to create your own icons and use them instead.

Note

When you use the Insert Object dialog box instead of the Paste Special dialog box, you do not need to have the object on the Clipboard.

19. Click on **OK** to close the Insert Object dialog box. The icon is added to your FRAME entry, as shown in Figure 11.16.

Figure 11.16 FRAME Entry with the Text Document Icon Added

You can rename and move the object as previously described. For example, you might want to rename this object to INFO1.

While the sign and the sign description are static embedded objects, the INFO1 object is a nonstatic embedded object.

20. Save the catalog entry by clicking on **File**, then clicking on **Save**.

21. Close the BUILD: DISPLAY window by clicking on **File**, then clicking on **Close**. When you are prompted whether you want to save the changes, click on **Yes**. The FRAME entry is saved and the BUILD: DISPLAY window closes.

Note

> Be sure that the BUILD: DISPLAY window is active before clicking on **Close**; otherwise, you could end up closing your entire SAS session.

When the driver's education student runs the SAS/AF application and double-clicks on the **Text Document** icon, the additional information is displayed, as shown in Figure 11.17.

Figure 11.17 Viewing the Text Represented by the Text Document Icon

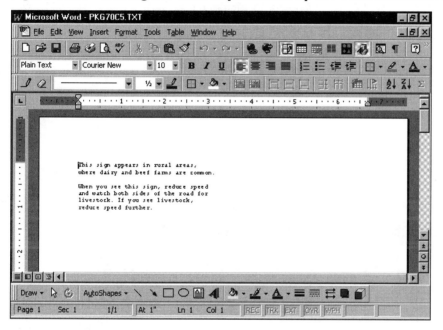

Note

> The Windows registry controls which editor application appears when you double-click on the Text Document icon. The editor is the one that opens .txt files. In Figure 11.17, the editor is Microsoft Word.

Obviously this is a small piece of the entire application; you need to add SCL code and other objects to your FRAME entries to enable students to progress from one sign to the next, do error checking, and so on.

Example 2—Using Linked Objects: Example 1 used embedded objects, both static and nonstatic. Embedded objects were useful in that example because the information did not change—the signs would always look the same, and the descriptions were finalized. In this example, you use linked objects. Linked objects are useful in applications where the information changes often, and you want your SAS/AF application user to have access to the latest changes or to be able to make changes to the information.

In this example, the SAS/AF application provides information about a company's construction project overseas. The application lets the user view the latest cost figures for the project, shows up-to-date floor plans, and even provides photos (updated weekly) of various parts of the project. While only a portion of the application is shown here, you get a good idea of how to create the other portions using the illustrated techniques.

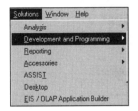

1. As with Example 1, the first step is to create a catalog and a FRAME entry. In Example 1, you used the BUILD command. For this example, you'll use the menus. Click on **Solutions** in the SAS System main menu, then on **Development and Programming**, then on **Frame Builder**. This opens an untitled FRAME entry in the WORK SAS data library, as shown in Figure 11.18.

Note

In the figure, the BUILD: DISPLAY window has been maximized.

Figure 11.18 Untitled FRAME Entry in the WORK SAS Data Library

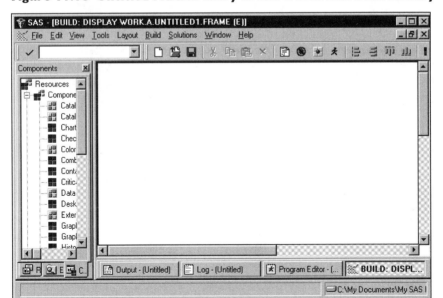

2. The first piece of the application we'll create is the floor plan for the project. These plans are updated periodically to reflect changes the engineers make. Therefore, you need to create a linked object so that each time the SAS/AF application runs, it accesses the most recent data.

    For this example, the floor plans are stored in graphics files created by Visio. You can use any other graphics program that supports OLE. Be sure that you've saved your graphics file before continuing.

3. After you've created and saved your floor plan graphics file, return to the BUILD: DISPLAY window. Drag an **OLE - Insert Object** component into the BUILD: DISPLAY window from the Components window. The Insert Object dialog box appears, as shown in Figure 11.19.

Figure 11.19 Insert Object Dialog Box

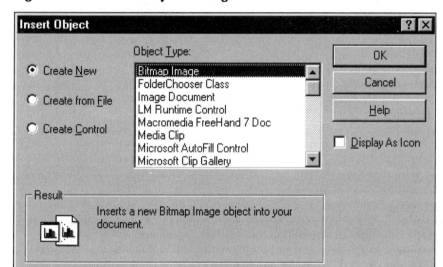

4. Click on **Create from File**, and type the graphic's filename in the text field. Also click on **Link** and **Display As Icon**. If you do not want to use the default icon, you must create your own icon using a bitmap editor, and use the **Change Icon** button to specify this new icon.

5. When you've finished with the Insert Object dialog box, click on **OK**. Now you see the object's icon, as shown in Figure 11.20.

Figure 11.20 Floor Plan Icon Added to the FRAME Entry

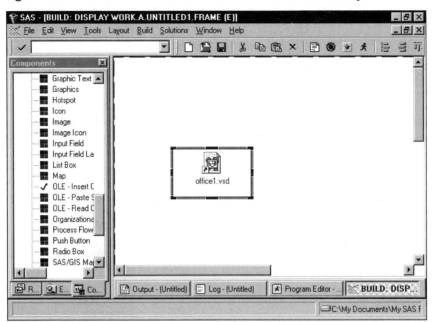

6. Rename and move the object as necessary. For this example, use the name FLRPLAN.

Note

> Some graphic file types do not support being used in this manner. You may need to experiment a bit with your graphics package to find a file type that works for you. Also, because the filename is displayed below the icon, it is best to have a meaningful filename.

By default, the link between your SAS/AF application and the data source (the graphics file) is automatic. That is, whenever the source is updated, the changes are reflected in the SAS/AF application. To view the object, the user of the SAS/AF application double-clicks on the object's icon. If the engineers have added a new wing to the existing plan, your SAS/AF application shows that wing.

7. To add a photo to your application, repeat steps 1-8, except that you may not want the photo shown as an icon—you may prefer to display the actual photo. It may be small, but the SAS/AF application user can double-click on the photo to open the graphics application, where the photo can be examined in detail.

Note

As with other graphics, some photo file types work better than others. For example, while JPEG files are detailed, they are also large and may use up too much RAM. The BMP and TIFF file formats are good choices for OLE because they preserve detail well, are supported by many programs, and create smaller files than some other formats.

8. When you finish adding objects to the FRAME entry, click on **File** in the SAS System main menu, then click on **Save As**. Because of the way you invoked the BUILD: DISPLAY window, you can save the FRAME entry in the WORK library only. Use the SAS Explorer window to move the FRAME entry to a permanent catalog after you close the BUILD: DISPLAY window.

9. Close the BUILD: DISPLAY window by clicking on **File→Close**.

You can use similar techniques to add a spreadsheet object to your FRAME entry (possibly using Excel or Lotus 1-2-3) that shows the current expenditures for the project. Another possible component of the application could be a timeline, created with a graphics package. You could also add more FRAME entries if necessary, and add SCL code to let the user move from one FRAME to the next. Using OLE and linked objects, your SAS/AF application users always have access to the latest data and information.

Running a SAS/AF Application: To run your SAS/AF application, you can use either the SAS Explorer window or the AF command.

To run a SAS/AF application using the SAS Explorer, right-click on the entry you want to start with. In the resulting popup menu, click on **Run**.

To use the Command bar to run a SAS/AF application, issue the following command:

AF *library-reference.catalog.entry.type*

library-reference.catalog.entry.type is the first entry of the application (the starting point).

To close the SAS/AF application and return to the Program Editor window, click on **File** in the SAS System main menu, then click on **Close**.

Using SAS/CONNECT® Software to Connect Your PC to Other Computer Systems

Introduction

V7 Hilites: In addition to the topics covered in this chapter, SAS/CONNECT features many enhancements that are beyond the scope of this book. Refer to your online and hardcopy SAS/CONNECT documentation for further details.

Except for Chapter 11, which discussed using SAS/AF software, this book has confined itself to discussing features of base SAS software. However, this chapter also discusses a separate product, SAS/CONNECT software. SAS/CONNECT software enables you to connect your Windows SAS session to SAS sessions running on other computer systems—perhaps an OS/390 mainframe, a UNIX workstation, or even another PC on your network.

The beauty of SAS/CONNECT software is that it enables you to access data stored on other machines and also to use more powerful machines to do "number-crunching" or other CPU-intensive programming tasks. This chapter shows, by example, the basics of using SAS/CONNECT software.

To use SAS/CONNECT software, you need some sort of connection between your computer and the other system and also some communications software (for example, Trumpet Winsock, Novell's Netware Requestor, IBM's LAN Support Program, or DEC's PATHWORKS software).

This chapter does not teach you how to install your communications software because there many configurations and options available. Nor does this chapter discuss all of the features and considerations of SAS/CONNECT software; it is intended only to get you started. If you plan to use SAS/CONNECT software extensively, read the latest edition of SAS Institute's documentation for SAS/CONNECT software.

As with most computer topics, communications between computers has its own jargon. So, this chapter first acquaints you with the terms that you encounter while using SAS/CONNECT software. Then, the chapter helps you conceptualize how SAS/CONNECT software works and how it can help you. Finally, five examples give you concrete experience using SAS/CONNECT software.

Learning Client/Server Terminology

SAS/CONNECT software is called "client/server" software. That is, it provides a bridge between your computer (the client), which requests data and services, and another computer (the server), which provides these data and services. Your computer is also referred to as the local computer, whereas the server computer is referred to as the remote computer. You need the SAS System installed on both the local and remote computer in order to use SAS/CONNECT software. After you have SAS/CONNECT software installed, you can send data in both directions between the local and remote computer.

As an example, suppose you have data stored on OS/390, but you want to analyze that data from your Windows SAS session. With SAS/CONNECT software, you connect your Windows SAS session to a SAS session on OS/390. You then submit program statements (such as DATA and PROC steps) to the OS/390 session. The OS/390 SAS session analyzes the data and passes the results to the Output window on your PC. Or, the OS/390 SAS session can pass data from OS/390 to your PC for analysis there. When you move data from the remote computer to your PC, you "download" the data. When you move data in the opposite direction, from your PC to the remote computer, you "upload" the data.

To establish the link between your PC and the remote computer, you use a "communication method." A communication method is a protocol for how two computers talk to each other. Examples of communication methods include TCP/IP, TELNET, RASYNC, and EHLLAPI.

Under Windows, several communication methods are available, depending on which remote operating system you want to connect to. See your SAS/CONNECT software documentation for a list of available communication methods.

If you are connected to the Internet under Windows, you probably already have some TCP/IP software installed. TCP/IP supports numerous remote connections. If you do not have communications software installed already, choose a product that supports connections to the remote operating systems that you want to connect to.

Understanding How SAS/CONNECT Software Works

V7 Hilites: The Signon dialog box has several new fields.

Remote Submit now opens a dialog box.

SAS/CONNECT software uses a "script file" that invokes the SAS System on the remote computer and defines the parameters of the connection between the local and remote SAS sessions. These script files are plain text files that are shipped with SAS/CONNECT software. You can use these files as-is, or you can modify them to meet your particular needs. There is a script file for every type of communication method supported by the SAS System under Windows, except for the APPC and DECnet communication methods, which do not require a script file.

When you set up a connection between the local and remote SAS sessions, you must specify the following information from the local SAS session:

- the script file

- the communication method to use

- an identification code for the remote SAS session (the remote session ID).

On the remote side, the SAS System must be configured properly for the connection. The configuration differs, depending on what operating system you are connecting to. For example, if you are connecting to OS/390, several SAS system options need to be set in the remote SAS session.

It is possible to connect to several different remote SAS sessions at the same time, using different remote session IDs. And while beginning SAS/CONNECT software users may prefer to specify the connection information using dialog boxes, it is also possible to specify this information programmatically, using SAS statements and system options. This enables you to use SAS/CONNECT software in batch mode. The last example in this chapter is a batch mode example.

Initiating the Connection: To initiate the connection, make the Program Editor window active. Click on **Run** in the SAS System main menu, then click on **Signon**. The Signon dialog box appears, as shown in Figure 12.1.

Figure 12.1 Signon Dialog Box

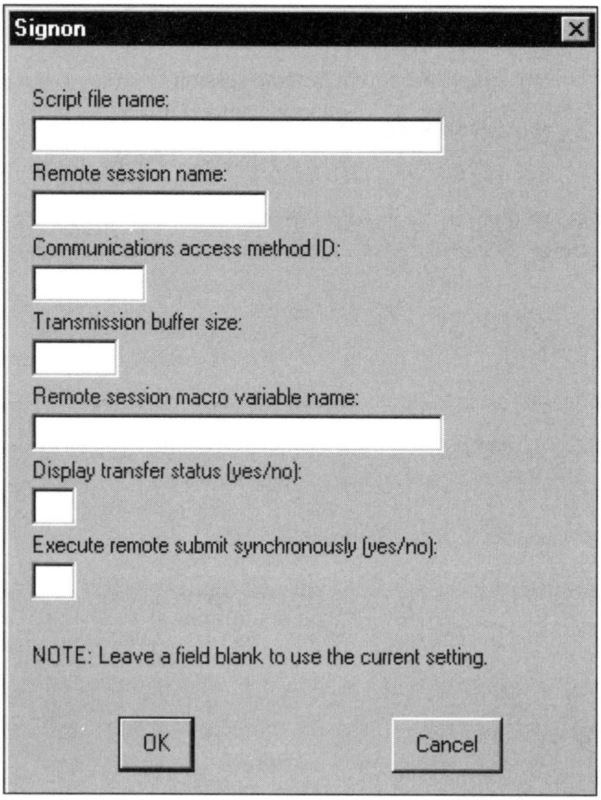

In the top field in the Signon dialog box, type the script file you want to use. By default, the SAS System looks for script files in C:\SAS\CONNECT\SASLINK. If your script file is located in another folder, be sure to type in the full pathname.

In the next field, type the remote session ID you want to use. The value of this field depends on which communication method you are using. It can be as simple a code as an "a" or a long Internet address. Your communications software documentation can help you determine this ID.

In the next field, enter the communication method. When you've typed the values, click on **OK**. (The default value for the other fields are sufficient for many users; a more detailed discussion of these values is beyond the scope of this book.)

Note

Completing the connection may take a few minutes, depending on the speed of your networks and the response time of the computer you are connecting to.

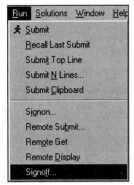

Terminating the Connection: To end the connection to a remote computer, make the Program Editor window active. Click on **Run→Signoff**. The Signoff dialog box appears, which is similar to the Signon dialog box. Specify the script file, remote session ID, and communication method for the connection you want to terminate, and click on **OK**.

Deciding How to Use SAS/CONNECT Software

When you submit SAS statements that execute on the remote system, you are using "compute services." When you access data stored on the remote system, you are using "data services." Which services you should use depends on your particular needs and how your computers are set up.

For example, if you have a PC that has minimum RAM and a slow processor and your data is stored on a mainframe, you probably want to use a combination of compute services and data services so that all the processing and number crunching occurs on the mainframe, and only the results get passed back to your PC. On the other hand, if your PC is a fast machine, you need to do lengthy data analysis, and your network is overworked, you may want to use only data services to download a copy of the data to your PC and do the computing there.

When you take advantage of data services, you can choose either to transfer the data between the remote and local SAS sessions, or you can access the data directly on the remote system, using "remote library services" (RLS). This means that you submit a LIBNAME statement that defines the SAS data library on the remote system. Then, you can use this library reference in any of your programming statements—either statements submitted on the local system or on the remote system. Think of data transfer as a moving van—the physical data are moved from one system to the other. RLS, on the other hand, is like a periscope from your PC to the remote system—you can see and use the data, but the data are not physically moved.

Figure 12.2 shows how SAS/CONNECT services can work.

Figure 12.2 SAS/CONNECT Services

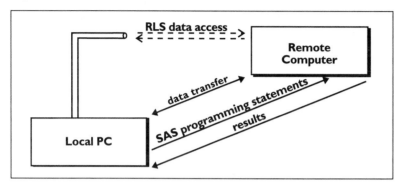

Understanding SAS/CONNECT Software's Compute Services

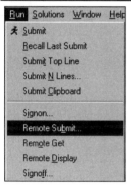

Submitting code that executes on a remote computer is as simple as submitting code on your own PC, after you have established the connection to the remote computer. Type the code into the Program Editor window. Then, click on **Run→Remote Submit**. This opens the Remote Submit dialog box, as shown in Figure 12.3.

Figure 12.3   Remote Submit Dialog Box

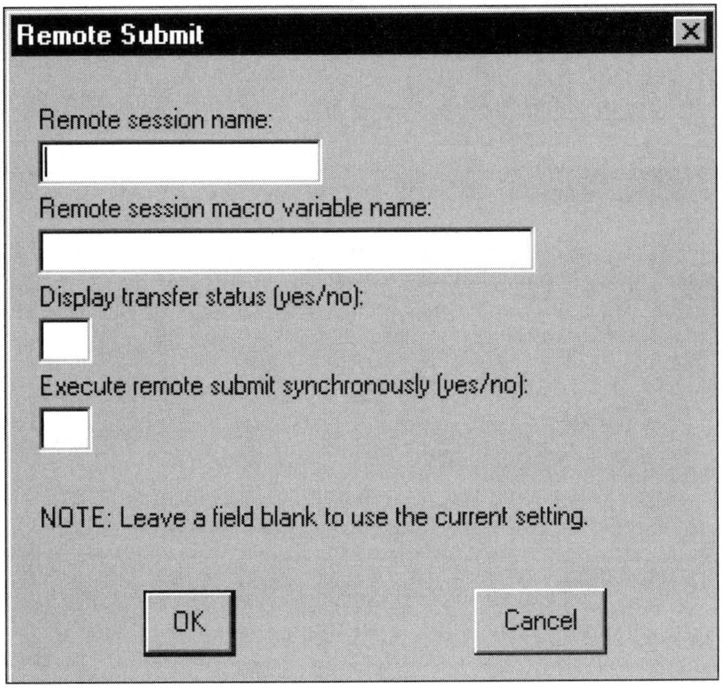

Because it is possible to have several remote connections active at once, you must enter the remote session ID in the top field of the Remote Submit dialog box.

Fill in the other fields as necessary; usually the default values are sufficient. When you are ready to submit the code, click on **OK**.

Note

Any library references, file shortcuts, and tables that you reference in remote submitted code exist on the remote computer—not on your PC.

If you prefer to use SAS statements instead of menus, use the RSUBMIT and ENDRSUBMIT statements to remote submit your code. Example 1 later in this chapter gives an example of using compute services, and Example 5 illustrates how to use the RSUBMIT and ENDRSUBMIT statements.

Deciding When to Use Compute Services: In general, use compute services when the remote computer has better, faster hardware resources than your PC. Also, use compute services to take advantage of printers and plotters connected to the remote computer. When you use compute services, you can use SAS components on the remote computer that are not installed on your PC (such as SAS/STAT or SAS/INSIGHT software).

Understanding SAS/CONNECT Software's Data Transfer Services

To copy data from the remote computer to your PC and vice versa, use the DOWNLOAD and UPLOAD procedures.

The DOWNLOAD procedure copies data from the remote computer to your PC; the UPLOAD procedure sends data from your PC to the remote computer. Both of these procedures can transfer SAS tables, SAS catalogs, and external files (for example, executable files, text files, and so on). By using subsetting features of the SAS System, such as the WHERE statement, you can move only the data you need.

Both the DOWNLOAD and UPLOAD procedures execute on the remote computer and must be submitted with the RSUBMIT statement or the Remote submit menu item. Any library references or file shortcuts used with these procedures must have been previously defined to the remote computer with remote submitted LIBNAME and FILENAME statements.

Example 2 later in this chapter illustrates using the DOWNLOAD and UPLOAD procedures.

Deciding When to Use Data Transfer Services: In general, use data transfer services when you are developing an application that repeatedly accesses data. If you do not download the data, you tie up the network every time you access the data. By downloading it, you use the network only once. Also, use data transfer services to make a backup copy of data.

Understanding SAS/CONNECT Software's Remote Library Services

Instead of using PROC DOWNLOAD to move data from the remote computer to your PC, you can use SAS/CONNECT software's Remote Library Services (RLS) to directly access data on the remote computer. What makes RLS unique is that it enables you to execute your SAS program on your PC, but use data, without downloading it, that reside on the remote computer.

Note

Not all communication methods support RLS. You need a program-to-program communication method. Examples of program-to-program communication methods include APPC, DECnet, NetBIOS, and TCP/IP.

To use RLS, you submit a special LIBNAME statement from your PC, which defines a library reference on the remote computer. This LIBNAME statement uses several keywords not used in a regular LIBNAME statement. Example 3 later in this chapter shows you how this LIBNAME statement and RLS work.

Using RLS with SAS Tables: RLS can access all types of SAS tables (including data defined by SAS data views and SAS/ACCESS access descriptors).

Using RLS with SAS Catalogs: RLS can access SAS catalogs only if both the local and remote computers use the same internal representations of data. This means that the local and remote operating systems must store both character and numeric data in the same way.

For example, both Windows 95 and Windows NT use the ASCII character set and store numbers in byte order, so you can use RLS to access SAS catalogs on a Windows NT machine. But OS/390 uses the EBCDIC character set and stores numbers in byte-reversed order, so you cannot access OS/390 SAS catalogs using RLS from your Windows SAS session. And even though both Win32s (the 32-bit version of Windows, required for Release 6.11 and later of the SAS System) and OS/2 store numeric data the same way, OS/2 uses a different version of the ASCII character set—so you cannot use RLS to access SAS catalogs on an OS/2 machine. The following operating systems use the same internal data representation as Windows and therefore support RLS catalog access:

- Windows (Win32s)

- Windows NT

- Windows 95 and subsequent releases, such as Windows 98.

Using RLS with SAS Stored Programs: RLS cannot access SAS PROGRAM files from any remote computer.

Deciding When to Use Remote Library Services: In general, use RLS when you need to execute your SAS program on your local computer but you need access to data on the remote computer and do not want to download the data. Remember that RLS requires use of the network every time you access the data, so if your network is slow or crowded, you may not want to use RLS.

Example 1: Using Compute Services

Your PC is connected to OpenVMS via the DECnet communication method. You want to use the SAS System on OpenVMS to execute your code because it requires a large table to be sorted. Because your PC is a slow 386 machine, the SAS System can sort the data faster on OpenVMS than on your PC. Here are the steps to work this example:

1. Determine your remote session ID. For DECnet access, the remote session ID usually takes the form of node "*username password*". However, the remote session ID must be eight characters or fewer. So, you must use a SAS macro to define a nickname for the remote session ID.

Suppose the node you need to access is WALKER, your username is SMITH01, and your password is MAGIC123. The remote session ID is WALKER"SMITH01 MAGIC123". The following SAS statement assigns the nickname SMITH to this ID:

```
%let smith=walker"smith01 magic123";
```

Submit this statement locally (for example, press F3).

2. Now initiate the connection: click on **Run→Signon**.

Leave the script file field blank because DECnet access does not require a script file. In the second field, type the nickname for the remote session ID (in this example, SMITH). In the last field, type DECNET. Now click on **OK** to initiate the connection.

3. Now you're ready to type the program you want to run under OpenVMS. Here is the program:

```
      /* Tell the OpenVMS SAS session to use */
      /* the HOST sort utility. /*
options sortpgm=host;
      /* Define a library reference on OpenVMS. */
libname panthers 'species::[florida.cats]';
proc sort data=panthers.kittens
      out=females (where=(sex='f'));
      by age idnum;
run;
proc print data=females;
      title='Female Florida Panther Kittens';
      by age;
run;
```

4. When the program is ready to submit, click on **Run→Remote Submit**. Type the remote session ID in the top field (SMITH). Now click on **OK**. The code is submitted to the SAS session on OpenVMS, and when it is finished, the Output window on your PC displays the results of the program.

5. When you are finished with the OpenVMS SAS session, terminate the connection by clicking on **Run→Signoff**. Type the same values you typed in the Signon dialog box, and click on **OK**.

Example 2: Using Data Transfer Services

Your PC is connected to OS/390 through the EHLLAPI communication method. You need to access some car emission data on OS/390. The table is not large, and you need only about half of it, but you do need to do repetitive analysis on it. So, you decide to download the table to your PC using PROC DOWNLOAD. Then you use PROC UPLOAD to send the results back to OS/390.

Here are the steps to work this example:

1. Determine your remote session ID. For EHLLAPI access, the remote session ID is the remote computer's session ID. You created this ID when you installed the communications software that enables your PC to connect to OS/390.

2. Now initiate the connection: click on **Run→Signon**. Type TSO.SCR in the script file field. For the second field, type the remote session ID from your communications software package. In the last field, type EHLLAPI. Now click on **OK** to initiate the connection.

3. Now you're ready to type the DOWNLOAD procedure statements. Here is the program. The WHERE statement pulls out only the data for vehicles made from 1975 to 1977 whose weight is larger than 6000 pounds and whose hydrocarbon emissions are greater than 750 parts-per-million.

    ```
              /* Define a library reference on MVS. */
    libname pollute 'vehicle.test.results';
    proc download data=pollute.large out=large;
        where year between 1975 and 1977
            and weight > 6000
            and hydcarb >= 750;
    run;
    ```

Note

It may be more efficient to use the WHERE= data set option in the previous example, instead of the WHERE statement.

4. When the program is ready to submit, click on **Run→Remote Submit**. Type the remote session ID in the top field (refer to your communication package for this name; it is the same name you typed into the Signon dialog box). Now click on **OK**. The code is submitted to the SAS session on OS/390. When it is finished, the temporary table LARGE is created on your PC. You can now analyze this data repeatedly, without tying up the network with further traffic.

5. After you have finished analyzing the data, send the results back to OS/390. Suppose the results of your analysis are in the temporary table HYDCARB. Type the following program into the Program Editor window:

    ```
    proc upload data=hydcarb
                out=pollute.hydcarb;
    run;
    ```

Click on **Run→Remote Submit**. Type the remote session ID in the top field (the same name you typed into the Signon dialog box). Now click on **OK** to submit the PROC UPLOAD step to OS/390.

6. When you are finished with the OS/390 SAS session, terminate the connection by clicking on **Run→Signoff**. Type the same values that you typed in the Signon dialog box, and click on **OK**.

Example 3: Using Remote Library Services

Your PC is connected to a UNIX workstation via the TCP/IP communication method. A table containing vehicle emissions data is stored on the UNIX machine. You need to access a small portion of this table to plot which vehicles had high carbon monoxide emissions. Because you need only a small portion of the data and you do not plan to repeatedly analyze the data, RLS is an efficient method of accessing the data.

Here are the steps to work this example:

1. Determine your remote session ID. For TCP/IP access, the remote session ID is the remote computer's Internet address. However, the remote session ID must be eight characters or fewer. So, you must use a SAS macro to define a nickname for the remote session ID.

    Suppose the Internet address for the remote UNIX machine is 1.20.327.45. The following SAS statement assigns the nickname TOUNIX to this ID:

    ```
    %let tounix=1.20.327.45;
    ```

    Submit this statement locally (for example, press F3).

2. Now initiate the connection: click on **Run→Signon**. Type TCPUNIX.SCR in the script file field. For the second field, type the nickname for the remote session ID (in this example, TOUNIX). In the last field, type TCP. Click on **OK** to initiate the connection.

3. To use Remote Library Services, you submit a special LIBNAME statement to your PC that identifies the remote SAS session. For example, the LIBNAME statement in the following program defines the library reference CO. The REMOTE option tells the local SAS session this is an RLS LIBNAME statement, and the SERVER option specifies the remote session ID for the UNIX SAS session, where the SAS data library resides. Submit this program locally (for example, press F3).

    ```
    libname co remote
        '/home/user/smith/vehicles/light/tests'
        server=tounix;
    data co.high_co;
      set co.year81;
      where carbmono > 1.2;
    run;
    ```

```
proc plot data=co.high_co nolegend;
   title1 '1981 Vehicles Weighing Less than
      6,000 Pounds';
   title2 'with High Carbon Monoxide Emissions';
   title3 '(Measured in Percentage)';
   plot vin*carbmono='*';
run;
```

The Output window on your PC displays the plot, although no data have been physically moved to the PC.

4. When you are finished with the UNIX SAS session, terminate the connection by clicking on **Run→Signoff**. Type the same values you typed in the Signon dialog box, and click on **OK**.

Example 4: Combining Compute, Data Transfer, and Remote Library Services

Your PC is connected to CMS via the TELNET communication method. Your application uses a combination of compute, data transfer, and remote library services. This application uses RLS to merge two tables (one on CMS, one on the PC) into a new one, then uses data transfer services to upload the new table to CMS. Then, the program uses compute services to do some tabulation, using CMS. The output of the TABULATE procedure appears on the local PC. TELNET access requires the remote session to run in line mode, which is fine for your needs. Also, although the communication method for the local machine is TELNET, the CMS session should be set up to use the RASYNC communication method.

Here are the steps to work this example:

1. Determine the remote session ID for the CMS session. For TELNET access, the remote session ID is the remote computer's Internet address. However, the remote session ID must be eight characters or fewer. So, you must use a SAS macro to define a nickname for the remote session ID.

    Suppose the Internet address for the remote CMS machine is tiger@cms.company.com. The following SAS statement assigns the nickname TOCMS to this ID:

    ```
    %let tocms=tiger@cms.company.com;
    ```

    Submit this statement locally (for example, press F3).

2. Now initiate the connection: click on **Run→Signon**. To initiate the CMS session, type TELCMS.SCR in the script file field. For the second field, type the nickname for the CMS remote session ID (in this example, TOCMS). In the last field, type TELNET. Now click on **OK** to initiate the connection.

3. The next step is to submit an RLS-type LIBNAME statement that refers to a SAS data library on CMS and a regular LIBNAME statement to define a library reference for a local SAS data library:

```
libname cms remote 'data a' server=tocms;
libname win 'c:\wildcat\info';
```

Submit these two statements locally (for example, press F3).

4. Now you are ready to merge the two tables (one remote, one local) together, to form a new, local table that contains both vital statistics (like weight and age) and location information for the various species of wild cats in the U.S. Again, these statements are submitted locally and create a temporary table, CATINFO, on the PC.

```
       /* First, sort each table by ID, so */
       /* the match-merge works. */
proc sort data=cms.vital;
   by id;
run;
proc sort data=win.region;
   by id;
run;
       /* Now create the merged table. */
data catinfo;
   merge cms.vital win.region;
   by id;
run;
```

5. Now you want to move the CATINFO table to CMS, using the UPLOAD procedure. Note that a new LIBNAME statement is necessary because this portion of the program is not using RLS. Submit these statements remotely by clicking on **Run→Remote Submit**) in the SAS System main menu, then typing the remote session ID (TOCMS) in the top field, then clicking on **OK**.

```
libname cat 'data a';
proc upload data=catinfo
     out=cat.catinfo;
run;
```

6. Because you want to do the tabulation on CMS, the PROC TABULATE step is also remote submitted (**Run→Remote Submit**, and so on):

```
proc tabulate data=cat.catinfo
              format=comma8.;
     title 'Tabulation of Wild Cat Information
         Organized by Species and Region';
     class species region;
     var weight age;
     table species*region,
     age*mean*f=8.2 weight*mean*f=8.2 age*n;
run;
```

This program tabulates the mean weight and age of each species of cat, organized by region. It also tells you how many cats are in each region. Even though the program was submitted remotely, the results of the TABULATE procedure appear in the Output window on your PC.

7. When you are finished with the CMS SAS session, terminate the connection by clicking on **Run→Signoff**. Type the same values you typed in the Signon dialog box, then click on **OK**.

Example 5: Using SAS/CONNECT Software in Batch Mode

V7 Hilites: RSUBMIT, SIGNON, and SIGNOFF statements now use the CONNECTREMOTE= option to specify the remote session ID.

Your PC is connected to OS/2 via the TCP/IP communication method. You have a batch program that uses SAS/CONNECT software to process some data on the OS/2 machine and download a resulting table to your PC.

SAS/CONNECT software works equally well in windowing or batch mode, and you can use compute, data transfer, and remote library services in both modes. The only differences between using SAS/CONNECT software in batch mode and in windowing mode are the following:

• how you specify the script file, remote session ID, and communication method

• how you initiate and terminate the connection

• how you remote submit programs.

Specifying the Script File in Batch Mode: Instead of typing the script file in the Signon dialog box, in batch mode use the special file shortcut RLINK by submitting a FILENAME statement that associates RLINK with the script file. Here is an example for the TCP/IP communication method between Windows and OS/2:

```
filename rlink
    'c:\program files\sas\connect\saslink\tcpos2.scr';
```

Submit this statement locally before you sign on to the remote computer.

Specifying the Remote Session ID in Batch Mode: Instead of typing the remote session ID in the Signon dialog box, in batch mode use the REMOTE SAS system option. Put this option in your CONFIG.SAS file or in an OPTIONS statement. This example uses an OPTIONS statement.

Follow these steps to specify the remote session ID in batch mode:

1. Determine the remote session ID for the OS/2 session. For example, for TCP/IP access, the remote session ID is the remote computer's Internet address. However, the remote session ID must be eight characters or fewer. So, you must use a SAS macro to define a nickname for the remote session ID.

    Suppose the Internet address for the remote OS/2 machine is 1.45.735.26. The following SAS statement assigns the nickname TOOS2 to this ID:

    ```
    %let toos2=1.45.735.26;
    ```

    Submit this statement locally before you initiate the connection to the remote computer.

2. Now use this nickname in the REMOTE system option, as in the following example:

    ```
    options remote=toos2;
    ```

    Put the OPTIONS statement in your AUTOEXEC.SAS file if you use SAS/CONNECT software regularly.

Specifying the Communication Method in Batch Mode: Instead of typing the communication method in the Signon dialog box, in batch mode use the COMAMID SAS system option. Put this option in your CONFIG.SAS file or in an OPTIONS statement. This example uses an OPTIONS statement.

For example, for the TCP/IP communication method, the value for the COMAMID option is TCP. Here is a sample COMAMID option specification:

```
options comamid=tcp;
```

Put the OPTIONS statement in your AUTOEXEC.SAS file if you use SAS/CONNECT software regularly.

Initiating the Connection in Batch Mode: Instead of clicking on **OK** in the Signon dialog box, in batch mode use the SIGNON statement. The SIGNON statement takes the remote session ID as an argument. Here is an example:

```
signon remoteconnect=toos2;
```

Submit this statement locally.

Remote Submitting SAS Statements in Batch Mode: Instead of using the **Remote submit** menu item, in batch mode use the RSUBMIT and ENDRSUBMIT statements in your code. Place the RSUBMIT statement before the first statement in the remote program; place the ENDRSUBMIT statement after the last statement in the remote program, as in the following example:

```
rsubmit connectremote=toos2;
    libname os2data 'c:\temp\july';
    proc sort data=os2data.hightemps;
        by date;
    run;
endrsubmit;
```

This example defines a library reference for an OS/2 SAS data library and performs an in-place sort on a table in that library.

Note

> By default, the RSUBMIT statement submits the code to the last remote session you have established. To submit the code to a different remote session, specify the CONNECTREMOTE= option in the RSUBMIT statement.

Terminating the Connection in Batch Mode: Instead of clicking on **OK** in the Signoff dialog box, in batch mode use the SIGNOFF statement with the remote session ID as the argument, as in the following example:

```
signoff connectremote=toos2;
```

Submit this statement locally.

Batch Example Code: Here is an entire sample batch program, with comments.

```
    /* Define a nickname for the remote session */
    /* ID. */
%let toos2=1.45.735.26;
    /* Set the remote session ID and */
    /* communication method. */
options remote=toos2 comamid=tcp;
```

```
   /* Assign the RLINK file shortcut to the
   /* appropriate script file. */
filename rlink 'c:\sas\connect\saslink\tcpos2.scr';
   /* Define a library reference on the local PC, where */
   /* the downloaded table is stored. */
libname windata 'c:\temp\july';
signon connectremote=toos2; /* Initiate the connection. */
   /* Begin the remote submitted block */
   /* of code. */
rsubmit connectremote=toos2 ;
   /* Define a library reference for an OS/2 */
   /* data library. */
libname os2data 'c:\temp\july';
   /* Create a temporary table that */
   /* contains the high and low temperatures */
   /* for July. */
data hilo;
      merge os2data.hi (drop=date place
                 rename=(time=hitime))
             os2data.lo
                 (rename=(time=lotime));
run;
   /* Download the merged table. */
proc download data=hilo out=windata.hilo;
run;
   /* End the remote submitted block of code. */
endrsubmit;
   /* Terminate the connection. */
signoff connectremote=toos2;
```

Appendix 1 Troubleshooting

Introduction

This appendix provides some hints for solving commonly encountered problems. The problems are organized into groups that match the chapters, such as printing, batch programming, and using SAS/CONNECT software.

If your problem is not addressed in this appendix, you may want to visit the Knowledge Base on the SAS Institute Web site (www.sas.com), under the Technical Support topic.

Learning to Do Windows and Performing the Basic SAS Software Tasks under Windows

Problem: The SAS System has caused a General Protection Fault (GPF).

Solution: Press CTRL-ALT-DEL. From the dialog box that appears, select **Task Manager**, where you can end any applications that are not responding, or select **Shut Down** to reboot your computer. The latter causes you to lose any unsaved tables and catalogs you created in your SAS session and in other applications as well.

Problem: Your keyboard has locked up and you cannot type or use the mouse.

Solution: First, press CTRL-ALT-DEL. If that does not work, turn off your computer, then turn it back on. This causes you to lose all unsaved data in all Windows applications.

Problem: Your mouse buttons do not work the way you expect.

Solution: Someone may have changed the mouse from a right-handed to a left-handed mouse or vice versa. Click on **Start→Settings→Control Panel**. In the Control Panel window, click on the **Mouse** icon, and use the resulting dialog box to reset your mouse's properties.

Problem: The Windows application you want to use is hidden behind several other open windows.

Solution: Click on the application's name in the Windows Taskbar.

Problem: The SAS window you want to use is hidden behind several other open SAS windows.

Solution: Click on the window's name in the Window Bar at the bottom of the SAS workspace. Alternatively, click on **Window** in the SAS System main menu, then click on the name of the window you want to see. If you have more than nine SAS windows open, click on **More Windows** to see a complete list of open SAS windows; double-click on the name of the window you want to see.

Problem: You cannot see the entire SAS window or dialog box—it seems to extend off the screen and buttons or fields are hidden.

Solution: Undock or close all docked SAS windows—this frees up more space for the window or dialog box. If you still cannot see all of the buttons or features of the window or dialog box, try making the entire SAS workspace bigger, then resizing the window or dialog box; this should enable you to see the entire window or dialog box.

Problem: You cannot see all the tools in the SAS tool bar.

Solution: Resize the tool bar by dragging the separator between it and the Command bar to the left. This makes the Command bar smaller and the tool bar bigger.

Editing and Working with Files

Problem: You cannot click in the Program Editor window. Every time you do, your computer beeps, and the mouse pointer is an hourglass.

Solution: You may have a synchronous DOS session active or have a dialog box open waiting for input (either in the SAS session or in another Windows application).

Look at the Windows Taskbar. If **MS-DOS Prompt** is listed, click on that task. Type EXIT at the DOS prompt to close the DOS session. To keep this from happening again, submit an OPTIONS statement in your SAS session with the NOXWAIT option.

If the Taskbar does not list any active DOS sessions, press ALT-ESC to toggle through all open windows to see if you have an open dialog box that needs input. If neither CTRL-ESC or ALT-ESC works, your Windows session may be hung—see the second problem under "Learning to Do Windows and Performing the Basic SAS Software Tasks under Windows," earlier in this appendix.

Problem: You want to customize your editing options but don't see the **Edit** or **Editor** choice in the **Options** menu.

Solution: Make one of the main SAS programming windows (Log, Program Editor, or Output) or another SAS text editing window (such as NOTEPAD) active before selecting **Tools→Options→Editor**.

Submitting SAS Code and Generating Output

Problem: Your program is in an infinite loop.

Solution: Click on the Attention icon on the SAS tool bar or press CTRL-BREAK. When the Tasking Manager appears, click on the appropriate line, then click on **OK**. Now the BREAK dialog box appears. Click on **Y to halt data step/proc**, then click on **OK**.

Problem: The **Recall Last Submit** menu item does not work.

Solution: You have probably cleared the window. Try using the UNDO command repeatedly to back through your actions. If this does not work, you must retype your text or reopen the file.

Problem: You cannot find your HTML output.

Solution: Check in the temporary directory for your SAS session, which by default is located as a subfolder of C:\DOS\Temp\SAS Temporary Files. Also check the **Results** tab of the Preferences dialog box to see which filename is specified there.

Problem: You are using the ODS statement to generate HTML output, but the output doesn't appear when you expect it to.

Solution: Before you can view your HTML output, you must use the ODS HTML CLOSE statement to close the output destination.

Printing

Problem: Your printer output does not look like you expect it to look.

Solution: Be sure you have selected the correct printer for your output. Also, you may have a form selected when you do not want to use forms, or the wrong form may be in effect. Check the Print Setup dialog box to see if the **Use Forms** option is checked. Use the FORMNAME command to display the current form. Also check the font and typesize settings, and check your SAS configuration file for LINESIZE, PAGESIZE, SYSPRINT, SYSPRINTFONT, and other system options that affect printer output.

Problem: Your SAS output looks funny and things do not align.

Solution: You may have chosen a proportional font for your printer output. Change the font to a monospace font such as Courier or SAS Monospace.

Problem: You get an error message when you try to print a bitmap file.

Solution: Check your free disk space—printing large files requires some free disk space for temporary files. Delete unnecessary files to free up more disk space.

Adjusting Your Windows Environment

Problem: You cannot resize or move the SAS workspace.

Solution: The SAS workspace is probably maximized. Check the maximize/restore button in the upper-right corner of the SAS workspace. If it is a single box, click on it once. Now you can resize or move the SAS workspace.

Problem: You cannot see all the tools in the SAS toolbar.

Solution: Resize the Command bar by dragging the separator (to the right of the Command bar) to the left. Now you will be able to see more tools.

Problem: You set colors in some SAS windows, but the next time you start the SAS System, the colors did not stick.

Solution: You may have forgotten to issue a WSAVE command from each window you changed. Make the changes again, and this time issue the WSAVE command from each window you change, or select the **Save settings on exit** option in the Preferences dialog box on the **General** tab.

Problem: You've closed one of the main SAS System windows, such as the Log or Program Editor, and want it back—but it's not listed in the **Window** menu.

Solution: Click on the SAS Programming Windows icon on the toolbar.

Problem: You try to move or resize the SAS Explorer or Results window, but cannot.

Solution: The SAS Explorer window is docked. To undock the window, select **Window→Docked**, so the checkmark next to **Docked** disappears. You can now move and resize the SAS Explorer window.

Problem: You want to customize your SAS Explorer options but don't see the **Explorer** choice in the **Options** menu.

Solution: Open a SAS Explorer window and make sure it is active before selecting **Tools→Options→Explorer**.

Managing SAS Files

Problem: You have accidentally deleted a file.

Solution: If the file was deleted using the Windows Explorer, look in the Recycle Bin on the Windows desktop to recover the file, as described in "Restoring Deleted Files" in Appendix 3.

If the file was deleted using the SAS System (from the SAS Explorer, for example), the file cannot easily be restored without a third-party file restoration utility such as Norton Utilities.

Problem: You know a file exists, but you cannot remember where you stored it.

Solution: Use the SAS Explorer to find the file. Alternatively, many dialog boxes in the SAS System (such as the Open dialog box) contain a **Browse** button. Click on this button to search through your computer's drives and folders until you find the file.

Another approach is to use Window's Find feature. Right-click on the **Start** button, then click on **Find**. In the resulting dialog box, type the filename in the **Named** field. If you want to search the entire root folder, click on the down arrow next to the **Look in** field, then click on the **C:** drive. Click on **OK** to start the search. The results of the search are displayed at the bottom of the Find dialog box.

Problem: You cannot perform a file operation, such as rename, move, or delete because you get a SAS error message about "insufficient authorization."

Solution: The file is protected by either the SAS System, Windows, or both. If the file is protected by the SAS System, you must specify the READ=, WRITE=, and ALTER= data set options and their respective passwords when you access the file. If the file is protected by Windows, use the Windows Explorer to display and change the file attributes. To do this, right-click on the file's icon in Windows Explorer, then click on **Properties**. The Properties dialog box appears, showing the file attributes.

Another possibility is that the file is being used by another Windows application. For example, you may be trying to access a text file that is already open in Word. If this is the case, close the file in the other application, then try accessing it with the SAS System again.

Problem: You can't remember which library reference points to which SAS data library.

Solution: Double-click on the **Libraries** icon in the SAS Explorer, then click on **View→Details**. The right pane now lists all active library references and the SAS data libraries they point to, along with the library references' associated engines.

Problem: You can't remember which file shortcut points to which external file.

Solution: Double-click on the **File Shortcuts** icon in the SAS Explorer, then click on **View→Details**. Resize or scroll the right pane of the SAS Explorer window until you can see the **Host Path Name** column.

Customizing Your Start-up Files and SAS System Options

Problem: The SAS System displays a message during initialization that it cannot find the SAS configuration file.

Solution: Add the CONFIG system option to your SAS command (for example, at the end of the **Target** field in the Properties dialog box). Be sure to specify the full pathname for the SASV7.CFG file.

Problem: The SAS System does not execute the AUTOEXEC.SAS file.

Solution: Add the AUTOEXEC system option to your SAS command (for example, at the end of the **Target** field in the Properties dialog box). Be sure to specify the full pathname for the AUTOEXEC.SAS file.

Problem: The SAS System complains about not being able to read the SASV7.CFG or AUTOEXEC.SAS files.

Solution: You may have syntax errors in these files. In the SASV7.CFG file, precede each option name with a hyphen, and do not use equal signs between the system option name and the value. Check your AUTOEXEC.SAS file for missing semicolons, comment delimiters, and mismatched quotes.

Another possible cause of this problem is that you may have inadvertently saved the SASV7.CFG or AUTOEXEC.SAS file in a non-ASCII format. If you have recently edited these files with a word processing program, check to see if you saved the files in a proprietary format. If so, this adds formatting characters to the file that the SAS System cannot interpret. Re-edit the files and save them as plain text (ASCII) files.

Using Batch Mode

Problem: You cannot start your SAS batch job; double-clicking on a SAS program file icon starts a windowing session.

Solution: Use the Options dialog box in the Windows Explorer to edit the default action for .SAS, .SAS7BPGM, and .SS2 files. See "Double-clicking on a File Icon in the Windows Explorer" in Chapter 9 for more details.

Problem: You get an error message PATHDLL not found or CONFIG file not found when you start your batch SAS job.

Solution: Try specifying the CONFIG system option in the SAS command (such as in the **Target** field in the Properties dialog box or in the **Open** field in the Run dialog box). If you already have the CONFIG option specified, be sure it references the correct pathname.

Problem: The LOG and LST files from your batch job are not where you expect them to be.

Solution: Check your program for PROC PRINTTO statements. Also, check your SAS configuration file for LOG, ALTLOG, PRINT, and ALTPRINT system options. Look in the SAS working folder and in the folder containing the batch SAS program to see if the log and list files ended up there. Also look in the folder C:\WINDOWS\DESKTOP (for Windows 95) or C:\WINNT (for Windows NT).

Problem: You are using PROC PRINTTO to send the SAS procedure output or log to a printer, but the print queue seems to be stuck.

Solution: You must issue an empty (no options) PROC PRINTTO step at the end of your program to close the printer file.

Executing DOS Commands and Windows Applications from Your SAS Session

Problem: When you submit an X statement or command, the SAS log displays this message: Shell escape is not valid in this SAS session.

Solution: The XCMD system option is turned off. Start SAS again, this time specifying the XCMD system option. (This option is not valid in the OPTIONS statement.)

Problem: The result of the DOS command that you executed via an X statement or command flashes by so fast that you cannot read it.

Solution: Submit the following OPTIONS statement:

```
options xwait;
```

Now resubmit your X statement or command. To return to your SAS session, press any key.

Problem: You started a Windows application via the X statement or command but now cannot use your SAS session while the application is open.

Solution: Close the application. Now submit the following OPTIONS statement:

```
options noxsync;
```

The next time you start an application with the X statement or command, it runs independently of your SAS session.

Problem: You used the X statement or command to start a Windows application but get an error message about being out of memory.

Solution: Each application you run takes up RAM. If your machine has a small amount of RAM available (such as 4 or 8M), you may be able to run only a few Windows applications at a time. Close unnecessary applications, and try the X statement or command again.

Problem: Your program uses the X statement but generates error messages or incorrect results. You are sure your programming statements are correct.

Solution: If the results of the X statement are not available before your program continues, it will not generate correct results. Specify XWAIT in your SASV7.CFG file, so your SAS program will not continue without your permission. Also, if you are starting another application such as Word, use the SLEEP function to pause your program long enough for the other application to start.

Sharing Data between Your SAS Session and Other Windows Applications

Problem: When using DDE, your data does not look like it should—all the data are in one cell, there are tabs where you do not expect them, or the data are truncated.

Solution: Remember that the SAS System expects tabs between columns. By default, it writes columns to separate cells when the data contain spaces. Use the NOTAB option in the FILENAME statement when you define the DDE file shortcut to suppress this default behavior. If the data contains spaces but is truncated, use the DLM statement option to define another delimiter.

Problem: When you submit your SAS DDE program, an error message says the SAS System cannot communicate with the other application.

Solution: Remember that the application must be open before you submit your DDE SAS program. Either manually start the application, or use the X statement or X command to start it. You may need to use the SLEEP function to pause your SAS program long enough for the application to start.

Problem: The macro you recorded with the Microsoft Word macro recorder does not work in your SAS DDE program.

Solution: If you are using a newer version of Word, such as Word97, the macros recorded by the Word macro recorder are in Visual Basic. However, you must use Word Basic syntax in DDE programs. To get help with Word Basic syntax, obtain a copy of the *Word Developer's Kit, 3rd Edition*.

Problem: The OLE objects in your SAS/AF applications do not reflect changes.

Solution: You may have forgotten to select the **Paste Link** option in the Paste Special dialog box or the **Link** option in the Insert Object dialog box, thereby creating an embedded object instead. Re-create the object, ensuring that this time you select the **Paste Link** option.

Problem: When you open a FRAME entry containing linked objects, you get a message that the link is unavailable.

Solution: Someone may have moved the source file for the object. Right-click on the object in the BUILD: DISPLAY window, then click on **Linked *xyz* Object** in the resulting popup menu (where *xyz* represents the object type, such as **Visio** or **Document**). In the second-level popup menu, click on **Links,** which opens the Links dialog box. Click on the link you want to modify, then click on **Change Source**. Type the new pathname in the **File name** field, then click on **OK**. Now click on **Update Now** in the Links dialog box to update the link. Finally, close the Links dialog box by clicking on **Close**.

Using SAS/CONNECT Software

Problem: You receive errors when you try to initiate a remote connection.

Solution: First, check the physical connection to the remote system—a cable may have come loose or broken. Also, check the syntax of your script file. If your network is busy, the connection may time out before it is complete. In the script file, look for a PAUSE or similar command and increase the time.

Problem: You try to access a SAS catalog using Remote Library Services but receive error messages.

Solution: Because of how characters and numbers are internally represented by operating systems, you can access SAS catalogs through RLS from the following operating systems only: Windows 3.1 (Win32s), Windows NT, and Windows 95 (and subsequent releases such as Windows 98).

Problem: You want to transfer an external file without the automatic conversion from one operating system format to another.

Solution: Use the BINARY option in the PROC DOWNLOAD or PROC UPLOAD statement, which prevents these procedures from converting the file format.

Problem: You need to transfer a text file whose record length is more than 132 bytes.

Solution: Use the LRECL option to set the record length in both the local and remote FILENAME statements.

Problem: You try to download or upload some data, but you receive errors in the SAS log.

Solution: The DOWNLOAD and UPLOAD procedures must be remote submitted. Use either the **Remote submit** item in the **Run** menu, or use the RSUBMIT and ENDRSUBMIT statements to remote submit your upload and download steps.

Appendix 2   Creating a Print File

Understanding Print Files

V7 Hilites: The Generic/Text Only printer driver is no longer necessary to create print files from the SAS System.

A print file is a file with special printer codes in it. These codes can be PCL codes (Printer Control Language) or PostScript codes, depending on which printer driver you use to create the file. Because print files contain these special codes, they are not ASCII files and cannot be viewed or edited with a text editor.

Creating a Print File in a Windowing Session

To print the contents of a SAS window to a print file, follow these steps:

1. If necessary, use the Print Setup dialog box to set the default printer.

2. Click on **File** in the SAS System main menu, then on **Print**. In the Print dialog box, click on **Print to File**. A text entry field appears by this option, as shown in Figure A2.1.

Figure A2.1   Print Dialog Box

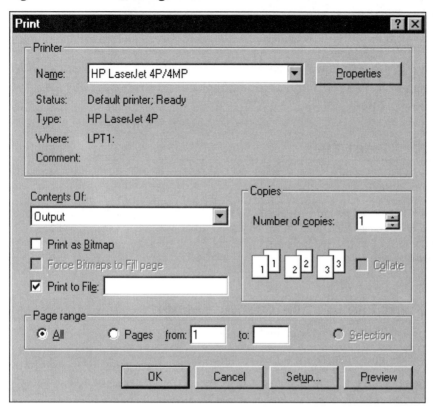

Type the name of the file you want to print to. If you do not want the file stored in the SAS working folder, specify the full pathname. You can use any extension you want, but normally you use .PRN for non-PostScript printers and .EPS or .PS for PostScript printers. Now click on **OK**. The SAS System creates the print file in the directory you specified.

Note

> To send DATA step output to a file, use the techniques discussed in "Creating a Print File in Batch Mode" later in this appendix.

Creating a Bitmap Print File

You can use the **Print to File** option in conjunction with the **Print as Bitmap** option to create a printer bitmap file. This does not create a bitmap file (such as the ones you open in Microsoft Paint, with an extension of .BMP); instead, it creates a file with special codes for the printer, telling it to interpret the information as a graphic. However, to make this combination work, your printer must support this technique. For example, you can use the WinFax printer driver provided with Delrina WinFax PRO 4.0 to fax bitmaps of SAS System windows.

Note

You can use this technique only in a windowing session.

Creating a Print File in Batch Mode

V7 Hilites: The syntax of the SYSPRINT option has changed.

You no longer need to specify the filename in the FILENAME statement.

In batch mode, you do not have access to the Print and Print Setup dialog boxes. But you can still create a print file. To do so, define the default printer and the print file destination with the SYSPRINT option, and define a file shortcut using the PRINTER keyword, as in the following example, which sends DATA step output to the print file:

```
options sysprint="HP LaserJet 4P/4MP" "c:\print.prn";
filename myfile printer;
data _null_;
      file myfile;
      put 'this is a test';
run;
```

You could also use the file shortcut in the PRINT= option in the PROC PRINTTO statement or in any other place in your code that creates output. For example, the following program sends the PROC PRINT output to the print file:

```
options sysprint="HP LaserJet 4P/4MP" "c:\print.prn";
filename myfile printer;

data a;
   x=1;
run;

proc printto print=myfile;
run;

proc print;
run;

proc printto; /* Close the print file. */
run;
```

When creating a print file, the file is always overwritten when new output is sent to the file; you cannot append output to a print file.

Note

> You can also use the ALTDEST= option in the FILENAME statement to specify the print filename; see the online help for the FILENAME statement for more details.

Printing to a Print File When You Don't Know the Printer Driver: You can use the SYSPRINT system option with a null printer driver name; this formats the print file using the default printer. Here is the syntax of the SYSPRINT option in this case:

SYSPRINT "" *"print-filename"*

For example, the following OPTIONS statement creates a print file named C:\PRINTFILE.PRN, which will be formatted for the existing default printer:

```
options sysprint="" "c:\printfile.prn";
```

Appendix 3	# Becoming Familiar with the Windows Explorer

Note

By default, the Windows Explorer does not show file extensions in the file list. To make the extensions visible, click on **View** in the Windows Explorer menu, then on **Options**. In the dialog box that appears, be sure the check box next to **Hide MS-DOS file extensions for file types that are registered** is not checked. (If you have Windows NT or a newer version of Windows, the selections in the dialog box may be worded slightly differently.)

While you can use the SAS System to rename, delete, copy, and move files, you may also want to use the Windows Explorer, which is a Windows application for managing files. Figure A3.1 shows the Windows Explorer displaying the SAS folder with its files and subfolders.

Figure A3.1 The Windows Explorer Listing the Contents of the SAS Folder

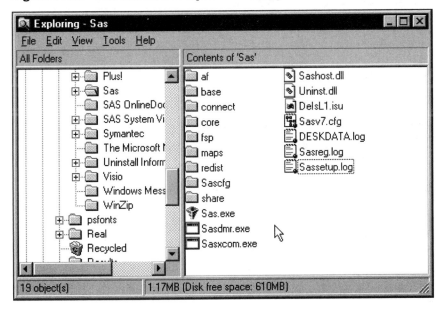

Your display may look different from this, depending on which SAS products you have installed.

To start the Windows Explorer, right-click on the **Start** button, then click on **Explore**. To see the contents of a particular folder, use the scroll bar in the center of the window to get to the folder you want to see. Click on the folder name—the contents of that folder are displayed in the right half of the window.

If you double-click on a folder in the left half of the window, any subfolders in that folder are displayed underneath the folder. This is called "expanding" the folder. Double-clicking on the folder again "collapses" the folder so that the subfolders are not shown.

The Windows Explorer uses different icons to indicate various file types. Some executable files have rectangular icons with a bar across the top; other executable files use a special icon associated with the program. If the file can be edited (such as a text file), the icon looks like a tiny page with fake text on the page. Folders and subfolders are indicated by little file folders.

To see the contents of a subfolder in the right half of the window, double-click on the subfolder name. The view changes accordingly. To change drives, scroll to the top of the left-hand Windows Explorer window and click on the drive you want to see.

Copying and Moving Files: You can use the Windows Explorer menus to copy and move files. For example, see Figure A3.2.

Figure A3.2 Preparing to Copy a File Using the Windows Explorer

Exploring - Sas	
File Edit View Tools Help	
All Folders	**Contents of 'Sas'**
af	af	Sashost.dll
base	base	Uninst.dll
connect	connect	DelsL1.isu
core	core	Sasv7.cfg
fsp	fsp	DESKDATA.log
maps	maps	Sasreg.log
redist	redist	Sassetup.log
Sascfg	Sascfg	append.sas
share	share	
SAS OnlineDoc	Sas.exe	
SAS System Vi	Sasdmr.exe	
Symantec	Sasxcom.exe	
The Microsoft		

1 object(s) selected   1.83KB

The file APPEND.SAS (a file in the SAS folder) is highlighted. Remember, to highlight a file, click on its name. To copy this file to a different folder, click on **Edit** in the Windows Explorer menu, then on **Copy**. The file is copied to the Windows Clipboard. Now display the folder where the copied file is to go, and highlight the folder name by clicking on it. After the target folder is highlighted, click on **Edit** in the Windows Explorer menu, then on **Paste**. The file is copied to the target folder.

Moving a file works exactly the same except that you choose **Cut** from the Windows Explorer **Edit** menu instead of **Copy**.

Renaming Files: To rename a file using the Windows Explorer, highlight the file by clicking on it. Click on **File** in the Windows Explorer menu, then on **Rename**. A box appears around the filename. Type the new name, and press Enter.

Deleting Files: To delete a file using the Windows Explorer, highlight the file by clicking on it. Click on **File** in the Windows Explorer menu, then on **Delete**. A dialog box asks you if you are sure that you want to send the file to the Recycle Bin. Click on **Yes** to complete the file deletion.

Note

Files deleted to the Recycle Bin are not deleted from the system. To completely delete a file, double-click on the Recycle Bin icon on the desktop, highlight the file in the file list, and press the Delete key. A dialog box asks you if you are sure that you want to completely delete the items. Click on **Yes** to complete the deletion.

Warning

Be careful when you move, rename, or delete files—some files, such as the SASUSER.PROFILE catalog, must have a particular name in order to work. In general, it is safe to move, rename, or delete catalogs and other files that you have created; do not move, rename, or delete files created automatically by the SAS System. Nor is it a good idea to rename SAS tables using the Windows Explorer because the table name is also stored in the table's header information.

Restoring Deleted Files: You can use the Recycle Bin to restore a file that you have recently deleted from a Windows Explorer window.

Here are the steps for restoring a deleted file:

1. Double-click on the **Recycle Bin** icon on the Windows desktop.

2. When the Recycle Bin opens, click on the file that you want to restore.

3. Click on **File** in the Recycle Bin menu, then on **Restore**. The file is restored to whatever folder it was originally stored in.

Warning

Files deleted from within the SAS System are not sent to the Recycle Bin—they are deleted completely from the hard disk. To recover these files, you must have a third-party file restoration utility, such as Norton Utilities.

Creating Folders: You may want to create new folders and subfolders to store the files associated with your work with the SAS System. For example, you might need separate folders for SAS programs, SAS logs, SAS output, and miscellaneous files.

To use the Windows Explorer to create a folder or subfolder, click on **File** in the Windows Explorer menu, then on **New**. When a list of choices appears, click on **Folder**. A new folder icon appears in the right half of the window, ready for a new name. Type the name and press Enter. The folder is now ready to store files.

Closing the Windows Explorer: To close the Windows Explorer, click on its Close button.

Glossary

active window: the application or part of an application that is ready to accept input.

application: a program with its attendant windows. Examples include programs such as the SAS System, Microsoft Word, and Netscape Navigator.

click: to press a mouse button once. Unless otherwise specified, click refers to the left mouse button.

client: an application that requests data or information from another application. For example, in OLE, the SAS System is the OLE client.

Clipboard: a Windows component that is like a pegboard—a place to store something until you need it again. Typically, the Clipboard is used to store text or graphics that you want to copy somewhere else.

close: to shut down an individual window or an entire application.

Close button: an X in the upper-right corner of an application's workspace. Clicking on the Close button closes the application. Every Windows application has a Close button, as do most windows within an application.

Control Panel: a Windows application that manages various aspects of your desktop, such as printers, colors, device drivers, the keyboard and mouse, and so on. The Control Panel is part of the **Settings** program group that is accessed through the **Start** button.

DDE: see Dynamic Data Exchange.

DDE triplet: used in a FILENAME statement when you are using DDE (Dynamic Data Exchange).The DDE triplet tells the SAS System how to access data at a particular point in a file.

desktop: your screen, where all applications appear and where you do all of your work with Windows.

dialog box: a type of window that solicits information from you. Usually, you must supply this information before you can continue using an application.

directory: see folder.

double-click: to press the left mouse button twice quickly.

download: to move data from a remote computer to a local computer.

drag and drop: a method of using the mouse to move an object on your desktop from one place to another. You can drag and drop text, file icons, and graphics. Usually, when you drop the object, some action is taken, such as copying text or submitting a file.

Dynamic Data Exchange (DDE): a method of sharing text-based data between Windows applications.

embedded object: an OLE object that is not linked to the server application. The object and its data are stored in the client application. Embedded objects can be static or non-static. Contrast with linked object.

file shortcut: a nickname the SAS System uses for an external file or folder. Define file shortcuts with the FILENAME statement or using the SAS Explorer. In Version 6 of the SAS System, a file shortcut was called a fileref.

folder: a collection of files.

full pathname: the complete physical filename, including drive, folder, subfolder, filename, and extension. An example of a full pathname is C:\SAS\SASUSER\APPEND.SAS.

icon: a pictorial representation of a Windows object. Examples of objects that can be represented by icons include entire applications, individual windows, and files.

library reference: a nickname the SAS System uses for a SAS data library. Define library references with the LIBNAME statement, the SAS Explorer, or the Active Libraries dialog box. In Version 6 of the SAS System, a library reference was called a libref.

linked object: an OLE object that is dynamically connected to its OLE server. When you paste a linked object into an OLE client application, only the object—not the data—is stored in the client application. The data remain independent of the client. Contrast with embedded object.

maximize: to cause an application or a window that is represented by an icon to restore to full size and take up the whole display.

menu: a visual method of executing commands in an application. To use the menu, click on a menu choice.

minimize: to cause an application or a window to become an icon.

mouse: the hand-held device you use to select and manipulate applications and text. The mouse activates the mouse pointer on the screen.

non-static embedded object: an OLE object that, when activated, can start its server application. Contrast with static embedded object.

ODS: see Output Delivery System (ODS).

object: something created by an OLE server that can be pasted into an OLE client application. Examples of objects are graphics, pieces of text, video clips, and sound files.

Object Linking and Embedding (OLE): a graphical method of sharing data between Windows applications.

OLE: see Object Linking and Embedding (OLE).

open editing: an OLE concept in which, when you edit an OLE object, the OLE server application starts in its own window, with its own menus and tool bars. Contrast with visual editing.

Output Delivery System (ODS): the portion of the SAS System that enables you to create different forms of output, such as SAS listing and HTML output.

point: to move the mouse pointer over a particular item on the screen, such as a menu item, a word, or an icon.

popup menu: a menu that appears when you click the right mouse button.

program group: a collection of application icons in the **Start** button menu.

Remote Library Services (RLS): a method of data access used with SAS/CONNECT software. RLS accesses data directly on the remote machine without physically transferring the data to the local machine.

right-click: to click the right mouse button once. Usually, this opens a popup menu.

RLS: see Remote Library Services.

SAS Explorer: a SAS window that lets you move, copy, rename, delete, and otherwise manage your SAS files (such as tables and catalog entries).

SAS table: synonymous with SAS data set.

SAS workspace: the borders within which an application operates.

screen tip: an explanation of a portion of an application's workspace (such as a tool or a field in a dialog box) that appears when you hold the mouse pointer over the area for a few seconds.

scroll bar: a method of moving vertically or horizontally in a document. Scroll bars have arrows on which you click to move the file view.

server: an application that provides data or services to another application. For example, in OLE, Word, Excel, or Lotus 1-2-3 can be OLE servers.

shortcut: a pointer or link to any object, such as a file, program, network folder, Control Panel tool, or disk drive.

StartUp folder: a Windows program group that contains programs that start immediately when Windows boots up.

static embedded object: an OLE object that is a picture. You cannot activate a static embedded object (that is, open its server application). Contrast with non-static embedded object.

subfolder: a collection of files that is part of a folder.

table: see SAS table.

Taskbar: a portion of the Windows desktop that lists by name all of the open Windows applications. To access an application, click on its name in the Taskbar.

title bar: the horizontal element at the top of a Windows application workspace that tells you which application you are running. Individual windows inside an application also have title bars.

tool bar: a visual method of executing commands in a Windows application. Each command is represented by an icon. To execute the command, click on the appropriate icon.

upload: to move data from a local computer to a remote computer.

visual editing: an OLE concept in which, when you edit an OLE object, the OLE server application menus and tool bars meld with the OLE client's menus and tool bars. Contrast with open editing.

Window Bar: a portion of the SAS workspace that lists all of the open SAS windows. To access a window, click on its name in the Window Bar.

Windows Explorer: a Windows application that lets you move, copy, delete, rename, and otherwise manage your files. The Windows Explorer can be accessed by right-clicking on the **Start** button and then clicking on **Explore**.

wizard: a Windows tool that guides you through a process, such as adding a printer to your system, installing new software, or importing data into a SAS table.

Index

Call your local SAS® office to order these other books and tapes available through the Books by Users℠ program:

An Array of Challenges — Test Your SAS® Skills
by **Robert Virgile** . . . . Order No. A55625

Applied Multivariate Statistics with SAS® Software, Second Edition
by **Ravindra Khattree**
and **Dayanand N. Naik** . . . . Order No. A56903

Applied Statistics and the SAS® Programming Language, Fourth Edition
by **Ronald P. Cody**
and **Jeffrey K. Smith** . . . . Order No. A55984

Beyond the Obvious with SAS® Screen Control Language
by **Don Stanley** . . . . Order No. A55073

Carpenter's Complete Guide to the SAS® Macro Language
by **Art Carpenter** . . . . Order No. A56100

The Cartoon Guide to Statistics
by **Larry Gonick**
and **Woollcott Smith** . . . . Order No. A55153

Categorical Data Analysis Using the SAS® System
by **Maura E. Stokes, Charles S. Davis,**
and **Gary G. Koch** . . . . Order No. A55320

Common Statistical Methods for Clinical Research with SAS® Examples
by **Glenn A. Walker** . . . . Order No. A55991

Concepts and Case Studies in Data Management
by **William S. Calvert**
and **J. Meimei Ma** . . . . Order No. A55220

Efficiency: Improving the Performance of Your SAS® Applications
by **Robert Virgile** . . . . Order No. A55960

Essential Client/Server Survival Guide, Second Edition
by **Robert Orfali, Dan Harkey,**
and **Jeri Edwards** . . . . Order No. A56285

Extending SAS® Survival Analysis Techniques for Medical Research
by **Alan Cantor** . . . . Order No. A55504

A Handbook of Statistical Analyses Using SAS®
by **B.S. Everitt**
and **G. Der** . . . . Order No. A56378

The How-To Book for SAS/GRAPH® Software
by **Thomas Miron** . . . . Order No. A55203

In the Know ... SAS® Tips and Techniques From Around the Globe
by **Phil Mason** . . . . Order No. A55513

Integrating Results through Meta-Analytic Review Using SAS® Software
by **Morgan C. Wang** and
Brad J. Bushman . . . . Order No. A55810

Learning SAS® in the Computer Lab
by **Rebecca J. Elliott** . . . . Order No. A55273

The Little SAS® Book: A Primer
by **Lora D. Delwiche** and
Susan J. Slaughter . . . . Order No. A55200

The Little SAS® Book: A Primer, Second Edition
by **Lora D. Delwiche** and
Susan J. Slaughter . . . . Order No. A56649
(updated to include Version 7 features)

Logistic Regression Using the SAS System: Theory and Application
by **Paul D. Allison** . . . . Order No. A55770

Mastering the SAS® System, Second Edition
by **Jay A. Jaffe** . . . . Order No. A55123

Multiple Comparisons and Multiple Tests Using the SAS® System
by **Peter H. Westfall, Randall D. Tobias, Dror Rom, Russell D. Wolfinger,**
and **Yosef Hochberg** . . . . Order No. A56648

Statistical Quality Control Using the SAS® System
by **Dennis W. King, Ph.D.** . . . . Order No. A55232

*A Step-by-Step Approach to Using the SAS® System
for Factor Analysis and Structural Equation Modeling*
by **Larry Hatcher** . . . . Order No. A55129

*A Step-by-Step Approach to Using the SAS® System
for Univariate and Multivariate Statistics*
by **Larry Hatcher**
and **Edward Stepanski** . . . . Order No. A55072

*Strategic Data Warehousing Principles Using
SAS® Software*
by **Peter R. Welbrock** . . . . Order No. A56278

*Survival Analysis Using the SAS® System:
A Practical Guide*
by **Paul D. Allison** . . . . Order No. A55233

*Table-Driven Strategies for Rapid SAS® Applications
Development*
by **Tanya Kolosova**
and **Samuel Berestizhevsky**. . . . . Order No. A55198

Tuning SAS® Applications in the MVS Environment
by **Michael A. Raithel** . . . . Order No. A55231

*Univariate and Multivariate General Linear Models:
Theory and Applications Using SAS® Software*
by **Neil H. Timm**
and **Tammy A. Mieczkowski**. . . . . Order No. A55809

Working with the SAS® System
by **Erik W. Tilanus** . . . . Order No. A55190

*Your Guide to Survey Research Using the SAS®
System*
by **Archer Gravely** . . . . Order No. A55688

Audio Tapes

100 Essential SAS® Software Concepts (set of two)
by **Rick Aster** . . . . Order No. A55309

A Look at SAS® Files (set of two)
by **Rick Aster** . . . . Order No. A55207

JMP® Books

Basic Business Statistics: A Casebook
by **Dean P. Foster, Robert A. Stine,
and Richard P. Waterman** . . . . Order No. A56813

Business Analysis Using Regression: A Casebook
by **Dean P. Foster, Robert A. Stine,
and Richard P. Waterman** . . . . Order No. A56818

JMP® Start Statistics, Version 3
by **John Sall** *and* **Ann Lehman** . . . . . . Order No. A55626

*Welcome * Bienvenue * Willkommen * Yohkoso * Bienvenido*

SAS® Publications Is Easy to Reach

Visit our SAS Publications Web page located at www.sas.com/pubs

You will find product and service details, including

- **sample chapters**
- **tables of contents**
- **author biographies**
- **book reviews**

Learn about

- **regional user groups conferences**
- **trade show sites and dates**
- **authoring opportunities**
- **custom textbooks**

Order books with ease at our secured Web page!

Explore all the services that Publications has to offer!

Your Listserv Subscription Brings the News to You Automatically

Do you want to be among the first to learn about the latest books and services available from SAS Publications? Subscribe to our listserv **newdocnews-l** and automatically receive the following once each month: a description of the new titles, the applicable environments or operating systems, and the applicable SAS release(s). To subscribe:

1. Send an e-mail message to **listserv@vm.sas.com**

2. Leave the "Subject" line blank

3. Use the following text for your message:

> **subscribe newdocnews-l** *your-first-name your-last-name*

For example: subscribe newdocnews-l John Doe

Please note: newdocnews-l ◄——— that's the letter "l" not the number "1".

For customers outside the U.S., contact your local SAS office for listserv information.

Create Customized Textbooks Quickly, Easily, and Affordably

SelecText® offers instructors at U.S. colleges and universities a way to create custom textbooks for courses that teach students how to use SAS software.

For more information, see our Web page at **www.sas.com/selectext**, or contact our SelecText coordinators by sending e-mail to **selectext@sas.com**.

You're Invited to Publish with SAS Institute's User Publishing Program

If you enjoy writing about SAS software and how to use it, the User Publishing Program at SAS Institute Inc. offers a variety of publishing options. We are actively recruiting authors to publish books, articles, and sample code. Do you find the idea of writing a book or an article by yourself a little intimidating? Consider writing with a co-author. Keep in mind that you will receive complete editorial and publishing support, access to our users, technical advice and assistance, and competitive royalties. Please contact us for an author packet. E-mail us at **sasbbu@sas.com** or call 919-677-8000, then press 1-6479. See the SAS Publications Web page at **www.sas.com/pubs** for complete information.

Read All about It in *Authorline*®!

Our User Publishing newsletter, *Authorline*, features author interviews, conference news, and informational updates and highlights from our User Publishing Program. Published quarterly, *Authorline* is available free of charge. To subscribe, send e-mail to **sasbbu@sas.com** or call 919-677-8000, then press 1-6479.

See *Observations*®, Our Online Technical Journal

Feature articles from *Observations*®: *The Technical Journal for SAS*® *Software Users* are now available online at **www.sas.com/obs**. Take a look at what your fellow SAS software users and SAS Institute experts have to tell you. You may decide that you, too, have information to share. If you are interested in writing for *Observations*, send e-mail to **sasbbu@sas.com** or call 919-677-8000, then press 1-6479.

Book Discount Offered at SAS Public Training Courses!

When you attend one of our SAS Public Training Courses at any of our regional Training Centers in the U.S., you will receive a 15% discount on any book orders placed during the course. Each course has a list of recommended books to choose from, and the books are displayed for you to see. Take advantage of this offer at the next course you attend!

SAS Institute Inc.
SAS Campus Drive
Cary, NC 27513-2414
Fax 919-677-4444

E-mail: sasbook@sas.com
Web page: www.sas.com/pubs
To order books, call Fulfillment Services at 800-727-3228*
For other SAS Institute business, call 919-677-8000*

* Note: Customers outside the U.S. should contact their local SAS office.